Essential interactionism

International Library of Sociology

Founded by Karl Mannheim

Editor: John Rex, Research Unit for Ethnic Relations, University of Aston in Birmingham

Arbor Scientiae
Arbor Vitae

A catalogue of the books available in the **International Library of Sociology** and other series of Social Science books published by Routledge & Kegan Paul will be found at the end of this volume.

Essential interactionism

On the intelligibility of prejudice

Barry Glassner
Assistant Professor of Sociology
Syracuse University

Routledge & Kegan Paul
London, Boston and Henley

*First published in 1980
by Routledge & Kegan Paul Ltd
39 Store Street, London WC1E 7DD,
Broadway House, Newtown Road,
Henley-on-Thames, Oxon RG9 1EN and
9 Park Street, Boston, Mass. 02108, USA
Photoset in 10 on 11pt Times by
Kelly Typesetting, Bradford-on-Avon, Wiltshire
and printed in the United States of America by
Vail-Ballou Inc
© Routledge & Kegan Paul, 1980
No part of this book may be reproduced in
any form without permission from the
publisher, except for the quotation of brief
passages in criticism*

British Library Cataloguing in Publication Data

Glassner, Barry

*Essential interactionism. – (International
library of sociology).
1. Social interaction
I. Title II. Series
301.11   HM291   79–41119*

ISBN 0 7100 0381 1

For Robert Boguslaw, Margaret Lee and
Richard H. Popkin, who let me learn

The Dutchman's not the kind of man to keep his
thumb jammed in the dam that holds his dreams in.
But that's a secret that only Margaret knows.
          Steve Goodman

Considerations of simplicity, power and precision,
scope and selectivity, familiarity and freshness,
are all relevant and often contend with one
another; their weighting is relative to our interests,
our information, and our inquiry.
          Nelson Goodman

Contents

Preface   xii

Introduction   xv

Part I   **Ontological considerations**   1

1   Causation and interaction   3
   Infusing correlations with causation   3
   An alternative relational concept   6
   Cause, interaction and dialectic   10
   Objections   11

2   Symbolic and essential interactionisms   14
   Idealism   14
   Symbolism   16
   Indeterminism   16
   Mead   21
   Essential interactionism   22

Part II   **Method**   25

Introduction   27

3   General considerations   29
   Expanding empiricism   31
   How subjective is phenomenology?   33
   What are essences?   34
   Objections to essences   36
   Essences in other inquiry strategies   39

CONTENTS

4	Literature as sites	41
	Vicarious phenomenology	41
	A fieldwork strategy: literature as sites	42
	Importance of literature sites inquiry	45
	Choosing sites	47
	Boundaries	48
	Is it an essence?	50
	Phantasy variations	52
	Essential relationships	53
	Meta analysis	54
	Verification and falsification	56

Part III First illustration of a method 59

Introduction 61

5	Maps and proposed essences	63
	Key informants	63
	Initial maps	64
	Definitions	66
	Determining possible essences	70
	Delimiting the experiment	73
	Summary	74
6	Elaboration of essences: I	76
	On functionalist sites	76
	A social psychological instrument: why?	78
	Aggression	78
	Simplification	80
	Why people stereotype	84
	Why people social distance	88
	Why people simplify affect	92
	A social psychological instrument: how?	93
	How people stereotype	94
	How people social distance	97
	How people simplify affect	98
	Interactions	100
	Summary	104
7	Elaboration of essences: II	106
	A social instrument: why?	106
	Intergroup competition	106
	Economic competition	110

	A societal tool: how?	115
	General entrenchment	115
	Target characteristics	118
	Entrenchment assistance by scientists and philosophers	120
	Identifiability	125
	Societal control of social psychological ways of prejudicing	126
	Summary	129
8	Possible applications	131
	Critiques of a functionalist proposal	131
	Classlessness and prejudice	136
	Normality of prejudice	137
	Essences of prejudice as general essences	139
	Concerning solutions	144
	Summary	145
9	Assessment and further development	147
	Methodological notes from the first illustration	147
	Next steps	151
	Missing literature sites	152
	Summary	156
	Appendix: Sample fieldnotes	158
	Notes	161
	Bibliography	165
	Index	181

Preface

Although arguments pro and con value freedom in research have a long and rich ongoing history, one point seems beyond question. Researchers and theorists always begin with conceptions about their methods and the subject matter they will study. This is a truism of the Sociology of Knowledge. As Durkheim (1954) noted and Mannheim (1954) elaborated, our thoughts and knowledge, our categories and the ways we categorize, derive in large part from our social experiences. I will have occasion to reflect upon appropriate ways to use and to revise this truism, but at no point will I deny the general sense of it.

Indeed, the 'value-freedom' thesis has encumbered sociologists' work unnecessarily. We are simply unable to conduct the business of sociology without making choices and taking actions which violate the demands of neutrality or objectivity. A summary of the reasons for this situation was provided by Friedrichs (1970: 89):

> The decisions we make regarding problem selections, the appropriate use of conceptual tools and their accompanying grammars and logics, the risking of hypotheses, the approximation of control, the impact of observation, the level of error admissible, the impact of prediction of future behavior, selectivity in communication, and the attitude we take regarding the application of the findings – all either demand or imply a value commitment that transcends the empirically given.

There can be no question that value commitment must exist – the scientist *qua* scientist makes value judgments (Rudner, 1961) – but much can be said about the appropriate use of one's commitment and the obligations to one's audience. Among these obligations is an attempt to reveal honestly how one came to the pertinent values and what these values are.

PREFACE

A major project in this book is to understand prejudice. Let me be brief but specific about the autobiographical bases of my value commitment to studying prejudice. I was raised Jewish in Roanoke, Virginia, an American town of 80,000 with a Deep South self-image, in a valley completely surrounded by the Blue Ridge Mountains and three hours by car from any other town of more than 20,000 population. Our home for much of my childhood was on what had been the grounds of a plantation. The Plantation House and Slaves' Quarters still exist three blocks from my parents' home.

Almost without exception, the only direct contact the social structure facilitated between blacks and whites consisted of black women serving as mammies or maids at white homes and their husbands and sons as custodial workers, or at lowest level positions within local businesses. From birth until sophomore year in high school the only blacks with whom I conversed for more than a couple of sentences were the family's maids. The maid's salary had reached $35 a week by the mid-1960s, and she worked about forty hours weekly for that salary, in addition to nearly an hour's commute each way on irregularly scheduled busses from 'colored town.' Not until I brought a Northern friend home from college did I realize that in other parts of the country middle-income families such as mine could not afford maids.

During the early years of the black civil rights movement, within my home I heard conflicting reports about prejudice. My maternal grandparents were from Selma, Alabama, where some of the family still lives. During the battles for voting rights in Selma, my parents received letters from a family member who expressed anti-black stereotypes and accusations of 'communist' influence in the civil rights movement. Simultaneously, my parents complained of Jews' exclusion from social affairs and neighborhoods in the South.

By the time I entered high school I had become a devotee of the civil rights movement, which was just gaining its full steam. I became editor of the high school newspaper, and wrote in support of public school integration. As a result, I was physically and verbally assaulted at the high school, excluded from social life there, and eggs and stones were thrown at my family's car and home. By the time I graduated, the school was still segregated.

As soon as I arrived at college in Chicago I was confronted with a dormitory in which the black students were demanding that they not be forced to room with whites; a state of affairs which thoroughly confused me. It was at that point that I began to read everything I could locate concerning prejudice.

I learned young and through first-hand experiences the destructiveness, complexities and contradictions of this phenomenon called prejudice. I do start with a value commitment to gain an

PREFACE

empirical and theoretical understanding about a phenomenon I dislike: What is it? What makes it possible? Under which conditions, and how often, is it destructive – usually, sometimes, seldom? What exactly *is* prejudice?

In my attempts to understand prejudice I have found no single literature (body of research, theory, etc.) that satisfactorily answers even one of these questions, although many reports contain bits of insight. Dismay at this state of affairs has lead to the second major project of the book, the development of methodological techniques to permit retrieval and development of the useful aspects of the literature.

In attempting to re-utilize existing literature I find myself dismayed at both quantitative and qualitative methods within sociology. Quantitative methods provide almost exclusively a correlational knowledge, do not give human groups or social phenomena a full or deep hearing, and are usually unfaithful to these phenomena by describing relationships in terms of causation. Qualitative methods suffer from confused determinism and a concentration upon small groups to the exclusion of both mass society and societal social phenomena.

I owe much to several people who have helped in the development of these value commitments and in the preparation of this book. David J. Pittman, Barbara Ponse, Robert Boguslaw, Gary Spencer, Manfred Stanley, Jonathan D. Moreno, Sharon Lehman, Richard Rudner, Richard H. Popkin, and Herbert Spiegelberg contributed valuable discussions and critiques of ideas and ways of exhibiting these ideas. Editor Peter Hopkins and his advisors at Routledge and Kegan Paul suggested changes that have improved the book substantively and technically. The manuscript was typed by Pam Boteler.

Introduction

This book suggests a solution to the dilemma of how to derive intelligibility of a social scientific phenomenon. Intelligibility has been derived in diverse ways by social scientists. Most customary approaches use commonsense, dictionary definitions, operationalization, or formal logic. Each is an attempt to make phenomena amenable to scientific discourse and is a response to the disarray of communication in social science. None of these customary approaches remain faithful, however, both to the social and scientific history of the phenomena and to the promotion of scientific discourse across theoretical and methodological boundaries.

Both the products and processes of science (Rudner, 1966: 8) are human actions. The products are human linguistic actions which result from processes of intellectual, social and other actions. Scientific literature is the reports of these actions. My proposal is to derive the intelligibility of a social scientific phenomenon by exploring the literature concerning that phenomenon, to study science as action.

We begin with some house-cleaning for sociological analysis and an underlying metaphysical assumption. Chapter 1 critiques causal analysis in order to indicate an alternative and more defensible basic relational concept for sociology: human interaction. The adequacy of this relational concept is argued through a survey of the social and philosophical history of causation and interaction, and through specific replies to the arguments of leading correlational causalists within sociology.

Consideration of symbolic interactionism emerges in light of my proposal that causal assumptions be replaced in large measure by interactionist assumptions. Symbolic interactionism is a leading interactionist sociology and very close to the sort of interactionism attempted throughout the remainder of the book. Chapter 2 takes a

INTRODUCTION

critical look at symbolic interactionism's confusing indeterminism and idealism, and its over emphasis on symbolism. Essential interactionism is proposed to meet the need to search for necessary properties of phenomena.

Development of a method for essential interactionist inquiries into large social phenomena is described in Part II. This is based primarily upon Husserlian phenomenological concerns, although enhanced from several other perspectives within the philosophy of science.

A proposed methodological strategy treats previous social scientific literature on any phenomenon as if it were fieldwork sites. Constant comparisons are made between these sites to determine which features of the phenomenon seem to be essential, to elaborate these features, and to describe their configurations. The special uses of key informants, site maps, and thought experiments ('phantasy variations') are described.

A first illustration or experiment with the method fills the remainder of the book (Part III). The method is applied to the phenomenon of prejudice via the social science literature concerning this phenomenon. The application is a detailed inquiry into prejudice and hopefully makes a contribution to sociological understanding of the phenomenon, while shedding some light on conflicting earlier theories and research reports. This is not intended as the full exploration of prejudice, however, nor even of a few essences of the phenomenon. Rather, the experimentation is conducted primarily to determine the ability of the research strategy to uncover and elaborate essences and provide descriptions of the configuration of these essences within the phenomenon.

part one

Ontological considerations

If social worlds were merely relative, that would be easy. If they were merely regular that would be easy. I find myself torn between a desire to savor humanity's myriad ways of being and to uncover how they are all the same. This makes my work difficult.

1 Causation and interaction

My concern in this chapter is that sociologists should make claims only for that which their research can actually reveal, with whatever degree of murkiness that entails. Certain causal assumptions have hindered allegiance to this maxim.

Critiques of causal sociology (in this chapter) and of rival interactionist positions (in the next) suggest the project of the essential interactionism proposed throughout the remainder of the book.

Infusing correlations with causation

The object of my critique is one notion of causation, an influential notion in sociology which we might call social-correlation causation.[1] Blalock (1964), Hirschi and Selvin (1967) and Hyman (1955) argue that correlations are causal when they meet these conditions: (1) they are statistically significant; (2) A produces a change in B; (3) A is prior to B; and (4) all other possible causal variables are held constant. Let us consider each condition.
1 A father of contemporary mainstream sociology is David Hume, who in the 1700s posited skepticism about concepts of causation in his *Treatise on Human Nature* but reiterated Sextus Empiricus's point (Bury, 1933: 337) that we must think in terms of causation. To resolve the contradiction Hume proposed that the closest we can get to causation is probability. 'The constant conjunction of objects determines their causation,' wrote Hume.

Of course, causal analysts recognize what Blalock calls 'the simple assertion that correlation does not prove causality (4).' To get around this problem, they take the other three circuitous routes listed above.
2 The route of recommending that 'X is a direct cause of Y if and only if a change in X produces a change in the mean value of Y' does

not do the trick. Blalock acknowledges Hume's point when elsewhere he notes that 'all we can observe is a change in X followed by a change in Y (19).' Talking of production simply avoids the issue. To say that 'X produces a change' is to replace one statement which cannot be observable with another. How, where and when can we in any way experience X producing any more than we can experience it causing?

3   In an *AB* conjunction which appears regularly, if *A* appears first, it is considered the cause of *B*. One can easily think of instances where the appearance can adequately be thought of only as simultaneous, however. My present writing activity is a case in point. It may be convenient to think of my hand as causing my pen to write, but to establish this we must rely on some grounding beyond order of appearance. My hand and my pen are moving together; the motion of neither is followed by the motion of the other. It would be false to say that the hand moves, stops, and then the pen moves. Equally false would be to say that the hand moves in quick jerks and each such brief motion is followed by a brief motion of the pen (Taylor, 1967: 65–6).

A more controversial example is Von Wright's (1971: 77), of a person who asks a friend to watch the neural events in his brain. He claims he will bring about the neural events for moving his arm *by* moving his arm. As his friend watches, he moves his arm, but before he moves it, the neural events occur in his brain and are seen by his friend. Von Wright argues that this is an example of an event which precedes its cause. A reply which could be offered is that the *decision* to raise the arm brought about the neural events, and the decision preceded the arm raising. But Von Wright seems correct that this begs the question, because intending to raise the arm does not bring about the neural events unless the arm is actually raised.[2]

In the second century AD, Empiricus attacked these temporal assumptions with logic (Bury, 1933: 343):

> to say that the Cause is brought into existence after the appearance of its effect would seem ridiculous. But neither can it subsist before the effect; for it is said to be conceived in relation thereto, and they affirm that relatives, in so far as they are relative, co-exist with each other and are conceived together. Nor, again, can it subsist along with its effect; for if it is productive of the effect, and what comes into existence must so come by the agency of what exists already, the Cause must have become causal first, and this done, then produces its effect.

Kelsen (1943: 237), argues that the tenacity of the asymmetrical assumption concerning cause and effect, that the cause must precede the effect, is a residue from prescientific meanings of cause and effect, which depended upon notions of retribution. Cause was originally the wrong and effect the punishment, and the latter could only occur in reaction to the appearance of the former.

4   The fourth circuitous route attempted from correlation to causation has been a process of elimination.[3] This reasoning maintains that if one eliminates all other things with which A could be correlated, one can assume that A's correlation with B is causal. Lundberg put it this way (1954: 20–1):

> cause is imputed to the independent variable or combination of variables when it shows a high probability-expectation in its concomitant variations with other factors or combination of factors, still other supposedly relevant conditions held constant.

This process of elimination argument was answered by MacIver (1942: 22):

> There are a vast number of situations in which, if you eat a poisoned dish, you die. Death is the normal, the common sequel. Other things being equal, you die. Here, then, is our formula – 'other things being equal' . . . It is a formula that admits of application only on the assumption of an invariant or static order . . . But where we are dealing with a phenomenon of change in a changing system – the typical problem of social causation – this device will no longer avail us.

Blalock's discussion surrounding his call for causation through elimination is illustrative of the increasing distance from observables necessary to support such an unsupportable argument. He tells us (1964: 16):

> Allowances for unknown causal variables that produce changes in the dependent variable thus make it possible to reconcile causal determinism with statistical laws.

In other words, Blalock asks us to seek causation empirically via statistics which entail invisible activities – after he has admitted that causation cannot be observed ('causal laws cannot be demonstrated empirically'). He then moves even further away from empirical grounding by adding that statistical formulations about such invisible causal variables (1964: 18) 'must involve definite assumptions about *how* the uncontrolled variables are operating.'

Both Hume and the causal sociologists believe that causation dominates the world and that the closest we can get to understanding causation is probability. They differ in that Hume chooses skepticism after his interactions with these beliefs, and the sociologists become dogmatists. Hume's conclusion is consequently a devastating critique of dogmatism (1888: 103):

Thus all probable reasoning is nothing but a species of sensation. 'This not solely in poetry and music, we must follow our taste and sentiment, but likewise in philosophy. When I am convinc'd of any principle, 'tis only an idea, which strikes more strongly upon me. When I give the preference to one set of arguments above another, I do nothing but decide from my feeling concerning the superiority of their influence. Objects have no discoverable connexion together; nor is it from any principle but custom operating upon the imagination, that we can draw any inference from the appearance of one to the existence of another.

This conclusion has some psychologistic biases, but at least it leaves us with important options for grounding of our relational talk. Before turning to a relational assumption which seems more appropriate than causation, a note is in order regarding one sense in which causation must be taken seriously by sociologists.

The persons we study often take causation to be real, and consequently in the important W. I. Thomas sense it is real. By purposely neglecting types of causation we make as serious mistakes as do those who always assume it. It *is* an empirical fact, for example, that people consider their own and others' deviancies to have an etiology. When labeling theorists disregard etiology, they also disregard a real aspect of deviance. What is needed here is recognition of the reality that Thomas's dictum has two sides. What people consider real will be real in its consequences, but if it is somehow unreal beyond their perceptions, this unreality will *also* have consequences. In the case of labeling theory, its lasting truth is that whether or not people conceive of their deviancies as having etiologies, an encompassing reality about deviance is that it results from labeling arising within interactions.

An alternative relational concept

My suggestion for a more adequate basic relational concept for sociology grows out of an investigation of the various conceptions of causation.

The Greek word for cause, *aitia*, also means guilt. Kelsen (1943: Chapter V), notes that in early Greek philosophy, as in the mythical thinking preceding it, nature was explained in terms of the prevailing social order. This order was one of direct justice from primitive times until the maturation of the State, which culminated in a pervasive criminal law and distributive justice, presumably for the entire world. Likewise, the justice of nature, causation, became a universal law.

In order to achieve dominance, Christianity placed the power of retribution, and with it causation, in the hands of God. Throughout the Christian era, causation retained its status as a norm, but it became God's norm. It is not surprising, then, that many persons we now consider founders of natural science operated from an assumption of divine, not natural, causation. Galileo viewed nature as 'an executor of God's orders,' Kepler explained the motion of the planets as God 'proceeding in a mathematical way;' and Newton believed that everything is God, that the laws of nature are established by his will (Kelsen, 1945: Chapter VI). Indeed, Newton viewed the whole structure of human history as ordained in the Biblical prophecies. Along with Hartley and Priestley, Newton spent much time demonstrating that Biblical prophesies are correct. These authors argued convincingly and in great detail that such events as the fall of the Roman Empire and the dispersion of the Jews were predicted and occurred (Popkin, 1976).

Hume's writings mark the beginning of a rejection of causation as God's rule and its replacement with causation as science's rules. We no longer seek verification for God's prophecies, or the work of Dike (the goddess of retribution), but rather for scientists' experiments. Rather than seeking to live according to the way God's rules necessitate that we live, we live according to the way that our scientific laws necessitate.

Inhering in all of these varieties of causation is the concept of *action*. These various forms describe different sorts of action, and different agents accomplishing the actions. Pre-Hume the action was always normative, and the agents were various gods. Post-Hume the actors became less visible, but remained present none the less.

It may be that we cannot conceive of cause except as action. Thomas Reid (1788), first noted this when he said that our notion of cause and effect in nature is modeled on an analogy between the human experience of an agent and his action. Gasking (1955: 483), specified this analogy:

> The notion of causation is essentially connected with our manipulative techniques for producing results . . . A statement about the cause of something is very closely connected with a recipe for producing it or preventing it.

Von Wright (1971: Chapter II), demonstrates that only a concept of action permits us to go beyond Hume's declaration that we never view causation, only constant conjunction. We can envision causation within a conjunction only in those instances in which we satisfy ourselves that, by manipulating one factor, we bring it about that the other is (or is not) there. This is typically accomplished by removing A from the conjunction of AB and finding that B vanishes as well, or by introducing *A* into a situation where *A* and *B* are missing and showing that *B* also comes about. The only traditional empirical method for accomplishing this removal or introduction is via controlled experiments (which obviates 'Causal Analysis in Non-experimental Research,' the title of Blalock's book). Of course, in cases where we cannot actually interfere with *A* and *B* we sometimes argue causation, but we do this via thought experiments which conclude that if we *could* produce *A* through our actions, *B* would also appear.[4] The empirical aspect of a conjunction is action; what we can 'point to' in relations considered causal are actions. In the case of the subject matter of interest to sociology, the conjunctions consist of interaction.[5] This becomes evident when we consider the broad subject matter of interest to sociology.

Two concerns are usually distinguished as being of interest to sociology: the structures and changes of human groups. Structures appear to many persons, including some Durkheimian, structuralist and other sociologists, to be objects capable of causal determinism. These views ignore the history of structures. Out of intentional actions and their unanticipated consequences emerge routines, which once established come to be viewed as objective and determinative by those persons and groups who singly can no longer affect the course of the routines if they so desire. Actions become subsumed within the reproduction of the routine structure. Human actions develop and maintain structures, then, and group structure varies according to the ways persons within the groups interact (e.g. primary vs. secondary groups) or by the interpretations arising from their interactions (e.g. being Rotarians).

Of changes of groups, we need only admit an ongoing dynamic process to comprehend that it is interactional (MacIver, 1942: 169 and 183):

> The role of the precipitant may vary enormously in significance, and . . . in each instance we can assess its causal importance only if we understand the whole dynamic system into which it enters. The causal efficacy we impute to any factor must always be contingent not only on the other factors but also on the dynamic interdependence of them all within the total situation . . . To explain social change we must always relate events to the order in which they occur. We must furthermore see the event as the culmination of a process or a new stage in the process.

To accept that explanation of the structure of social groups depends upon interaction is finally to accept that conjunctions depend upon actions and that by definition human groups consist of two or more persons. To accept that explanation of social change depends upon interaction is finally to accept that social processes are dynamic and that conjunction is defined in terms of action.

What causal analysts consider effects, then, in terms of interaction analysts are events within interaction; typically events which occur at the end of a group of interactions (Blumer, 1969: 54):

> The reluctance, and indeed the failure, of social scientists and psychologists to pay attention to the formation of social action by the acting unit is astonishing in view of the fact that such formation is what actually goes on in empirical social life. This failure is an interesting example of scholars being committed to a collective view, in this instance a view that sees social action as product and that jumps to antecedent factors as explanatory causes . . . social action must be studied in terms of how it is formed; its formation is a very different matter from the "causes" of the social action and is not covered by any specification of such causes.

This refracts Empiricus's objection to causal assumptions on the grounds that the separation of cause and effect is empirically impossible (Bury, 1933: 339):

> It is, for example, impossible to conceive the Cause before apprehending its effect as *its* effect; for we only recognize that it is causative of the effect when we apprehend the latter as effect. But we cannot either apprehend the effect of the Cause as *its* effect unless we apprehend the cause of the effect as *its* Cause; for we think we know that it is its effect only when we have apprehended the Cause of it as its Cause . . . the fallacy of this circular mode of reasoning proves both to be inconceivable . . .

Blalock's most often cited source in favor of causation is Bunge, who put our case beautifully (1959: 156):

> That causation is often a one-sided approximation to interaction is rather obvious in biology; and more so in social matters. Take sociopolitical ideologies: they grow in a given social and cultural matrix, they are effective solely to the extent to which they adapt themselves either to the prevailing social structure or to social movements engaged in attempting its modification; but besides being the children of objective social situations, ideologies may react back on the system of social relations in the midst of which they grow, helping either in the conservation or in the modification of the very conditions that had elicited their emergence . . . Despite the almost obvious fact that the various aspects of social life act upon one another, most sociological

theories and metahistories assert a one-way action of one of the factors over the remaining ones.

We should note in passing that MacIver's (1942), classic statement in favor of social causation is less susceptible to the criticisms noted here specifically because MacIver's argument is for interactive suppositions about relations, though he wants to consider these relations a 'causal nexus.' Throughout his book he calls for sociological research to concern itself primarily with interactive processes which are in a state of change. This is illustrated by his remarks about Weber's *Protestant Ethic* (1942: 177):

> [Weber] takes the position, for example, that the Protestant ethic was in a special way the solvent of the traditional restraints on business enterprise and monetary acquisition and thus a primary cause of the rise of capitalism in Western Europe and America. But it might easily be claimed that the rise of the Protestant ethic itself, with its stern individualism, its 'worldly asceticism,' and its doctrine of stewardship, was the expression in the religious sphere of a pervasive change of social attitudes corresponding it and causally interdependent with a changing socio-economic order.

Cause, interaction and dialectic

This reliance upon interaction can be grounded in a separate way as well. Within the Hegelian dialectic, cause and effect are two poles of an interaction category, or as Engels put it, cause and effect 'become confounded when we contemplate that universal action and reaction in which causes and effects are eternally changing places, so that what is effect here and now will be cause there and then, and vice versa.' Although Hegel recognized the mind as a decisive factor or primary agent, and his materialist followers often emphasized matter as a primary factor, causation is implied in their writings to be an antiquated concept in relation to specific types of interaction.

In a letter from Engels to Conrad Schmidt, this point was specified. Engels was replying to some of his critics (*Correspondence*, 484):

> What these gentlemen lack is dialectic. They never see anything but here cause and there effect. That this is a hollow abstraction, that such metaphysical polar opposites only exist in the real world during crises, while the whole vast process proceeds in the form of interaction (though of very unequal forces, the economic movement being by far the strongest, most elemental and most

decisive) and that here everything is relative and nothing is absolute – this they never begin to see. Hegel has never existed for them.

Hegelian and Marxist thinking emphasizes laws, but they are conceived in a manner not unlike what I will call essential interactionism. For Hegel the idea of law is primarily that of intrinsic or necessary connection which can be grasped through specific methods of reflecting. This becomes translated in some Marxist writing as depending upon dialectical thinking of development through thesis, antithesis, and synthesis. As will be seen in the following chapters, my call for essential interactionism accepts systematic modes of reflection in addition to the dialectical method. But the crucial point to be made now is that the dialectical assumption is not causalistic. 'Effect contains nothing whatever which Cause does not contain. Conversely Cause contains nothing which is not in its effect,' Hegel (1929: Vol. II) noted. He illustrated this with the case of rain which 'causes' dampness. The same water which is rain is dampness, and it is only by our convenient conventions of speaking that we can make the water at one time the cause and at the other the effect. 'The cause is no richer than the effect,' Hegel put it (1929: Vol. II). Hegelian and Marxist ideas of law rely upon necessary interactions which in the former are grounded conceptually or logically and in the latter are grounded historically.

These points can be demonstrated more clearly in relation to the foregoing discussion of the necessity for thinking in terms of action when talking about causation. As noted there, the 'visualization' occurring in causal thinking is that of manipulation of parts: 'If I change A, then B will change.' Such thinking boils down to inductive generalizations (predictions) established through observation, thought experiment or active experiment. Hegelian and most Marxist work does not predict in this way, but rather attempts understanding of the nature of the case at hand.[6]

Objections

This interactionist assumption may be disputed in at least four ways. First, it may be that action cannot be understood unless causation is already understood, given that a part of my argument holds that action emerges as the empirical aspect of causation. To this I would reply that action is what can be pointed to in conjunctions *regardless* of whether or not these conjunctions were originally labeled as causal. In addition, the history of causation can also be read as suggesting the possibility of radical change. Is the change from conceiving causation as guilt to conceiving it as natural order any less extreme than the change from natural order to action?

The second objection is that some conjunctions we consider causal do not involve action by any conceivable agent. Consider, for example, 'the tides are caused by gravitational forces of the moon.' Can we imagine controlling the gravitational pull of the moon (Taylor, 1967)? In fact we do conceive of the moon pulling the tides only in terms of our own experiences of gravitation. We experience the pull of gravity on our bodies and can imagine the tides being so pulled as well. We know that with the proper manipulation we can remove ourselves from the pull of gravity, and we can imagine the same being applied to the tides. Our very notions of 'pull,' 'force,' etc. are derived from that which we ourselves do.

The third objection concerns the move from action to interaction. I have argued that what we can point to in conjunctions and other types of processes is action, and that the social depends upon more than one person, consequently a relational concept which can be grounded for sociology is interaction. But what about those social situations in which one person or one group is doing all or nearly all of the acting, and the other persons or groups are largely recipients of those actions? When a dictator rounds up a group of people and kills them, where is the interaction?

This third point is the central one raised by Bunge (1959: Chapter 6), against interactionism as a universal relational assumption. He wants to use the case of 'irreversible productivity' to demonstrate that causal assumptions are sometimes necessary for adequate understanding. It is readily apparent, however, that even within such conjunctions we cannot point to causes in any manner, only to actions, though they may seem to be unidirectional. Hence, my position and Von Wright's concerning action as the primary concept for empirical inquiries still holds.

But this objection does throw into question the *inter*actionist argument. It is difficult, however, to think of unidirectional relations in *social* life, even if they do exist elsewhere. Unidirectional relations would seem to entail a type of dictatorship. But dictators must employ agents to carry out their plans. Once these intermediaries are involved, who have the freedom and machinery to accomplish their missions, the intermediaries can turn against the dictator as well. Alistair McIntyre argues that this is why it was inevitable that Bukharin and Rabovsky were accompanied in their mission against Stalin by police chiefs Yagoda and Yezhov.

Some might argue that social structures also achieve unidirectional relations upon persons and groups. Our earlier discussion would suggest, in contrast, that such assumed determinism of social structures is actually a description of persons redirecting their actions into those activities which support and reproduce the routines we call 'structures.'[7]

Probably Boguslaw's (1965) concepts of established and emergent situations are the relevant ones for putting this third objection into perspective. In established situations of unidirectional action, it would make no sense to attempt to understand via interactionist assumptions. But since no situations remain established or arise already established, there is, within every 'established' situation, emergence. Within emergence one inevitably finds interactional relations.[8]

The fourth criticism of interactionism will require a radical revision in the way in which sociology has typically employed interactionist assumptions, and in large part the remainder of this volume is devoted to suggesting that revision.

This criticism was noted early by Sextus Empiricus (Bury, 1933: 337):

> if cause were non-existent everything would have been produced by everything and at random. Horses, for instance, might be born, perchance, of flies, and elephants of ants.

From before Empiricus's time to the present the major relational and deterministic concept has been causation. Equally true, however, is that during all of this time causation has been inadequate for these purposes. As Empiricus put it, 'A cause is no more existent than non-existent' (Bury, 1933: 343).

I have argued that interactionism can be empirically grounded and is a viable alternative relational concept to causation. But how can it deal with determinism: how can it explain why horses are not born of flies and elephants of ants? Some varieties of interactionism *cannot* deal with such questions, as the next chapter will indicate for forms of symbolic interactionism.

2 Symbolic and essential interactionisms

The type of interactionism I will develop throughout this book emerged out of experiences with symbolic interactionism. Rather than reiterate the central tenets of symbolic interactionism, which I accept, the following discussion is intended to point out some places in the works of Mead, Blumer and their followers in which some issues are inadequately considered. My central concern is that regular or essential features of social phenomena have been ignored or relativized at times by symbolic interactionists. This I discuss via considerations of idealism, symbolism, and determinism in some major symbolic interactionist works. This discussion is intended as an introduction to the types of concerns which are addressed at length by the revised form of interactionism, essential interactionism.

Idealism

Symbolic interactionists have been known to posit a sociologists' version of Bishop Berkeley's sort of idealism, which holds that all we know of objects is the idea we have of them. Berkeley appropriately named his philosophy immaterialism, or a world conceived without matter. When logically extended (first by Fichte), an end is subjective idealism which holds that the universe is nothing but my own mind and its ideas; or when 'socialized,' the world is nothing but *our* ideas or definitions of it (Blumer, 1959: 10–11).

> The position of symbolic interactionism is that the 'worlds' that exist for human beings and for their groups are composed of "objects" and that these objects are the product of symbolic interaction. An object is anything that can be indicated, anything that is pointed to or referred to . . . The nature of an object – of

any and every object – consists of the meaning that it has for the person for whom it is an object.

Idealism has been throughout the recent history of thought an alternative to materialism, the doctrine that to understand the world one must understand the nature of objects apart from minds. The difficulty with choosing in every case to conduct inquiries from either idealistic or materialist assumptions is to ignore that both can be demonstrated faulty to some extent, just as both can 'prove' themselves. The case against strict materialism was most thoroughly presented by Hume, who demonstrated that all we directly experience is our mind. 'We have no perfect idea of anything but of a perception. We have, therefore, no idea of a substance,' Hume wrote. But then, the materialist retort has pointed out that idealists are too certain of the validity of their perceptions, which may be the result of the material world in the first place and at the least are often changed by the world outside of oneself.

That both sides of the question have worth is also suggested by the vigor and dedication with which they are proposed throughout the history of thought. The pertinent and difficult question becomes one of determining how far to go with each, under which conditions, and in what manner.

To avoid confronting this issue by instead taking a firm side results in positions which can quite easily be demonstrated inadequate. For instance, when Blumer argues that 'the environment consists *only* of the objects that the given human beings recognize and know,' he falls into this kind of error. Whether or not a person knows she is amid bacteria or not, she may well become ill as a result of having interacted with them. Whether or not a German Jew recognized or knew Hitler, he was likely to become dead or harmed as a result of Hitler.

Blumer's out-of-hand idealism contradicts itself, even within single paragraphs (1969: 22):

> The traditional position of idealism is that the "world of reality" exists only in human experience and that it appears only in the form in which human beings 'see' that world. I think this position is incontestable . . . the empirical world can 'talk back' to our pictures of it or assertions about it – talk back in the sense of challenging and resisting, or not bending to, our images or conceptions of it.

If the worlds exist only in our experiences as we see them, what's doing the talking back to us?

Symbolism

A difficulty with symbolic interactionism is the first word of its name. Charles Morris notes this in his introduction to Mead's *Mind, Self and Society* (1934: xiv):

> There is a question whether in identifying mind with the operation of symbols it must be held that such symbols are all language symbols of a social-vocal origin. If this is not so there may be individual aspects of mind in men and animals that do not come within the scope of Mead's terminology. In current terms, the question is as to the generic priority of sign-situations (non-language symbols) and symbol-situations.

The gist of the symbolic interactionist argument is that social reality grows out of social process. As my foregoing discussion should have made clear, I not only agree with this, but consider it an important discovery and in contrast with mistaken concepts currently used by other sociologists. But to concern oneself largely with verbal symbolism is to ignore many other aspects of interactions. Interactions consist of at least the following: events, states, phenomena, and processes. None of these can be reduced completely to analysis of symbols. Processes consist of phenomena within various events, which at each point make up an existing state amid other states.

Indeterminism

Consider the following statement from Blumer (1969: 12):

> Objects have no fixed status except as their meaning is sustained through indications and definitions that people make of the objects. Nothing is more apparent than that objects in all categories can undergo change in their meaning. A star in the sky is a very different object to a modern astrophysicist than it was to a sheepherder of biblical times; marriage was a different object to later Romans than to earlier Romans; the president of a nation who fails to act successfully through critical times may become a very different object to the citizens of his land. In short, from the standpoint of symbolic interactionism human group life is a process in which objects are being created, affirmed, transformed and cast aside.

This relativism of symbolic interactionism is very important in contrast to static sociologies. But in Blumer's deterministically obscure form it neglects that social phenomena have genetic-like compositions, which prescribe their potential for social status within bounds. To make this clear, we need only exchange the locations of some of the items Blumer mentions. Although what he says about stars, marriages and presidents is true enough, can a star ever become a marriage, or a president a marriage, or a sheepherder a star, and so forth? Positions such as Blumer's have been termed 'mereological inessentialism' by Chisholm, who notes that such positions are manifestly absurd (1973: 584):

> This would be the view that, for any whole w, w could be made up of any two things whatever. For, given such a view, one could say, of *this table*, that it could have been made up of the number 36 and the property blue.

A sociological equivalent would be to say of capitalism that it could have been made up of equality and a non-competitive economy. The point to be made is that objects are determined by social processes within the bounds set by their essential natures.

The neglect of essentialism by Blumer also leads to a very inadequate way of dealing with interaction patterns which remain stable or which repeat themselves (1969: 18):

> We have to recognize that even in the case of pre-established and repetitive joint action each instance of such joint action is to be formed anew . . . Repetitive and stable joint action is just as much a result of an interpretative process as is a new form of joint action that is being developed for the first time.

Blumer ignores the feature of social life which J. L. Moreno (1953), appropriately termed 'cultural conserves.' Although it is often true that people decide which conserves to use, or whether or not to use conserves at all, this is the case only for some people under some circumstances. Moreno correctly noted that creativity and spontaneity are to be developed and trained, and that persons do not by any means act creatively from their capacities for spontaneity in all of their affairs. Persons sometimes use cultural conserves for conducting interpretive processes themselves and for negotiating what will become social facts. Indeed, repetitive and stable joint actions are characterized by the use of cultural conserves, and they are often best understood as such. To understand the everyday workings of a bureaucracy, for example, is to understand the repetitive processes at work repeating repetitive processes. The line workers who start 'interpreting' these are likely to find themselves fired for inefficiency or disrespect. The pertinent questions are why and how interpretative processes and cultural conserves exist in given periods and states.

Likewise, Blumer is wrong in a crucial respect when he extends his 'no fixed status' thesis to groups (1969: 19):

A network or an institution does not function automatically because of some inner dynamics or system requirements; it functions because people at different points do something, and what they do is a result of how they define the situation in which they are called on to act.

Although the first part of this statement is supportable, the second part is true only within a range of possibilities. At any given time, in light of the essential properties of the phenomena with which they are working, people can define within only a given range. On an obvious level this is exemplified by the fact that a line worker in a factory either works in the ways he is expected to work or is somehow demoted, regardless of how he defines the situation. To tell him he has equal definitional power with the bosses may seem humanistic at first blush, but it is dishonest. Although through political organizing he may in fact be able to change the conditions by changing definitions of the situation, to inform him that what he does is the result of how he defines the situation is to tell him a dishonest truth. The more honest approach (and thereby the more humanistic) is to tell him the parameters of his powers and those of his bosses and the possible processes which are open to him and those being used upon him.

At a more basic level, Blumer's error can be demonstrated by another type of example. I may go to the store because I define that action as necessary to obtain food to keep me alive. Or I may go to the store because I feel like taking a walk. My outward behaviors may be exactly the same in each case. I may put on the same shoes, walk at the same pace, buy the same number of items, and think the same thoughts. Although there is a kernel of truth to the proposal that I do what I do because of the way I define the situation, explanations of this variety in some circumstances do not give very deep explanations or exclude possibilities.

When these difficulties with idealism, symbolism and determinism in symbolic interactionism are carried over to actual theories and research, they are compounded. An example is the case of labeling theory, which despite its critics (ranging from Marxists to positivists to phenomenologists) has been able to sustain itself. In some ways labeling theorists necessarily make mistakes and miss important features of the social worlds they study. The most blatant of these errors occurs when labeling theorists posit that deviance is 'whatever social processors define it to be,' and thereby imply that it can be anything. This position cannot be maintained, and consequently labeling theorists resort to poorly grounded determinations of labeling. These have tended to be whatever is most immediate in the small-scale social interaction the labeling theorist investigates, or whatever the official version may be. Consequently labeling theorists have been criticized along these lines:

> it does not see deviance as deriving from specified master institutions of this larger society, or as expressing an active opposition to them (Gouldner, 1968: 107).

> writers of this field still do not try to relate the phenomenon of 'deviance' to larger social, historical, political, and economic interests. The emphasis is still on the 'deviant' and the 'problems' he presents to himself and others, not on the society within which he emerges and operates (Liazos, 1972: 104).

> by locating deviance in 'traditional' areas, labeling sociologists take the perspective of officials. They further take the perspective of officials by defining deviance as what officials perceive as deviance . . . (Warren and Johnson, 1972: 81).

Works such as *Wayward Puritans* (Erikson, 1966), and *Boys of Boise* (Gerassi, 1966), were largely labeling in their perspectives and concerned themselves with larger institutions and with labeling by persons other than officials. Nevertheless, labeling studies have tended to concentrate on traditional areas of deviance and upon official labeling (Warren and Johnson, 1972).

Concurrently, labeling theorists necessarily place great force in labels, and as their parent symbolic interactionism would dictate, they tend not to search for which types of power the label has, but to attach causal power to the label. Within labeling theory the label is still thought of as a cause and the resulting deviant behavior as an effect. It is interesting that this state of affairs could arise, in light of leading symbolic interactionists' cautions against causal analyses (e.g. Blumer, 1969: 57). But it is quite understandable that such a position continues, given that symbolic interactionism offers no more acceptable way for dealing with determinism.

In addition, labeling theorists do not recognize much of what inheres in labeling, largely as a result of their over emphasis on symbolism to the exclusion of essential features of interactions. Among the assumptions they have held without adequate support are the following: (1) that rules are enforced against only actual (or perceived) deviants; (2) that successful labeling effects only those labeled; and (3) that whether the label 'sticks' depends primarily on the interaction which occurs between the designated recipient of the label and those involved in the application. A difficulty with these positions was noted by Thio (1973: 7):

> when a small minority of powerless people are successfully

labeled as deviants . . . by the law enforcers, the majority of powerless people are likely to be labeled by the general public as potentially deviant when compared to the powerful.

A search for the essential features of 'label' would likely avoid these sorts of errors. The label is not some vague symbolic object out in the world, which persons construct anew out of equally vague social interactions. It is employed in specific types of interactions, under specific conditions, and in specific ways.

By shifting to essential concerns, one can locate missing links in the labeling perspective. An example is *potential labeling* (Glassner and Corzine, 1978). Labeling is a social tool which actors can use as they deem appropriate, and they can use it in a variety of ways. By thinking of labeling in terms of potential labeling, we are offered a link for the study of deviance among different social classes. While members of the upper classes are not typically redefined as deviant, even when the criminal law is breached (Sutherland, 1949; Geis, 1968), evidence indicates that they do employ similar methods of masking their questionable activities as do members of the lower classes. Documented cases include price fixing in the electrical industry (Schur, 1969), and the Watergate conspirators. Many of the actions of both Richard Nixon and the closet homosexual can be better understood in terms of responses to the potential that they will be labeled.

Another line of critique also points at problems within symbolic interactionism. Causal analysts and macro theorists have been fond of accusing symbolic interactionists of ignoring the regularities and relationships within mass societies, in order to concentrate on small group interactions (Glassner, 1976b). This critique was specified by Gouldner (1970), Liazos (1972), and I. Taylor *et al.* (1974), in relation to symbolic interactionists' ignorance of the role which powerful elites play in controlling small group interactions by controlling society's central master institutions. Recently, some symbolic interactionists have set out to demonstrate that they are not compelled to ignore such features. Among the efforts is Harvey Farberman's (1975), excellent participant observation study, 'A Criminogenic Market Structure: The Automobile Industry.' Farberman found specific ways in which the largest Detroit automobile manufacturers compelled low level employees at their dealerships to engage in fraudulent service operations, kickback systems and 'short sales.'

In terms of further specifying how alienation and crime are inherent in this market structure, Farberman's paper is invaluable. But the paper does not tell us about the regularities of this market structure, or to be more accurate, it cannot tell us the essences of the market structure, or even the essences of crime and alienation in the particular market. For all we know from the paper, the activities described may be flukes within a particular state of capitalism. This is evident in several ways. Most simply, the practices Farberman uncovered may disappear entirely within several months, and then his symbolic interactionist research serves no purpose beyond temporary description, and it would be necessary to go back to the field to find the new features every time things changed. Additionally, if one notes carefully Farberman's text, it is apparent that these practices were occurring, as far as the author can specify, at no more than 20 per cent of the agencies studied.

Farberman's paper clearly contains more explanatory power than would a study which correlated crimes with agencies or types of market structures (and would probably conclude that the relationship is 'insignificant'). It also gives us several ideas about the nature of crime within capitalism. But the paper does not reach the type of strong explanation which tells us, e.g. the necessity of crime as a defining characteristic of this market structure.

Mead

The purpose of this critique has been to introduce the importance of conducting essential analyses as part of interactionist research. This has been attempted through some criticisms of major practitioners of symbolic interactionism.

It should be noted, however, that the difficulties found among practicing symbolic interactionists do not necessarily inhere in the work of George Herbert Mead. Space does not permit an adequate analysis of Mead's work relating to these points; but let me offer a series of his statements to illustrate how they differ from some contemporary practices.[1]

Idealism Mead seems an idealist of a different sort than those noted above, if he can be classified as an idealist at all (1934: 122f and 188):

> The meanings of things or objects are actual inherent properties or qualities of them; the locus of any given meaning is in the thing which, as we say, 'has it'.

(This is an excellent statement for the importance of conducting inquiries into essences.)

> I want to avoid the implication that the individual is taking something that is objective and making it subjective. There is an actual process of living together on the part of all members of the

community which takes place by means of gestures. The gestures are certain states in the co-operative activities which mediate the whole process. Now, all that has taken place in the appearance of the mind is that this process has been in some degree taken over into the conduct of the particular individual.

On the other hand, statements such as the following may lead to the kind of idealism we have noted by Mead's followers (1938: 417):

> The living being acts to reach a certain result in the future, the realization of its act. In this action it may be said to select its own time system and the space that this involves. It thus determines the world within which it lives.

Symbolism One would be hard pressed to argue that Mead did not emphasize the importance of symbolism; it was a major concern of his life's work. But there are indications that he saw the importance of conducting inquiries into essences as part of this concern. For example (1934: 146):

> Our symbols are all universal. You cannot say anything that is absolutely particular; anything you say that has any meaning at all is universal. You are saying something that calls out a specific response in anybody else provided that the symbol exists for him in his experience as it does for you.

Determinism Mead recognizes determination as arising from interactions (1938: 153):

> The individual and society are selectively and causally determinative of the environment, and this determines the individual or the society – neither can be explained in terms of the other except as the other is determined by it. The attempt to proceed otherwise leads to an impossible solipsism or to an equally impossible determinism.

He sees uniformities as inherent features of reality, but ones which must be dug out (1936: 479):

> To have uniformity you must have it in that which is not uniform; that which the genius of research is able to get out of the world are uniformities in the midst of that which is not uniform. You cannot have the one without the other.

Essential interactionism

We have noted that interactions consist at least of the following: events, states, phenomena, and processes. Interactions may be described as processes made up of phenomena within various events, which at each point make up states amid other states.[2] Causal (correlational) analysis locates particular local states, taking phenomena for granted. For instance, correlational analysts have examined the conjunctions of frustration, race, socio-economic position, educational attainment, marginality, etc. with prejudice. In so doing, they take these phenomena for granted and do not study them in-themselves, but rather construct operational definitions of the terms being correlated, in order to concentrate on the direction, type and magnitude of the conjunctions. On the other hand, from their idealism, emphasis on verbal symbols, and indeterminism, symbolic interactionists underemphasize phenomena. This was dramatized for the author when one of America's best-known symbolic interactionists informed him in a private conversation, 'You cannot study prejudice, only settings and symbols in which prejudice exists.'

Both correlational analysis and symbolic interactionism assume implicity that we already know about the phenomena which the former finds constantly conjoined and which the latter finds within events. But it is impossible to learn about a phenomenon itself by seeing only how it interacts with other phenomena. We also require understanding of phenomena themselves—of their composition and possibilities. To do this we must look for the essential make-up of phenomena, and hence I call the enterprise essential interactionism. This endeavor is a systematic attempt to accomplish the old ontological dictum that 'the knowledge of possibilities must precede that of actualities.'

An appreciation of the need for essential interactionism sheds some light on why so much theorizing based primarily upon correlational analysis is so easily replaceable. Thus, the history of social science theories concerning prejudice reveals that a new theory of prejudice develops every time prejudice manifests itself in a slightly different manner from its previous exhibition. Through an essentialist understanding of prejudice we can hope to avoid this syndrome of dealing solely with manifestations of a phenomenon rather than with the phenomenon itself. Through essential interactionism we can see that what we find at the moment to be 'the real social world' is only a special case of possible social worlds.[3]

part two

Method

Customary 'how to' manuals are usually insulting, but wise 'how to' manuals seldom teach how to.

Introduction

This Part will propose a strategy for essential interactionist research into pervasive social phenomena which have been widely studied by other types of researchers in the past. Part III will then apply this strategy to the social phenomenon of prejudice.

Clearly this is not the only sort of research which can or should be conducted by essential interactionists, and I trust that methodological strategies for other sociological concerns will be developed.[1] Chapter 3 is intended to be useful for such future methods for essential interactionism as well as for development of the immediate methodological strategies. The chapter is devoted to general and impressionistic discussions of some major entities and procedures which seem important for any sort of essential interactionist methodology.

Chapter 4 translates the general concerns into a strategy for conducting research upon large bodies of material from previous (not essential interactionist) researchers. The goal will be to offer a strategy for producing grounded theory from these desperate and often conflicting earlier works, to re-utilize literature.

This strategy for essential interactionism is finally a methodological heuristic. Parallel efforts include C. Taylor's (1971), attempt to determine intersubjective assumptions within a pattern of social practice; etymological studies of social scientific concepts; and development of a formal lexicon for social science based upon rules for the admission of primitives into a system (thus far an unpublished effort by Professors Richard H. Rudner, Robert Wolfson and Robert Barrett).

The project of the present book owes its intellectual allegiances primarily to Aristotelian and Husserlian notions of essences as those elements without which the phenomenon cannot be imagined. We do not concern ourselves with ontological problems of essentialism in its various forms. Thus, the discussions of Husserl's eidetic and transcendental reductions are not considerations or critiques of Husserl's endeavors, but are used to develop our unique form of essentialism. The goal is to devise a strategy for locating essences of social phenomena, by looking closely at the (perhaps unconscious) agreements among a variety of uses of a phenomenon by social scientists and persons they study. We seek to elicit intellectual consistency.

3 General considerations

Once one's goal becomes that of describing the essences of something there are few places to turn for methodology. As we have seen both causal and interactionist methodologists have taken for granted social phenomena and their compositions. A movement within Western thought which has concentrated, in contrast, upon internal understanding of phenomena has been phenomenology, and for this reason I have turned especially to phenomenology in developing this method for essential interactionism.

Although the term phenomenology was used as early as 1765 and appears several times in Kant's writings, it did not obtain a technical meaning or come to be practised until Hegel. Hegel's concern was essentially that of reaching Absolute Mind, or as he phrased it, *Phenomenology of Mind*. Some of the preceding and some of the following discussions rely upon Hegel's insights. However, when contemporaries speak about phenomenology, the central figure is Edmund Husserl, who formally laid out what phenomenology would look like in practice and conducted a variety of phenomenological inquiries into consciousness and into phenomenology itself.[1]

Within sociology, phenomenology has a long history. In addition to having its impact on others' sociologies (notably that of Georges Gurvitch), early phenomenological sociologists produced complete works of their own. Among these are Alfred Vierkandt's *Natural and Cultural Peoples* (1895), and *Theory of Society* (1922), and Theodor Litt's *Individual and Society* (1919). At present phenomenological sociology is usually associated with the work of Alfred Schutz and those who have been influenced by his work (e.g. Harold Garfinkel). These movements have been concerned almost exclusively with investigating meaning in order to understand social life.

Although Husserl emphasized the importance of meanings, this was not the central focus of his phenomenology.[2] Throughout Husserl's work the goal was to determine methods for conducting inquiries into the essences of phenomena, and to conduct such inquiries. Husserl's own essence inquiries were for the most part into consciousness, and during these inquiries he argued that 'everything else *has* meaning; the ego, through its conscious intentionality, *bestows* meaning' (Carr, 1977). Husserl identified such concepts as the following: 'intersubjectivity,' the radical possibility of seeing as another or others sees; 'intentionality,' the necessity for consciousness always to be directed toward something; 'constitution,' the make-up of thought objects; and 'the life world,' the everyday world in which persons (and consciousnesses) operate. These essences can be studied via investigations of meanings held by persons and groups within social worlds. As a leading textbook for this sort of phenomenological sociology put it (Phillipson, 1972: 87):

> If one adopts the position that the peculiar character of the social world, that which differentiates it from the object – or natural-world, is its inherent meaningfulness, then this not only directs attention to the central subject matter and problems for sociology but at the same time provides a criterion for judging the range of competing sociological perspectives. The ontological presuppositions of phenomenological philosophy, posit of a social world constituted and sustained through meaning . . .

A defect of some meaning-centered sociological literature is that meanings are viewed as the supreme determiners of social life. As noted in Chapter 1, although W. I. Thomas was correct that men's definitions of reality are real in important ways, this is only one side of a dialectical dictum. Even when men define something as *unreal*, if it has essential reality it will have consequences for them. No matter how desperately some groups of German Jews initially defined Hitler's power as inconsequential, it was consequential.

While essential interactionism does not deny the importance of meaning, it attempts to look at the other essences of social life in addition to meanings. In short, 'phenomenological sociology' has often been limited to investigations of some of the essences identified by Husserl, while essential interactionism is Husserlian-based in its search for essences.

A general introduction to phenomenology would be impossible here in fewer than several hundred pages,[3] and such an introduction is not my intention in this chapter. Rather, I hope to present general considerations of method for essential interactionism. Many of these considerations derive directly from Husserlian phenomenology, but thinkers as possibly distant from Husserl as Nelson Goodman, Aristotle, and Marx will play significant roles in the development of these methods.

Expanding empiricism

A major goal of essential interactionism is to provide an expanded empiricism. To sociologists who have been blinded by correlational empiricism and have come to believe that it is the only possible variety, a proposed expansion of empiricism may seem at first a proposal to *abandon* empiricism. Actually the thrust of phenomenological analysis throughout its history has been a two-fold strategy for refining empiricism. The negative side of this strategy consists of turning away from crystallized beliefs and theories handed down by tradition, in J. L. Moreno's terms, away from 'cultural conserves' of the sciences and social sciences. This means a scrupulous identification and deliberate elimination of existing constructs in order to return to the phenomenon itself. Such an emancipation from preconceptions is a very difficult matter indeed, as will be made clear in the chapters describing specific strategies for accomplishing this feat. A complete accomplishment of the task is impossible, of course, and this is recognized even before a strategy is presented. But this impossibility is built into the strategy and partially ovecome by way of a constant meta analysis procedure.

The positive side of phenomenology's strategy for refined empiricism consists of its own ways of turning back toward the phenomenon in order to investigate it in particular, its general essence, the essential relationships among essences, its modes of appearing, its constitution in consciousness and in the lifeworld, and its meaning (Spiegelberg, 1965: 656–9).

Traditional empiricism takes for granted that a small group of experience types (usually experimentation and correlation) are appropriate for investigating all types of phenomena. In contrast, a phenomenologically directed empiricism tries to determine the appropriate use of appropriate methods according to the nature of the phenomenon being investigated and the nature of the methods (*Ideas*, 78):

> If by *Positivism* we are to mean the absolute unbiased grounding of all science on what is 'positive,' i.e., on what can be primordially apprehended, then it is *we* who are the genuine positivists. In fact we permit *no* authority to deprive us of the right of recognizing all kinds of intuition as equally valuable

sources of the justification of knowledge, not even that of 'modern natural science'.

Some traditional empiricists have criticized phenomenology on the ground that intuition cannot provide useful data. The point at issue is what Spiegelberg (1965: Chapter 659), calls 'the sense organ bias of traditional empiricism.' This bias consists of eliminating from one's inquiries anything which cannot be assigned to a specific sense organ of humans' biological makeup. Spiegelberg notes physical phenomena such as force and distance perception as examples which have been studied phenomenologically and the research has been rejected by traditional empiricists on the basis that sense organ data was not that which was chiefly employed in the inquiries.[4]

In the social sciences an excellent case is the phenomenon under scrutiny in the following chapters, that of prejudice. As will be repeatedly pointed out, traditional empiricists have studied prejudice solely from their sense organ biases, while prejudice is clearly a phenomenon of consciousnesses. Although behaviors such as discrimination may be investigated by seeing and hearing what people do, this provides only one aspect of the phenomenon of prejudice.

Simply put, essential interactionism recognizes that there is more to experiencing of evidences than traditional empiricists have accepted. When I intuit something I am experiencing a type of evidence. Indeed, I am 'seeing' perhaps the most immediate evidence available to me.

Husserl's notion of intuition is different in two ways, however, from that of the conventional use of the term. First he specifies systematic routes to intuition; and second, his aim through these methods is to allow the thing under investigation to present itself as clearly as possible. The fundamental call from Husserl is to be as attentive to the item under investigation as possible, without prejudgments of theories, in order to let the thing present itself to one's mind. Husserl denied both the image and sign theories, which state that we have available to us only images or signs of things, not the things themselves. He insisted that we are consciously aware of a thing in its embodied forms, that 'we are not given an image or sign in its place' (1962: Section 43).

Intuitions bcome very important when we recognize that they are the building blocks for any type of analysis whatsoever. Thus, induction must rely upon something which is given to us in intuition or the memory of something previously given to us in intuition. Likewise, verification relies upon intuitions, because the verifier is intersubjectively checking whether to accept the intuitions of the original researcher (1970b, Section 34). It therefore becomes crucial that we be especially careful about our intuitions in any inquiry, at least as careful as about the second order uses to which we put them.

How subjective is phenomenology?

The talk above (and throughout Husserl's *Crisis*) of objective reality may make phenomenology sound totally subjectivistic. Introductory sociology texts refer to phenomenology as subjectivism. Actually, Husserl never denies objective reality, though he does take a critical look at previous notions of objectivity (1962: 14) and (1970b: 96):

> Our phenomenological idealism does not deny the positive existence of the real world and of Nature – in the first place as though it held it to be an illusion. Its sole task and service is to clarify the meaning of this world, the precise sense in which everyone accepts it, and with undeniable right, as really existing.

> What is, in respect to sense and validity, the 'objective world,' objectively true being, and also the objective truth of science, once we have seen universally with Hume (and in respect to nature even with Berkeley) that 'world' is a validity which has sprung up within subjectivity, indeed – speaking from my point of view, who am now philosophizing – one which has sprung up within *my* subjectivity, with all the content it ever counts as having for me?

Probably the clearest notion of the Husserlian position on the subjective-objective question is Spiegelberg's (1973), which holds that phenomenology's type of subjectivity is that of *subject-related*. This usage is rather different from the two more common usages: the merely personal (varying from person to person); and dependent upon a subject (without a subject objects cannot exist). Subject-related suggests the interwoven nature of the subjective-objective 'split,' and is well compared to an image in a mirror, which is dependent upon the subject but also upon the object.

One who reads bits and pieces of Husserl's work is not likely to find such a clear usage of subjectivity and objectivity, however, because this weaving of the two poles was a lifetime dialectic for Husserl. In his earlier works, the focus was upon ways in which we conceive the objective world. This continues in the *Crisis* as well, but in new ways. History becomes important in *Crisis* as Husserl traces the conversion in Greece of notions of 'knowledge' and 'truth' into those of 'objective truth,' which in the modern period becomes further transformed as that which is the product of universal science (Section 33). At the same time, Husserl emphasizes that scientific work and products must come from, and thereby be grounded in, the everyday world of experiences and what we take to be self-evidences, but that this is a dialectical truth, because science and scientists are also part of (and producers of) the everyday world.

What emerges is this interwoven subject-relatedness. 'The concrete life-world; then, is the grounding soil of the "scientifically true" world and at the same time encompasses it in its own universal concreteness' (1970b, 131). In other words, Husserl's view becomes a fusion of his early concerns with constitution and intentionality and his later investigation of science. The subject constitutes the world of objects, but does so through consciousness, which consists of *essential* structures. These essential structures are the same for all consciousness.[5] Hence, the 'merely personal' conception of subjectivity becomes inaccurate, and the "subject-dependent" conception becomes a sub-possibility within the 'subject-related' conception (Spiegelberg, 1973).

Phenomenologically oriented work (such as essential interactionism) is left, then, with a task far more difficult than a 'subjectivistic' discipline might entail. We must determine intersubjectively valid essential structures.

What are essences?

The best image I have been able to locate of 'essence' appears on the first page of Husserl's preface to the English edition (1962: 5):

> Whatever facts present themselves serve only as examples similar in their most general aspect to the empirical illustrations used by mathematicians; much, in fact, as the actual intuitable dispositions of numbers on the abacus assist us, in their merely exemplary capacity, to grasp with insight, and in their pure generality the series 2, 3, 4 . . . as such, pure numbers as such, and the propositions of pure mathematics relative to those, the essential generalities of a mathematical kind.

Essences are the immutable and necessary complex of characteristics without which the phenomenon cannot be conceived. These characteristics are not the phenomenon themselves, however (1962: 49). 'The Essence is an object of a new type. Just as the datum of individual or empirical intuition is an individual object, so the datum of essential intuition is a pure essence.'

It is important to note immediately, however, that essences are not the same as ideal types or as generalities. Husserl does not limit himself to talking about ideality or to opposing essences to the 'this-here.' He considers it inadequate to raise the individual phenomenon to the general or to the ideal.[6] Rather, in the determinations of the phenomenon there is seen to be a hierarchy which has its own grades of clearness. In other words, the essences of a phenomenon are its necessary and immutable structure, not its ideal or general structure. The essences are what make the phenomenon what it is. The search for essences therefore becomes a kind of meta-empiricism: a search for that which is the principle of the phenomenon beneath its everyday properties.

A clear but simple example of these points about essences can be seen with the concept of sound. In order for a sound to have a determined intensity, timbre and pitch, it must possess the essences timbre, intensity and pitch. An essential interactionism would seek to specify these essences.

It may also be useful in this general introduction to put essences (and essential interactionism) into non-Husserlian terms. Within the history of Western philosophy, essentialism is usually traced to Aristotle, and defined as by Quine (1966b: 173):

> Aristotelian essentialism. This is the doctrine that some of the attributes of a thing (quite independently of the language in which the thing is referred to, if at all) may be essential to the thing and others accidental.

Aristotle in the *Posterior Analytics* defines science in terms of this essentialism (90b):

> Scientific knowledge is judgment about things that are universal and necessary, that the conclusions of demonstration and all scientific knowledge follow from the first principles.

Probably the most serious deficiency in Aristotle's essentialism from our view is his fusion of necessity and sufficiency. He ends up equating attributes whose retention is sufficient and those whose retention is necessary, to keep a thing in existence (N. White, 1973). Our own concern is to locate these necessary attributes and their essential configurations, and through an understanding of these to offer insights into the possibilities as well for the other (e.g. sufficient) attributes within the total phenomenon.

Some distinctions by N. Goodman (1951), also help place our discussion in perspective. Goodman notes first a distinction between phenomenalistic systems, which deal with what he calls qualia (qualitative elements), and physicalistic systems, which deal with things, processes, etc. In both cases, one employs perceptible individuals for achieving the analyses. Our research for essences is much like a search for qualia, and therefore within what Goodman calls the phenomenalistic tradition. Specifically, we fall into the second of Goodman's following types of phenomenalistic systems: realistic and particularistic. Realistic systems begin with qualia and attempt to build concrete individuals, while particularistic systems begin with concrete individuals and attempt to build qualia (Chapter IV). Goodman notes that both systems are appropriate strategies and probably compliment one another. In one case, we must force ourselves to abandon the habit of looking upon qualities as constituent parts of concreta and in the other we must force ouselves to regard qualia, which are in some regards less visible than concreta, as literal individuals (Chapter VI).

But to regard qualia as somehow less distinguishable than concreta Goodman correctly notes is difficult to defend. Although it is true that a quale cannot be lifted out of the stream of experience, it is also only through our convenient usage that we can think of so removing a concrete object. I can mentally just as completely remove the essence 'red' as I can remove an individual red object. In both cases I am still living in a stream of ongoing places, times, etc. I am just as capable of distinguishing one from the world around it as of distinguishing the other (148).

Objections to essences

The objection raised by relativists against essences is that what is found to be an essence by one person or one group is not so for another. The great lesson of cultural anthropologists during the first half of this century has been to demonstrate that the facts for one culture may be the fictions of another, and that the methods for verifying facts are likewise variable.

This position was adequately answered earlier in regard to symbolic interactionism, where I noted that in fact specific objects and processes do not become identified within an infinite range of possibilities, but rather within a finite range. This was phrased in more Husserlian terms by Strasser (1974: 75), when he noted that items have 'sides,' which permit them to appear differently to distinct persons. But it is demonstrated repeatedly in everyday experiments that through discussions persons can come to see additional 'sides' than the one(s) with which they begin. A Husserlian may certainly recognize that in everyday life persons may be aware of only a few of these essences, or may even consider as determining essences things which are not.

I reintroduce this discussion here to bring out a point which will become important in the next chapters: an excellent route to locating essences is through intersubjective experiences, or sharing others' subjective experiences and unique angles. As Husserl put it

(*Crisis*, 139), 'the lifeworld does have, in all its relative features, a *general structure*. This general structure, to which everything that exists relatively is bound, is not itself relative. We can attend to it in its generality and, with sufficient care, fix it once and for all in a way equally accessible to all.'

But these arguments against essences can be dismissed more directly. Those who argue against essences must rely upon essences. Symbolic interactionists find symbols and interactions to be the essences of social life. Similarly, functionalists find the organic analogy to be an essence of social life. Both admit to essences implicitedly, while rejecting them explicitely. As Paul Simon put it during his *Live Rhymin'* concert: 'After changes upon changes we are more or less the same.'

A related objection is that essences are 'merely concepts.' This objection holds that many different concepts can be identified as essences of a phenomenon, and that consequently essences are merely concepts. But such a critique ignores the point at issue. Certainly, of the number One I can have many concepts: O-n-e, U-n-o, An Apple, 1 . . . And these are 'mere concepts.' But behind them is the essence of One or the essences of One, to be determined through systematic investigations of necessary and immutable properties of One, which none of the above would fit (i.e. spelling varies according to language, an example is not a number, etc.).

Santayana answered these relativistic criticisms in a couple of separate ways (1927: 23 and 66):

> Essence so understood much more truly *is* than any substance or experience or any event: for a substance, event or experience may change its form or may exist only by changing it, so that all sorts of things that are proper to it in one phase will be absent from it in another. It will not be a unit at all, save by external delimitation . . . Essence is just that character which any existence wears in so far as it remains identical with itself and so long as it does so . . .

> By one of the uses or abuses of the word *is*, one thing is often said to be another. This absurdity (as a pure logician might think of it) flows out of the natural relation of essences with things and serves clumsily to express it. A thing naturally has many appearances – lights, sounds, temperatures, perspectives; and it may conventionally have many names. Each of these essences, as it crosses the field of intuition, is verbally identified with that thing; but good sense, unless a sophistical attempt at accuracy trips up its honest intentions, will easily see that none of these names or appearances *is* the existing thing . . .

Throughout the history of its usage, essentialism has frequently occurred in indefensible forms.[7] Among these are the spurious essentialisms of these arguments: (1) 'Jack is a teacher, necessarily teachers are degree holders, therefore Jack necessarily holds a degree;' and (2) 'The word "Homer," as we use it, connotes or intends being a person who wrote the *Iliad*; therefore Homer, if he existed, was such that he necessarily wrote the *Iliad*.'

Rather, we are speaking of what Chisholm calls 'mereological essentialism' (1973: 583):

> We are saying . . . that there exists an x, a y, and a z such that: x is identical with this table, y is identical with this stump, z is identical with this board, and x is such that, in every possible world in which x exists, it is made up of y and z.

This type of essentialism neither restates the obvious nor makes any claims about how humans may look upon the objects or phenomena in question, and consequently it says nothing about the ways in which people happen to describe the objects. And despite its immediate appearance, it does not suggest changelessness. At least four changes are possible: coming into being; passing away (wholes do both); joining together with other wholes; and disjoining to form separate wholes.

But, as Chisholm notes, even if we avoid spurious essentialism difficulties can be raised. These are basically of the form: 'My automobile has parts (or could have parts) it did not have last week. The principle of mereological essentialism implies that, if anything is ever a part of my automobile, then that thing is always a part of my automobile.'

Our reply is that this statement confuses essential and nonessential parts. To have made our statement above about the table was not to exclude the possibility that a, b, c . . . could not be the parts of *any* table. Rather, we were stating that our y and z could not be replaced by a, b, or c if we are still to have table x. The distinction is between what Chisholm calls 'part in the strict and philosophical sense,' and part in the popular sense. Of the automobile, if in fact we have argued successfully that a part is an essential one, and it has changed, then we would have to say that we then have a different automobile (or another different entity). As Chisholm sums up (1975: 481):

> The extreme form of the principle of merelogical essentialism (of strict parts) is quite compatible with the existence of vulgar objects and their inessential nonstrict parts. The important thing, if what I have said is correct, is that, even if there are the

common sense or vulgar objects, each of them is constituted by a nonvulgar primary object.

Essences in other inquiry strategies[8]

Blindness to ideas is a kind of psychic blindness, which through prejudices renders us incapable of bringing into the field of judgment what we have already in our field of intuition. Our critics in truth see, and so to speak continuously see, 'ideas,' 'essences' – make use of them in thought, formulate judgments concerning essences – only from their epistemological 'standpoints' they explain the same away. Self-evident data are patient, they let theories chatter about them, but remain what they are (*Ideas*, 80).

The earlier chapter on causation noted the dependence of causal analysts upon action. And a few pages back we noted some essences of symbolic interactionism and functionalism. Similarly, it can be seen in a more general way that inquiries which do not concern themselves with essences must depend upon essences.

The most general sense in which this is true is that noted by Husserl, that physical scientists take the world of everyday life as the 'forgotten sense foundation of physical science' (*Crisis*, 48). Husserl illustrates the importance of this point in several examples concerning Galileo's, Einstein's and Michelson's works. Thus, when Einstein repeats Michelson's experiments in his laboratory with instruments copied from those of Michelson, he takes for granted what these instruments are, what instruments are used for by humans generally, what a laboratory is, etc. All of this is based on his uncritical acceptance of aspects of the everyday world around him. We may wish to consider this acceptable for Einsteinian method, but we *cannot* consider his conclusions as grounded anywhere but in this everyday world that he accepts uncritically. (On the other hand, Einstein and the others are considered great contributors to human knowledge because so often they *do* place the commonsense assumptions in doubt; to develop new instruments, theories, etc.)

Husserl also notes this importance of taken-for-granted essences in his discussions of mathematics (throughout *Crisis*, notably Part II). As he puts it, (53), 'For in spite of all that is new (in modern physics), what is essential in principle, it seems to me, remains: namely, nature, which is in itself mathematical; it is given in formulae, and it can be interpreted only in terms of the formulae.' In Husserl's view what has made the great progress of modern physics possible is that Galileo, through systematic reduction, noticed that the ontology of nature is to be found in the geometry and mathematics developed in antiquity (see *Rigorous Science*).

Strasser (1974: Chapter 8) points out that another level at which essences are crucial to the scientist is at the point of presenting 'theoretical' (as opposed to 'substantive') findings. What these persons attempt to present are further specifications of assumed essences. For example, a sociologist of religion takes for granted that religion is 'functional' or 'the opium for the masses,' etc., and *then* makes theory about them. He talks about the ways in which it is functional or an opiate. This is perhaps the reason that many specifications of 'macro theories' can be rejected although the initial insight often cannot. We can reject extensions, specific researches or unsupported statements of a conflict theorist, for example, but we cannot reject the essence which conflict theory describes: that social life is regularly characterized by groups in battles with one another. In other words, most sociologists are attempting further specifications of essential insights, without recognizing them as essences among other essences.

More fundamentally, the very strategy in positing laws of deduction (*à la* Hempel) is founded upon intuition of essences. Levinas (1967) expressed this when he noted that 'the necessity of the conclusion of a syllogism is founded upon the formal essence of its premises in which it is grasped as evident.' Deduction consists of reducing a non-evident truth to a series of terms which are self-evident. We could say that the law view of science takes essences for granted, but relies upon them to build its highly valued products, its laws.

'Operationalizing'[9] also requires assumed essences. P. W. Bridgman (1954), the founder of operationalism, is simply suggesting essences when he operationalizes. For instance, he claims (91) that 'identity is determined by the operations by which we make the judgment that this object is the *same* as that one of my past experiences.' In so doing, he names sameness as an essence of identity. Or when he says (5) that 'the concept of length is . . . fixed when the operations by which length is measured are fixed' he is saying that being measurable is an essence of length. Further, by putting everything in terms of operations that are performed, he is positing that an essence of definition is operationalizability.

Bridgman takes many essences for granted. As Martin Heidegger (1962: 61f) notes, it is within taken-for-grantedness that one most appropriately searches for essences. Heidegger recognized that the apparent familiarity of something is a mask which conceals that entity from full view. Recognition of this fact requires one to embark upon a hermeneutic type of inquiry, or a systematic interpretation of the familiar which through its familiarity has become unknown.

4 Literature as sites

The method to be proposed in this chapter consists of a search for essences of interactions through other persons, of what Herbert Spiegelberg (1964) has named 'phenomenology through vicarious experience.' Such an investigation attempts an intersubjective appreciation of others' understandings of the phenomenon in order to develop and ground proposed essences.

Vicarious phenomenology

Phenomenology is customarily interpreted as the direct study of phenomena as given to the phenomenologist. Is it not true, then, that by attempting phenomenology through vicarious experience essential interactionism abandons the original project of phenomenology?

Perhaps the most accurate answer is that we do not abandon the original project any more than did Husserl himself. Husserl makes marvelous use of historical material for his own final work, the *Crisis*. More generally, in his meditations on the problem of intersubjectivity Husserl was unable finally to decide whether phenomenology has adequate direct access to others and their worlds or whether they are only indirectly presented by what is directly given (Spiegelberg, 1964). Husserl confronts these questions in the fifth of his *Cartesian Meditations* and in some material in *Husserliana I* (trans. Cairns, 1960). At some points he contends that the other person stands before us directly (1960: 124):

> What we really see is not a sign nor a mere analogon or in any ordinary sense a likeness . . . The other is seized in real originality.

This statement refracts his earlier statement about our access to things generally (1962: 123):

> The special thing which we see is, despite all its transcendence, perceived, we are consciously aware of it as given in its *embodied form*. We are not given an image or a sign *in its place*.

At other points, Husserl confesses (1960: 108f):

> it must be conceded that, properly speaking, it is not the other ego, his experiences and his phenomena which we are given originally, and that the givenness of the other in our intentional acts has a certain indirectness.

Spiegelberg has proposed a five-point program for going beyond Husserl's dilemma and giving phenomenologists some access to others' subjectivities, via a phenomenology of vicarious experience:

1 The investigator imagines himself as occupying the actual place of the other and tries to see the world as it would present itself from this other perspective.
2 This transposal is not merely a type of 'if I were you' seeing. Rather, one's original and historical self is left behind during the transposal. This may mean learning new abilities or abandoning existing ones.
3 The investigator must not attempt to 'go native.' Rather, he must move back and forth between his own place and understanding and that of the other. 'If we lost ourselves head over heels in his place we should no longer be expanding our phenomenological grasp.'
4 Clues are sought from the situation into which we have put ourselves imaginatively, in order to build the others' world and self as she is likely to do.
5 Throughout the process we must revise and reconsider our imaginative constructions in light of new clues from the other's behavior or our own constructions while trying to assume her perspective.

Social scientists will note that these steps which philosopher Spiegelberg describes read like textbooks on qualitative sociological or anthropological field methods, with the possible exception of the emphasis on imagination (discussed later in this chapter). The phenomenology of vicarious experience seems to be of necessity a type of fieldwork.

A fieldwork strategy: literature as sites

Let us consider two strategies for conducting phenomenology

through vicarious experience. The first is through fieldwork with persons who have experienced the phenomenon and been a part of it in various ways, eliciting understanding of the phenomenon in order to attempt to determine for oneself the essences of the phenomenon. Such a strategy would employ the traditional fieldwork methods, such as participant observations, interviewing, role-playing, etc. within a group or groups the researcher can adequately contend experience the phenomenon in its only forms. For example, to study the essences of homosexuality one might want to determine the variety of gay groups (closet, open, bar going, 'friendship group,' etc.) and enter these as a participant observer.

In many cases of essential interactionist research, however, such a strategy will not offer the researcher as many angles for examining the phenomenon as would another strategy. Where one is dealing with a large social phenomenon, which exists in a myriad of groups, historical times, and locations, a different type of research site may prove more appropriate. These sites consist of previous research concerning the phenomenon in question. As Glaser and Strauss (1967: 163), note:

> There are some striking similarities – sometimes obvious although often overlooked – between fieldwork and library research. When someone stands in the library stacks, he is, metaphorically, surrounded by voices begging to be heard. Every book, every magazine article, represents at least one person who is equivalent to the anthropologists' informant or the sociologists' interviewee. In those publications, people converse, announce positions, argue with a range of eloquence, and describe events or scenes in ways entirely comparable to what is seen or heard during field work.

Although this methodology is mentioned by Glaser and Strauss, its potential has not been explored beyond their initial descriptions, neither theoretically nor in actual fieldwork. Part III of the present work explicitly will consider previous research as the fieldwork sites. Proceeding from this assumption, qualitative fieldwork among these researchers will be undertaken, much in the traditional fashion (summarized by Bogdan and Taylor, 1975; Wax, 1971; Filstead, 1970; and others.)

Several important comparisons and contrasts are necessary between traditional fieldwork sites and the prejudice literature sites.

The prejudice literature sites differ from many traditional sites in that what is being attempted by social actors at the site is the handling of a single phenomenon: in this case prejudice. This contrasts markedly with such sites as street corners, bars, and neighborhoods, where many social phenomena dominate the interactions. The prejudice literature sites do resemble on this criterion some other traditional sites, however. Thus, an 'Alcoholics Anonymous' group is an example in which generally a single phenomenon is being dealt with, albeit in a variety of ways.[1]

Factions tend to emerge in almost all fieldwork settings as individuals come to perceive that they possess not only the principal phenomena in common, but also share with some of the other persons either external commonalities or similar perspectives on internal issues. Within the prejudice literature the parallel divisions are according to theories, with subdivisions such as 'socialization determinism,' 'neoFreudianism,' and 'Authoritarian Personality framework.'

A way in which literature sites compare favorably with traditional sites is in their ability to deal with historical questions. Traditional qualitative analysis has been criticized for being ahistorical. This is a problem which fieldworkers in literature sites can often avoid. The qualitative method demands that fieldworkers report primarily their first-hand involvement with people at the sites. Since fieldworkers in traditional sites are able to visit only those locales and groups existing during the time of the research, by definition they cannot report much about sites from other periods. Traditional fieldworkers are able to visit only those sites which are separated by space, not those separated by time. The researcher employing literature sites is able to visit historically separate sites as well.[2]

In the present case of prejudice sites, historical divisions may be quite important in trying to determine the essences of prejudice. Many of the theories arose largely in reaction to historical manifestations of prejudice: e.g. the theories involving *The Authoritarian Personality* (Adorno, 1950), were in large part reactions to Nazism, while 'shared coping' theories (Collins, 1970), developed amid the American civil rights and integration movements.

Literature sites also have inherent disadvantages. The prejudice literature sites were constructed by persons who often had cross-purposes to that of phenomenologically oriented fieldwork. Most of the sites were built by persons attempting to construct a positivistic environment. As Cicourel (1964), points out, this environment tends to include assumed correspondence between (1) indicators used by the man in the street to identify meaningful objects and events and those used by sociologists to so identify, and (2) the actor's point of view and the observer's point of view. In many cases, the only material remaining with which to participate and observe may be 'data collected such as to leave the respondent with no other possibility but to respond in terms of the options made available to him,' 'ambiguous responses fitted into the context of the observer's framework,' or 'glosses managed in terms of the interpretive procedures of the sociologist' (Walsh, 1972: 27).

To say the above is to say that the literature sites exhibit a specific variation of a common fieldwork problem. Sites are seldom if ever constructed with the fieldworker in mind. They are built by the participants, for the participants' own needs, upon the participants' own customs and languages. These features obligate the fieldworker to constantly translate back and forth among languages and to expect varieties of fabrications from participants' accounts. In the case of literature sites, however, one is usually unable to use such fieldwork methods as observing how persons talk about the same topic among a variety of listeners, or asking a question again at a later time or in a different way.

Other good methods exist for dealing with the above problems, however. Careful fieldworkers come to expect people to tell lies or to offer partisan accounts for good reasons. The statement of individual participants can be further checked through comparisons with others at the sites, through observations of other activities at the sites, and through phantasy variations (described later in this chapter).

Importance of literature sites inquiry

Phenomenology has often been mistaken by practitioners and critics alike for a new version of simple subjectivism. We noted in the last chapter that this danger exists within phenomenology, but that it can and should be avoided through a subject-relatedness. In the specific case of essential interactionist inquiries into large social phenomena, research into literature sites is a strategy for combatting these dangers and for maximizing the angles available for locating essences.

Most basically, the literature sites inquiry is a recognition and use of others' honest attempts to understand prejudice and of the current researcher's own inability to view the phenomenon from all of the many times in which it has existed, or 'through the eyes' of the many who have participated and observed it. Such an appreciation or use would not at all conflict with Husserl's own intention for phenomenology. Husserl emphasizes in the *Crisis* (Section 54), the importance not only of others' perceptions and existences, but of the reality that the 'I' is an I among many I's, which constitute 'all of us' among whom I am but one 'I'. Given this situation, the 'all of us' or the 'many I's' became for Husserl inevitably interwoven in each individual 'I.'

Further, we have all had experiences of turning other I's into I-myself. When we think about ourselves at some point in the past (or imagine ourselves in the future), we are taking other I's and considering them as if they were present I's, despite the fact of our present 'I' which is constantly performing this operation. We achieve this transcendence of another's subjectivity through similar procedures. When we walk through a store and see an unfamiliar object, we attempt to understand this new object in part by becoming a variety of I's. If we are alone or do not wish to talk with others, we may do this by looking at it first from one angle then from another; first from one theory then from another; first as if we were an artist then as if we were a scientist, and so forth. In other words, I see the new object as it might be differently seen by other persons (Ricoeur, 1954). To put this on a fundamentally sociological level, it can be posited, as did Strasser (1974: 83), that 'man's essence is an orientation to others.'

The matter becomes thorny in conflict situations, however. To stick to the above example, suppose we ask two people about the new item we have seen, and they disagree. Confronted with just this predicament, Merleau-Ponty has critiqued Husserl's project as impossible, alleging that any conclusions we reach could be considered ridiculous within another time, group or place.

But here we have another unwarranted variety of the relativistic critique noted previously. For if we probe the conflicting persons as to the processes through which they arrived at their conclusions and the interpretations of their conclusions, we can expect the conflict to evaporate. To stick to our previous example, suppose our first informant responds that the new item we are seeing is a box full of demons, while the second replies that it is a television set. We would seem to have a conflict. In fact, neither of these replies tell us anything about the new item's essences, and upon further questioning we could expect to gain essences from both persons. The essences might turn out to be that the new item is such that if a person does actions A_1–A_n the item may reveal pictures B_1–B_n, and if one tears it apart through actions C_1–C_n one can see how items D_1–D_n and processes E_1–E_n make up pictures B_1–B_n. Despite the differences along the way, one can derive the essences from others' accounts through an intersubjectivity in which one sees others' processes of understanding and from them permits one's own 'I' to derive the essences of the object. As can be clearly seen from the above example, however, it is important to obtain all relevant perspectives. If we spoke only to the demon theorists we might never look at the circuitry, and without the demon theorists we might miss identifications of the range of possible pictures and actions.

Choosing sites

A problem which may seem monstrous for inquiries into literature sites as large as that concerning prejudice is the choice of sites for doing one's fieldwork. It would be impossible to spend long periods of time on the several thousand books and papers which have been written concerning prejudice. The problem is no larger, however, than with most traditional fieldwork projects, if we are honest about these other projects. If one wishes to study alcohol treatment facilities through fieldwork, one requires neither a visit to every center nor a random sample of centers, but rather an understanding of the types of centers which exist and adequate fieldwork in representative centers.[3]

Wherever one begins research, what becomes important is to gain from the participants themselves a conception of the sites available and what distinguishes them, and then to encourage oneself to go to those sites which would seem likely to offer an understanding of problems one is investigating.

We can posit that an early 'step' for essential interactionist fieldwork at literature sites is to determine from informants which sites exist, and how they are distinguished from one another. In practice this means extensive use of card catalogs, book indices, periodical indices, literature guides, etc. Such a search takes the form of a spiral, with the first book's references employed to lead the fieldworker to others, whose references are also used. Quick visits ('skimming') must then be employed to determine into which groups the various individual sites fall, both according to the description of their group memberships and others' descriptions. Such divisions tend to run according to theories, and debates within theories.

After this point, one may choose either of two options: (1) going to one site and letting possible essences emerge, then investigating them further at other sites; or (2) attempting to visit those sites that participants consider representative of each group. The inability at this point to know which informants to trust concerning representativeness of sites indicates that (2) may lead to mistaken assumptions from the beginning, and assumptions which may be hard to revise once one is locked into these sites and becoming an insider. This strategy may also result in only cursory acquaintance with many sites, rather than depth understanding of any single site. But (1) has pitfalls as well. The fieldworker may build into the research the impossibility of investigating entire groups of sites (i.e. if the essences found in the first site are very distant from those one would have found at other sites).[4]

My own attempted solution will be to visit representative sites

METHOD

and allow essences to emerge from these. During these visits I will attempt to detect hints that I have been grouping sites poorly or that visited sites are atypical, according to the ways in which participants speak of other sites and of their own site, and by my observations at the sites.

But my first work in the field will be to conduct large-scale tours of as many sites as possible, to accomplish two feats: a broad appreciation of the field, of which sites exist, how, when, and where; and locating key informants. Beginning with 'Doc' in Whyte's *Street Corner Society*, key informants have been crucial to the success of fieldwork. Key informants do fieldwork themselves, though in different ways and for different reasons than the social science fieldworker. Usually the key informants do their fieldwork to obtain leadership positions for themselves or to protect their positions within the sites. They are usually old-timers within the field and the most knowledgeable participants. Key informants are especially useful in introducing the fieldworker to knowledgeable persons and giving the fieldworker tours of the various factions and subdivisions within groups of sites.

From my fieldnotes during these visits, and from information obtained from key informants, I will then construct maps of the field (Bogdan and Taylor, 1975). These maps will divide the sites into groups and identify the sites considered most important within these clusters by participants at other sites and by the key informants.

Research into essences can then commence. The first search for essences will be accomplished simultaneously with the first attempt at an intersubjective understanding of the phenomenon. I will attempt to identify what the participants at the major sites within the various groupings consider to be essences of the phenomenon. This entails the construction of a list of definitions the participants offer for the phenomenon. Whether they do so on the basis of their own research into prejudice or to have 'operational definitions,' definitions the participants offer are their views of the briefest explanation of prejudice which can include all forms which the phenomenon takes.

These suggested essences are only the starting points for our own query into essences. We expect to refine some, eliminate others, and use still others solely as touchstones for new groupings of sites.

Boundaries

Beyond the first groupings, determination of the inner and outer boundaries of sites or site-groups is no more nor less objectively pre-given for literature sites than for traditional fieldwork sites. The fieldworker studying gay bars may defensibly limit his observations to 'the back room with the stage and chairs' when the topic is drag shows. The site may be even further reduced to one row of seats when the topic is 'straights' reactions to drag shows. Yet the site may later become a surburban home when the topic is 'drag show straights' at home, and this site may be abandoned after additional fieldwork, in favor of those homes scattered throughout a metropolitan area which the fieldworker has determined to be connected by telephone conversations.

A literature site may be the report of a single study exploring the substantive question at hand, and this site may be replaced or expanded in favor of a dozen studies separated in time or space but all dealing with the same topic. For example, the Sherif (1966), study of intergroup prejudice at a summer camp may be examined as a site unto itself concerning the process of change from friendship-with to prejudice-against, since Sherif's summer camp environment uniquely produced this change. In looking at the question of group norms, however, the Sherif site would be only one area among many within the site, which would include several other areas where group norms have been central concerns.

Or the boundaries of a literature site may be determined not by substantive questions, but by theory or method. Theories or methods may themselves offer essences of a phenomenon, quite apart from the substantive issues they share with other theories or methods. Thus, one might take conflict theory (as developed by Simmel, 1955; Coser, 1956; Dahrendorf, 1958; and James, 1968), in its richness, perhaps even to the exclusion of its believers' specific works on prejudice. The goal would be to see if essential interactionist analysis performed on this social theory offers essences of the specific social phenomenon in question. Among the questions which might arise from this inquiry are: Is conflict inevitable? If so, is it not possible that prejudice is also inevitable, as the necessary attitude nexus for conflict? What about the dispute between functionalist conflict theorists and Marxist conflict theorists – is prejudice system-supportive, system-destructive, neither, both?

An example of a method as a site would be consideration of those studies which request subjects to answer questions about target groups on the basis of feelings scored from one to ten. One might ignore the actual questions asked during these studies and concentrate upon the response patterns. Do the subjects tend to respond to each question far to the lower end of the scale, far to the upper end, far to both ends, towards the middle? Does a clear response pattern indicate the direction of prejudice? Does the response pattern reveal the method of prejudice (e.g. negative end tendencies, dichotomous thinking, neutral opinions)?

METHOD

Is it an essence?

When a potential essence is found at a site, its necessity and immutability must be considered through the methods of phantasy variation and constant comparison, which constitute the next part of essential interactionist fieldwork.

The technique of constant comparison has been used informally in sociology and anthropology for many years (e.g. Shils, 1963 and Glaser and Strauss, 1967).

A complete history of this method would take us all the way back at least to Aristotle, who lists three types of inferences: deductive, inductive, and abductive (sometimes translated 'reduction,' Husserl's term for his own method). Pierce (1931) described these three inferences:

> (Induction) sets out with a theory and it measures the degree of concordance of that theory with fact. It never can originate any idea whatever. No more than deduction. All the ideas of science come to it by way of Abduction. Abduction consists in studying facts and devising a theory to explain them. Its only justification is that if we are ever to understand things at all, it must be in that way. Abductive and inductive reasoning are utterly irreducible, either to the other or to Deduction, or Deduction to either of them . . . (Section 146).

> Deduction proves that something *must* be; Induction shows that something *actually is* operative; Abduction merely suggests that something *may be* (Section 171).

We will not be constructing theories in the same sense as Pierce envisions them, but our constant comparisons will constitute a type of Abductive strategy, in that we will look at 'facts' and cases and attempt to determine the essences within them. We do so with a recognition that we are not offering final explanations or complete elaborations of essences, but rather soliciting essences of the phenomenon at its current stage of development.

The techniques of constant comparison might be compared to those of the jazz musician, while many traditional sociological methods would be comparable to those of the classical orchestra musician. The former borrows a bit from here and there when various elements of a composition present themselves to him, while the latter sticks to predetermined scripts. As a result, the jazz musician sometimes borrows from blues, sometimes from classical music, sometimes from field hollars, and sometimes from other jazz compositions. When successful, the final product is a rhapsody in blue, or a mood identical to none the musician or audience had previously experienced. When unsuccessful, the jazz product is unaffecting, or affecting in ways the musician or audience did not intend. The classical musician when successful performs the prescribed piece as it is intended, with just enough changes to distinguish him from other players. When unsuccessful, the classical product is very different from its presentation in the past. The advantage to the former strategy is that one has more freedom: of discovery, of what to do with the product, etc. The advantage of the latter is that one knows in advance pretty well what one is going to get for one's time and money (Bledsoe, 1975).

Two types of constant comparisons can be distinguished, both within Husserl's work and within the work of sociologists who follow Glaser and Strauss (e.g. Hadden and Lester, 1976). The first is horizontal (synchronic), as Husserl employed in his earlier works such as *Logical Investigations*. Horizontal comparisons treat material as it presents itself to the investigator at the present moment. The second type, vertical comparisons, treats the material as existing at a variety of times, as having a history. The vertical method is sometimes called genetic phenomenology, and is evidenced by Husserl's 'The Origin of Geometry' in the *Crisis*, in which he retraces the conceptual decisions and turning points made by geometers (Levin, 1975: 74).

For our purposes, the horizontal constant comparative method will be employed by taking the essence which has been suggested to the fieldworker and seeing if it exists at other literature sites when the phenomenon under investigation exists. If in fact we have discovered an essence, it should exist at all of the sites in some form (it should exhibit immutability).

For vertical comparisons we take an essence to the various sites and try to observe how it arose. Through this attempt to untie the knots of conceptual decisions, vertical comparisons offer fresh information about the phenomenon by showing the ancestral concepts as decisions, and as resolutions to webs of experience. We thereby reactivate these webs to see the numerous alternative 'readings' that are possible and perhaps choiceworthy.

We will note in detail later in the chapter that all essential interactionist analysis must involve meta analysis. The immediate importance of this while doing constant comparisons is that we must not expect to find the essence as "single layered." An illustrative example is the essence red. Were we conducting an inquiry into the essences of color, we would do well to anticipate layers of red, and thereby be able to make sense of pink, for example, when we find it in another color-site.

A value of the constant comparative method for investigating large social phenomena is that it further obligates the fieldworker continuously to visit many sites and thereby to probe more deeply into the sites, have additional opportunities for redescribing into which groups they belong, and discover other essences or information about the essence at hand. Indeed, while checking one essence at a site where it did not originate, a careful fieldworker will be observing and taking notes on other possible essences.

Phantasy variations

The discussion of intuition in the previous chapter suggests that we do not ground an essence empirically merely through constant comparative fieldwork at the sites. The essence is further grounded through phantasy variations, a process during which one constructs possible worlds, i.e. social structures one would expect under specific conditions which do not happen to be present at currently available sites. Through phantasy variations we are able to further enrich the data by building directly into the methodology a strategy for going beyond what appears as fact, and working with it as possibility. Rather than limiting our vision to a site as it presents itself at the moment, we can imagine specific changes in that site through possible or likely interactions in the future and possible ramifications these changes could have for the essences we are investigating.

What phantasy variation offers that other parts of our method do not is a chance to look at the essence itself with less constraint than when we must pay attention to its ways of presenting and ways of acting amid others. In phantasy variation we concentrate upon the essence *qua* essence and allow ourselves to change it in any ways which seem possible, or to change its surroundings in ways which seem possible (*Ideas*, Sec. 4). Only in this way are we able to vary the form of the essence without limit and place it in different locations, times and circumstances. In such a way we detect at what points the essence is varied beyond its concrete possibility, and thereby loses its ability to exist as an essence of the phenomenon at hand. We also see whether or not it *is* an essence (Levinas, 1967: 95–6):

> The predicates of the object may vary without jeopardizing the possibility of the object, it is only the *essential* predicates which do not tolerate a variation. And what is more, it is precisely their constancy which allows the variation of the other predicates: each variation, indeed, presupposes something constant which makes it possible. In this way we come again upon the definition of essence which we have already formulated according to which essence is constituted by an ensemble of predicates which the

object must materialize for the other predicates ever to be able to belong to it.

Phantasy variation is a strategy both for discovery and for verification, then. We verify that we have an essence through phantasy variations by imagining the phenomenon without the essence, with the essence changed in various ways, or within various possible manifestations of the phenomenon.[5] Thus, in examining the phenomenon 'triangle' we might verify our essence statements through phantasy variations by determining whether three sides, three angles, and certain shapes and sizes of these sides and angles are necessary and immutable for triangles to exist, or whether they are merely compatible with it. We would go through phantasy variations to answer such questions as whether a triangle without these elements would become another figure, and whether a figure without these essences is impossible, since it would include incompatible ingredients (Spiegelberg, 1965: 680).

Sticking to this example, we can also answer a common criticism of the technique of phantasy variation. We do not vary possible worlds at random or needlessly. We would not, for instance, consider phantasy variations for the essences of triangles in worlds where straight lines cannot exist, or where all angles are larger than 360°. For every phantasy variation we must be able to demonstrate how the world so conceived could actually come to exist. Phantasy variations upon empty sets would be fruitless.

Essential relationships[6]

Neither essences nor phenomena are disconnected entities floating in space and time. Both are connected to other entities in essential ways. Essential interactionist investigations must determine (1) the essential relationships among the essences of the phenomenon and (2) the essential relationships between the phenomenon and other phenomena.

We sought in the previous steps to distinguish the essences of a phenomenon from those properties which appear under certain manifestations but not under others. Next we attempt the same process of elimination for relationships between essences. Typically, essences will be found in various configurations within the variety of manifestations of a phenomenon. Through the methods of constant comparisons and phantasy variations, we try to determine which of these relationships among the essences are essential. This consists in practice of rearranging the essences or connecting them in different ways and noting (1) whether the fundamental structure of the phenomenon remains unaffected by the rearrangements or new connectors, thereby demonstrating that the arrangement or connector was not essential; (2) whether the fundamental structure changes, but only into another of its possible forms; or (3) whether the phenomenon 'explodes,' or its gestalt ceases to exist, amid the incompatibility of the new arrangements.

A phenomenon is likely to be determined no less by the arrangements of its essences than by which essences it entails. The simple example of a triangle demonstrates this point. The three sides, range of possible angles, etc. are no more determining than are the essential ways in which they are placed and connected.

This step is not applied to the essences, of course, until the fieldworker has derived and elaborated enough of the essences that she can posit descriptions at least of segments of the essential compositions of the phenomenon.

The second part of this operation – investigation of essential relationships between the phenomenon and other phenomena – we accomplish by bringing the phenomenon to stand on its own, as a possible essence itself of other phenomena, and in its essential relationships with other phenomena. Obviously, this part of the inquiry can be done only as part of a larger inquiry into the essences of a group or groups of social phenomena, because it is necessary that one knows the essences and essential compositions of the other phenomena being considered. In this step we investigate how the activities of phenomena with other phenomena are internally determined.

Meta analysis

An essential interactionist recognizes essences as already there, but that people can do many things with these already-present essences, including the attachment of interpretations. This is one reason that the essential interactionist attempts to listen to as many of these variations on the object as possible, to enrich his descriptions of essences and to increase the number of essences he discovers (Merleau-Ponty, 1967: 365):

> The most important lesson the reduction teaches us is the impossibility of a complete reduction. This is why Husserl is constantly re-examining the possibility of reduction. If we were absolute mind, the reduction would present no problem. But since, on the contrary, we are in the world, since indeed our reflections are carried out in the temporal flux on which we are trying to seize . . . there is no thought which embraces all thought.

Husserl[7] notes this need for many layers of essence analysis in his discussion of generalization, via the example of a triangle, which is an essence in some cases, but is subordinated under another essence, spatial shape. In turn, the particular triangle may be found to contain the independent essence red, which entails further essences, and so forth (*Ideas*, Sec. 13).

Even further, in his *Logical Investigations*, Husserl recognizes that vagueness may itself be an essence of certain objects and phenomena, and must therefore be accepted and reported by the phenomenologist. This is the significant difference between the essences of phenomenologically-oriented social science, including essential interactionism, and similar conceptions such as Weber's notion of ideal-types (1970c: 245):

> The spatial figure of the tree, exactly taken as it is present in the corresponding perception, that is to say as a moment of the intentional object, is not a geometric formation; neither is it ideal nor exact in the sense of exact geometry. In the same way an intuited color is not an ideal color.

A goal of phenomenologically based inquiries is to investigate social reality as it exists for participants, which is from a variety of angles and a variety of shades of exactness, each capable of revealing essences or information about essences. That these essences sometimes are not precise in the case of social phenomena need not disturb or surprise us anymore than in phenomena from science and mathematics – such as diabetes, force, or flight – which likewise are essentially inexact.

We also recognize that our own and others' intuitions of essences may not be singular, even when they have been properly elaborated. Strasser (1974: 255) remarks that 'human perception has the character of an endless (in principle) series of acts rather than of a definitive, absolutely satisfying intuition.'

In short, as essential interactionists we approach social phenomena expecting varying degrees of vagueness and many essences, which themselves are available in varying degrees of clearness. Even were we able to locate all of the essences currently present, that would be only the beginning of our meta-analysis, in light of the suggested dialectical essence of the social: our own analysis in one sense becomes still another part of the phenomenon.

Further, the persons who wrote the literature we will use as sites need not be specifically aware of an essence we name in order for a case to be made that it is indeed an essence of the phenomenon. These essences are parallel units to the outcomes which other qualitative fieldworkers call 'problems' (Wax, 1971), 'hypotheses' (Bogdan and Taylor, 1975), and 'dimensions' (Ball, 1970). Thus, the ghetto participants at Suttles' (1968), sites may not have been

METHOD

aware of 'the social order of the slum' or of 'the ecological basis of ordered segmentation'; medical students at Becker's (1961), site may not have been aware of their 'idealism'; and the school children Glassner (1976), witnessed may not have been aware of their 'kid society.' In all of these cases, the very contribution of the fieldworker's research and theorizing was to bring these features to light.

Verification and falsification

Most of this chapter has concerned discovery, and methods of discovery for essential interactionism have been proposed; but what about verification and falsification of these discoveries?

An essential interactionist interpretation of verification is similar to that of Hanson (1971: 76), that 'to the degree that sociologists and cosmologists, by their special theories and techniques of inquiry, can explain perplexing aspects of their intricate subject matters, and can render intelligible what might otherwise have been a chaotic confusion of conceptual concerns – to that degree such disciplines will justifiably be said to be verified.'

That statements must have built into them the possibility for their falsification is a criterion made popular by Popper.[8] The theses of Popper and his students are as follows:

1 Those hypotheses that are most refutable but have not yet been refuted are preferred to those that are less refutable.
2 Those hypotheses that are most refutable are the ones that are most simple.
3 Refutability is a sufficient and necessary condition for separating science from nonscience (Popper, 1969).

Of the first two statements, we can fairly easily show that the most refutable is not necessarily the most desirable. Consider the statements, 'All humans are social animals' and 'All humans from Missouri are social animals.' The latter is more refutable than the former (considering the smaller sample), but the former we may consider the 'better' statement because it tells us more. And the second statement is less simple than the first, thus creating difficulties for Popper's second thesis. Popper's second thesis also seems worthy of rejection because we know from everyday experiences that the simplest route is not necessarily the best. The simplest route from point A to point B is a straight line, but the best route may be circular, zig zagged, etc., if such a route avoids troubles along the way.

Simple statements of existence create difficulties with Popper's third thesis. The following statement would be non-scientific according to Popper: 'At least one person is alive on earth today.' No amount of possible evidence could conflict with this statement.

In summary, attempts at verification and falsification are attempts at gaining certainty, which is a special way of gaining confidence in one's work. Essential interactionists seek confidence in their work as well, but through *clarity of possibilities* rather than *certainty of facts*. Such clarity is achieved by processes of phantasy variation upon essences and constant comparisons amid alternative existing sites.

To say the above is not to say that products of essential interactionism are irrevocable or closed to external testing. Not only is it possible for others to apply essential interactionist methods to the same phenomenon, they may also apply these methods to the previous inquiry, or to parts of the previous inquiry. Despite the misunderstanding of some of his critics, this is not a possibility ruled out by Husserl. He recognized in *Cartesian Meditations* and in Sections 50 and 51 of *Ideas* a social unity or community world which he calls *Kulterwelt* and which grows out of his notions of intersubjectivity. Within these concepts exist the possibility for what we might call 'intersubjective verification' (see Lauer, 1958: Chapter 8 for a more complete discussion). Such an exercise, one must note immediately, is a type of 'comparing of notes,' of saying 'I did such-and-such to such-and-such ends, and you are invited to do the same and see if you end up with the same.' This is precisely what objectivistically oriented researchers do when they verify.

Further, Goodman's (1951: Chapter IV), work points out that essences[9] are revocable on specific grounds. Although any essence takes on the trappings of a decree, and is therefore incapable of being challenged by itself, when it is placed amid other essences (as in the study of phenomena) it is open to revocation according to the criteria of workability and compatibility.

Under workability, an essence is tested to see how much difficulty it will give us if we accept it as a possibility. Goodman's example (100), is of perversely considering an essence of an apple to be the color of the sky on a clear day. This will create difficulties as soon as I begin describing the essences of the sky, or work with the sky and the apple together. I would have to abandon either the unitary color of a clear sky or the unitary color of the apple, and transitivity of identity is a concept which would seem so valuable that I would instead be obligated to see my previous essence statement as unworkable. This example also illustrates revocation by compatibility. An essence of an apple (and also of a sky) is its possession of transitivity of identity, and our new essence may be rejected on the grounds that it is not compatible with this other essence.

As Goodman put it (101), if an essence (quale) 'survives because

METHOD

it is psychologically satisfactory and workable, and because it is compatible with the body of other accepted statements, it may be said to be well verified.'

Our context of validation is not limited, however, to logical validation. Empirical validation is possible through application to essential interactionist research strategies of traditional procedures. Thus, in fieldwork with a large body of literature sites, one may divide the sites and measure intercoder reliability. Or the sites may be divided such that one is the control and the other the experimental group, on the basis of systematic differences in authors, content, or other aspects.

part three

First illustration of a method

A return 'to the things themselves' requires a return to the persons who construct the things.

Introduction

This Part is an initial illustration of the essential interactionist method described in the previous chapters. The procedures noted in Chapter 4 will be applied to the phenomenon of prejudice via the social scientific literature concerning this phenomenon, by treating the literature as sites. The process begins by locating and mapping the various sites and determining which properties the participants at the sites consider essential.

Then we begin vertical and horizontal comparisons to determine whether the essences suggested by these previous researchers hold up. Some of these can be promptly discounted through illustrations of sites at which the property is not present. Those features which remain are considered possible essences, and we make extensive rounds throughout the sites to specify how and why each of these essences operates or appears not to operate. We try to determine not only whether these possible essences are to be accepted as essential, but also to describe and understand them as fully as possible.

Only one of the possible essences actually will be examined in depth in this book, however. The goal is not to present a complete theory of prejudice, but to provide an illustration (first experiment) with this particular method for essential interactionist research. It is hoped that significant theoretical insights will be obtained through this illustration (including additional possible essences). But more important to the overall goal is to uncover inadequacies of the method through its initial application. Indeed, the book is intended as a methodological study more than as a study of prejudice.

The Part concludes with a chapter discussing some initial theoretical statements about prejudice and prejudice reduction that can be made on the basis of the illustration of the method. This is followed by a final chapter assessing the method in light of its initial

FIRST ILLUSTRATION OF A METHOD

application and suggesting further research necessary for the development of an adequate theory of prejudice.

5 Maps and proposed essences

In line with the methodological strategy suggested in Chapter 4, the first work was to search and take notes on listings for 'prejudice' in several university and community libraries' card catalogues, in current *Books in Print* volumes, and in *Sociological Abstracts*. On the basis of suggestions found therein, the same search was made of listings for 'discrimination.' From these searches, lists were constructed of about 125 titles of social science books dating to the 1800s and sociology and social psychology papers of the last ten years. Nearly 90 per cent of these materials were located and read, and notes were kept concerning their basic contents.

Key informants

On the basis of the initial fieldwork notes, three key informants emerged. Each of these persons has been involved for most of his adult life with numerous prejudice-literature sites and with the many people of these sites. Gordon Allport, James Jones and Howard Ehrlich each put together detailed books which offer tours and analyses of the social science literature on prejudice. Each attempts to summarize the literature to date on prejudice.

Allport's *The Nature of Prejudice* (1958), is referred to at many other sites as 'the classic work on prejudice.' Allport considers prejudice from several angles, including the types of persons who are considered prejudiced, objects of prejudice, theories of prejudice, formation of prejudice, personality features in prejudice, reducing prejudice, cultural elements of prejudice, stereotyping, and traits of object groups. An important point which emerged in reading Allport is the need for a variety of types of maps, rather than simply one dividing the sites according to theory. As this key informant so clearly demonstrates in his tours and analyses, persons at the sites also see themselves and are seen by others to belong to clusters according to the aspect of prejudice which they examine.

Jones's *Prejudice and Racism* (1972) is divided into two parts, each dealing with half of the title. Jones distinguishes the latter from the former as prejudice solely based upon race and often entailing more than individual or group action by becoming deliberately institutionalized. In our terms, Jones appears to be distinguishing types of manifestations of prejudice, but we will have to examine at some point the question of whether prejudice and racism are two phenomena (1) that share some essences; (2) of which one is an essence of the other; (3) that are actually the same phenomenon in different manifestations; or (4) are entirely distinct phenomena.

Jones divides his discussion somewhat differently than does Allport. Parts of the book consider historical periods, others discuss theories, and the chapters on racism offer the locations thereof (e.g. 'Institutional Racism – Education,' 'Institutional Racism – Justice').

Ehrlich's *The Social Psychology of Prejudice* (1973) divides the prejudice-literature sites according to what the author defines as the components (or dimensions) of prejudice: cognitive, conative, and affective, plus what he calls 'supporting mechanisms' (e.g., 'Child-Rearing Practices,' 'The Reference-Other Matrix').

Between the three key informants' bibliographies one finds mention of nearly all of the sites from my original list from the catalogues and abstracts, plus about 500 additional sites. Ehrlich attempts to be exhaustive in his inclusion of all available sites, and there is every evidence that he was close to successful in locating those dealing with the aspects of prejudice stressed in his book. This makes it possible to turn to Ehrlich first for sites up to 1973.

Initial maps

On the basis of reports from the three key informants and from fieldnotes during the initial visits to sites, the sites have been divided into lists equivalent to spatial, temporal activity and other mapping used in more traditional fieldwork investigations. In the case of literature sites, these maps take the form of outlines and do not describe points in space, but rather divisions and affiliations according to criteria which exist within the sites.

The first mapping is according to *theoretical positions*:

Map 1

I Psychoanalytic
    A Projection: scapegoating I
    B Frustration-aggression-displacement: scapegoating II
    C The authoritarian personality
    D Child-rearing practices

II Historical
    A Marxist
    B Industrialization
    C Situational

III Behavioristic
    A Stimulus object
    B Earned reputation

IV Functionalism
    A Functional
    B Dysfunctional

V General sociocultural determinism
    A Socioeconomic status and mobility
    B Education
    C Socialization
    D Self-and-other attitudes
    E Pluralism vs. assimilationism
    F Contact: intergroup relations determiners (and conflict theory)
    G Marginality

Two major groups seem curiously missing from this map, symbolic interactionism and phenomenological. No sites were located during my own search nor reported during those of the three key informants for either variety of theorizing. Both Allport and Jones do mention the possibility of phenomenological theories of prejudice, but neither specify any existing work in these areas. Other missing categories will probably present themselves during the course of the fieldwork. It is clear that we may need to go to some general theorizing from these missing areas and to research within these frameworks to see if the positions have anything to say about prejudice.

The second mapping is according to *way of prejudicing*:

FIRST ILLUSTRATION OF A METHOD

Map 2

I   Cognitive: stereotyping
II   Conative: social distancing
III Affective: behavior intentions and emotions
IV Anxiety
      A Sexual
      B Self-esteem
      C Inner conflicts
V   Authoritarianism
VI Dichotomization
      A In-groupings and out-groupings
      B Self-other
      C Reference-other
VII Linguistic features
      A Labeling
      B Sentence structuring
VIII Social functions and dysfunctions
      A Economic
      B Competition control
      C Labor supplies
IX Scapegoating

Other maps may be needed, notably one for methods for reduction, and one for the victims of prejudice. Within each map I have attempted to locate representative major sites, on the bases of my own observations from the visits, the reports of the three key informants, and reports from persons at the sites visited (reports about other reports). These maps will seldom be mentioned directly in the following chapters. They are constructed for the fieldworker's organizational needs, and used to locate sites during actual horizontal comparisons.

Definitions

As noted in the previous chapter, our next major task is to list definitions from the major sites. This is an attempt to begin our essence search with those attributes which the participants themselves consider essential and also to avoid a standard problem in fieldwork, of starting at a major site or group of sites and never considering other important sites. Starting with definitions also permits us to begin hermeneutically, by searching for essences within the taken-for-granted beliefs of the participants. Care must be taken, however, not to be blinded by these definitions. An attempt is made to combine the traditional fieldwork dictum that 'features should emerge from the fieldwork, not be brought by the fieldworkers' with our goal to uncover and elaborate essences. To that end the definitions are aproached critically and with the expectation that brief constant comparisons and variations will eliminate some. Although the definitions contain for the most part only those features which the participants at the sites consider essential, the participants are not speaking of essentialism in our terms. A result is that an essential interactionist analysis is not obliged to reply to each such statement on its own grounds, but rather to sift from these definitions the possible essences.

Lengthy rounds were conducted through key sites, and prior to that, brief visits occurred at a majority of the approximately 600 sites. As might be expected, the same elements of prejudice were repeated in the definitions at several sites. From the fieldnotes of definitions at the key (about 100) sites, the following comparably short list includes all of the elements offered by these definitions:

An interpersonal hostility which is directed againt individuals based on their membership in a minority group (Jack Levin, 1975).

A pattern of hostility in interpersonal relations which is directed against an entire group, or against its individual members; it fulfills a specific irrational function for its bearer (Ackerman and Jahoda, 1950).

Prejudice is defined as hostility or aggression toward individuals on the basis of their group membership (Buss, 1961).

Ethnic prejudice is an antipathy based upon a faulty and inflexible generalization. It may be felt or expressed. It may be directed toward a group as a whole, or toward an individual because he is a member of that group. The net effect . . . is to place the object of prejudice at some disadvantage not merited by his own misconduct (Allport, 1954).

Race prejudice is a social attitude propagated among the public by an exploiting class for the purpose of stigmatizing some group as inferior so that the exploitation of either the group itself or its resources may both be justified (Cox, 1948).

We are now in a position to understand the anti-Semite. He is a man who is afraid. Not of the Jews, to be sure, but of himself, of his own consciousness, of his liberty, of his instincts, of his responsibilities, of solitariness, of change, of society, and of the world – of everything except the Jews (Sartre, 1965).

Prejudice is a negative attitude toward a socially defined group and toward any person perceived to be a member of that group (Collins, 1970).

Prejudices are social attitudes which are developed before, in lieu of, or despite objective evidence (Cooper and McGaugh, 1963).

A feeling or response to persons or things which is prior to, and therefore not based upon, actual experience. It may be positive or negative, and it may be directed to any one of a large variety of objects (Klineberg, 1954).

An unfavorable attitude toward an object which tends to be highly stereotyped, emotionally charged, and not easily changed by contrary information (Krech, Crutchfield, and Ballachey, 1962).

Prejudice could well be regarded as 'social neuroticism' in the sense that it is an adjustment which reduces the efficiency of a society by draining off physic and physical energy and preventing successful collective achievement (Martin, 1964).

Preconceived judgments toward persons, beliefs, or objects (McDonagh and Richards, 1953).

Literally, prejudice means prejudgment, a judgment before knowledge (Peterson, 1958).

An attitude that considers selected categories of people in terms of stereotypes, usually for some purpose (conscious or unconscious) believed to be of advantage to the person who has the prejudice (Rose, 1965).

. . . a facet of the normative system of culture. Prejudice is built into the culture in the form of normative precepts . . . which define the ways in which members of the group ought to behave in relation to the members of selected out-groups (Westie, 1964).

In comparing this list with the previous maps one can see that some elements from the maps are missing. This is because the definitions present only those elements participants consider crucial (which usually translates to 'most important'), whereas the maps are constructed with all divisions I and my key informants found among the sites. We would have recourse to look at the items noted there during my full elaboration of essences, however, as it is entirely possible that essences would emerge from other items on the maps.

The components of these definitions may be mapped as follows, according to the *overall crucial features as defined by the participants*:

Map 3

I Activity toward target(s)
   Behaviors toward   Attitudes toward
   1 Hostility   Direction:
   2 Aggression   1 Negative
                             2 Positive
                             Type:
                             3 Social
                             4 Sick ('social neuroticism')
                             5 Emotional
                                (a) Fear of self
                                (b) Antipathy
                             6 Not easily changeable
                             7 Stereotyped
                             8 Without (or before)
                                information
                                (a) Objective evidence
                                (b) Actual experience

II Types of targets
    1 Individual
    2 Individuals on basis of group membership
    3 Minority groups(s)
    4 Belief holders
    5 Objects

III Functions
     1 Advantage for possessor
     2 To meet normative demands
     3 Reduced efficiency by reducing collective achievement

Our goal in working with these definitions is both to simplify and to elaborate the notions of prejudice contained therein. We first simplify by seeking from the third map those items to consider as posible essences, and this is accomplished by eliminating items that exist within prejudice only in certain of its manifestations. To constitute a potential essence of prejudice an item must potentially exist in any manifestation of the phenomenon; it must have a chance of meeting the necessity requirement. It must not be immediately susceptible to elimination from the phenomenon with the phenomenon still capable of existing after its elimination.

We elaborate these possible essences in the next two chapters, wherein they are investigated through the types of fieldwork described in Chapter 4.

Determining possible essences

The items from map 3 were considered in terms of their necessity, and lengthy notes taken concerning the items. When required, the items were investigated at relevant sites, according to the possibility of prejudice existing at these sites without the item. On the basis on these investigations, the following proposals are offered:

1 Of the attitude and behavior dimensions of activities toward targets, the behavior dimension should not be included in constructions of possible essences. A person may be prejudiced when the target of prejudice is not nearby and therefore no behavior toward the target is possible. Key informant Allport reminds us that persons often implode rather than explode, and thereby direct their aggressions and hostility at themselves. This may suggest that they redirect the prejudice against themselves, or that *some* target for aggression or hostility necessarily must be present during prejudicing. These questions will be important for us in other contexts. The immediate ramification is that persons may be prejudiced against targets without exercising hostility or aggression upon them. This brings up a distinction between prejudice and discrimination. Persons do discriminate against others without any particular thoughts or feelings about those people, but rather with the sole concern of achieving some end for the discriminator.

Merton (1949), suggested on the basis of his review of prejudice and discrimination sites a four-fold typology of prejudiced discriminators, prejudiced nondiscriminators, nonprejudiced discriminators, and nonprejudiced nondiscriminators. Other sites indicate that persons choose when they prejudice and when they discriminate without regard for a positive correlation between the two. An example is Lohman and Reitzes (1952), who talked with 151 white steel workers in East Chicago, Indiana. The men were members of a racially integrated union in which blacks held several major offices. Only 12 per cent of the whites verbalized what the researchers termed 'low acceptance' of blacks in the work situation. But 86 per cent rejected the idea of allowing blacks to live near them. Just the converse is the case at Pilcher's (1972), site, which looked at nonprejudiced discriminators among Portland longshoremen.

2 As the variations and contradictions on the map indicate, the

attitude dimensions which prejudice may take vary according to the conditions under which prejudice manifests itself. These are described as positive or negative, sick or simply emotional. Although prejudiced persons do tend to stereotype, we cannot list this as immutable. Ehrlich demonstrates in his tours through the literature sites that for some persons prejudice consists not of holding stereotypes, but instead consists of conative responses (behavior intentions) or affective responses. We also must not include the condition of 'not easily changeable,' since various persons in various situations will hold their prejudiced attitudes with greater or lesser vivacity and therefore be more or less easily changeable.

3 The item concerning possession of information cannot be retained in its present forms. Prejudicing toward something (or accomplishing anything toward something) is impossible without some information. One must be able in some way to identify what the target is. Such information can come only through objective evidence; if we take the meaning of 'objective' as in Websters', 'of or having to do with a known or perceived object as distinguished from something existing only in the mind of the subject.' And information about the outside world mut be via 'actual experience.' Furthermore, informant Barry Collins (1970), summarizes numerous contact situations in which prejudice did not diminish after the prejudicing persons had contacts with the targets of their prejudices.

These objections notwithstanding, one can intuit that this category relates to prejudice, in the original sense of the concept 'to prejudge.' This we will need to explore.

4 An item which remains is that prejudice is social; prejudice is directed toward an other or others. This possible essence of 'toward others' is not a simple one. Although prejudiced persons typically direct their prejudice toward other persons and groups, many examples at the sites indicate that minority group members sometimes direct prejudices at themselves. Among these are reports of dark-skinned black troops in the United States Army taking out their aggressions against light-skinned blacks and vice versa, with the two groups referring to each other as 'spooks,' 'shiftless' and 'ignorant' (Allport, 1954: 149). Various reports suggest that a person who is prejudiced against himself is prejudiced on the basis of his membership in a group he considers an out group. Whether or not this is the case we must check through constant comparisons and variations when we investigate the possible essence we term 'toward others.' This essence will obviously have to be described more specifically, to include cases where one's self becomes the target of the prejudice (unless this is done by making the self into an other).

71

Apparently the larger essence involved here concerns self-other possibilities in general. This can also be seen on the map under 'emotional.' Here we find some persons at the sites declaring that prejudice entails fear of oneself (Sartre says as much). But this appears to conflict with a whole body of literature concerning 'Social Distance' (beginning with Bogardus, 1925), that prejudiced persons want to stay away from those against whom they are prejudiced.

5   Of the types of target, a simple glance at map 3 indicates that no single type of target could enter as an essence. The targets vary according to specific manifestations of prejudice – on a variety of bases from group membership to belief holding. This category may contribute some thickness to the possible self-other essence above by specifying how prejudicing persons construct objects to receive their prejudice.

6   The third category, 'functions,' is the clearest case of a possible essence which can be derived from map 3. Unlike the others we have noted, this category cannot be discounted or radically revised in any simple manner, despite several apparent difficulties which can be noted:

First, the items 'advantage for possessor' and 'reducing collective achievement' may seem to contradict. It is tempting to discount each item as a possible essence by noting the other item. In this way we could argue against the necessity of 'function' by noting cases in which the possessor thinks she is achieving an advantage over others through prejudicing, when actually harming herself and her targets through reducing group or societal efficiency, solidifying false consciousness, etc. Conversely, we could discount the reduction of collective achievement by suggesting that even while it is being reduced individuals are increasing their own achievements. But beneath this sort of discussion exists a potential essence that holds up. Prejudice is perceived as useful; prejudice seems to be an *instrument* for the accomplishment of social life. It may be used by individuals to put others at a disadvantage, it may be used by capitalistic monopolists to obtain cheap labor or keep workers fighting with one another, etc., but whether 'functional' or 'dysfunctional' it is an instrument.

A related problem with functions we also avoid by viewing instrument as the possible essence. The initial functionalist conception is of an entity within a social system, the social system being conceived analogous to a living organism. Although social systems may appear to have such lives of their own, persons are the 'working parts' which make them run, and they do so via intentionality. We can easily avoid, then, the imprecision of the mechanistic or organic analogies, but still retain the possible essence within this section of map 3.

A third difficulty is the item 'to meet normative demands.' This proposes that the ways in which social instruments can be used are determined through normative structures. From a hermeneutic viewpoint, we must search out ways in which persons take the moral order as true, or are obligated to accept as fact what others accept as fact, including the potential inhering in instruments. On the other hand, our essentialism specifies that we look concurrently at the essences of social instruments in general and how these affect the normative order's power over the instruments.

7 Finally and similarly, we must look at 'reduces efficiency by reducing collective achievement' in light of the foregoing. Ordinarily, instruments can both increase and decrease efficiency, depending upon how they are used. One can certainly find prejudice used to increase efficiency. The Sherif (1961) site is an apparent example. The two groups developed at Sherif's summer camp used prejudice against one another to increase their efficiency at competing with one another. Each group thereby increased the efficiency of its collective achievement. Only if we consider the two groups as one can we consider what happened at the summer camp as reducing efficiency by reducing collective achievement.

Delimiting the experiment

The previous chapters have specified a few concurrent goals crucial to the sort of phenomenological sociology of which essential interactionism is a part. First, we seek a critical examination of taken-for-granted features of the lifeworld (i.e. a hermeneutic inquiry). Second, we seek essences of social phenomena. And third, we seek understandings of these essences in their richness, rather than thin descriptions which permit simplified appreciations, fewer pages of description, and precise statements. It follows that our first experiment – which constitutes the remainder of this book – should concern itself (1) with as thick a description and analysis as resources permit of only one or two essences; (2) that the initial essence be one which is uncritically assumed at many of the sites to be true; and (3) that we investigate not only to determine whether something is an essence, also its potential to reveal other essences.

Of the possible essences which emerged from fieldwork with the above definitions the one which seems best to meet these criteria is the instrument essence. Most of the sites are functionalist or Freudian in orientation, and both groups take for granted that prejudice is an instrument. The other possible essences which have emerged from the fieldwork discussed in this chapter would have to be considered in depth as well, however, for any full essential interactionist theory of prejudice.

Some will perhaps find it ironic or worse that I would concentrate on a functionalist concern at a time when 'sociology has finally thrown off the chains of functionalism.' As T. S. Eliot expressed in his *Four Quartets*:

We shall not cease from exploration
And the end of all our exploring
Will be to arrive where we started
And know the place for the first time.

Summary

Details are offered of the lengthy search for a complete list of social science literature in English dealing with prejudice. Each paper or book within this literature will be treated as a fieldwork site during the first illustration of the method suggested in Part III. From approximately 600 titles uncovered, key informants Allport, Ehrlich, and Levin emerged, each of whom has written a book summarizing the literature on prejudice.

Maps of the sites were constructed according to (1) theoretical positions, (2) ways of prejudicing, and (3) crucial features. The third map became central to our initial illustration of the method, and resulted from definitions at the sites. The features that persons at the sites considered essential were used to determine which suggested essences would be investigated in the initial experiment with the method.

The remainder of the chapter offered quick visits to sites and simple phantasy variations to rule out as possible essences many of the features noted in the definitions from the sites. In this way we were able to demonstrate that the following features do not hold up in all manifestations of prejudice (or apparently even in most): (1) behavior, and concurrently hostility and aggression; (2) a single direction for prejudicing (negative or positive); (3) a single type of attitude (sick, emotional, not easily changeable, stereotyped, without objective evidence or actual experience); (4) any particular type of target (individuals, individuals on basis of group membership, minority groups, belief holders, objects); and (5) specific functions (advantage for possessor, meeting normative demands, reducing efficiency by reducing collective achievement).

These initial comparisons revealed some features which remain from those recommended by the sites, and which we will consider possible essences, as follows: (1) pre-judging, (2) toward others, and (3) instrumental.

The initial experiment with the method to be carried out in the following chapters was delimited to investigation via one possible essence: the suggested instrumental essence. Major goals for the experiment are (1) to provide a thick description and analysis of only a few essences, (2) to begin with a possible essence uncritically assumed at many of the sites, and (3) to permit elaboration of this essence to result in specification of other possible essences.

6 Elaboration of essences: I

This chapter and Chapter 7 examine the suggested instrumental essence of prejudice. We do so by bracketing at first whether or not instrumental *is* an essence of prejudice, in order to concentrate directly upon instrumentalism. As described in Chapter 4, such a strategy allows us to assume not that instrumental is an essence of prejudice, nor that it is not, but rather to examine prejudice *as if* it were an instrument (an item used as a means for achieving desired ends).

This strategy permits us to approach prejudice in its thickness, to describe the ways in which it can operate under various conditions. While working with the bracketed essence 'instrumental' we seek the potential *whys* and *hows* of prejudicing in general: Why do people prejudice? How do they prejudice? These questions we attempt to answer both social-psychologically and sociologically.

Such elaborated strategy is called for by the impossibility of discounting the proposed instrument essence through simple comparisons of variations, as we did with such proposed essences as discrimination, not-easily-changeable, and others in the preceding chapter. After this elaborated fieldwork we can then evaluate our comparisons among the sites and our phantasy variations on the sites to see if cases are possible in which prejudice need not be instrumental.

On functionalist sites

We begin with the group of sites concerned directly with the instrument essence of prejudice, namely, the functionalists. One can expect, however, that the demands of our horizontal comparisons will frequently and quickly take us to nonfunctionalist sites during this inquiry.

Before discussing material from the functionalists, this is perhaps a good time to state explicitly what was already suggested in previous discussions concerning the possibility of using work by theorists without accepting their theory. The tendency in sociology has been to throw out the baby with the bath water: when serious deficiencies are indicated in a theory, large groups of sociologists abandon that theory and all of its contributions to understanding social life. In reading social theory and research and in talking with social theorists and researchers one is struck by the vivacity with which they believe what they are positing. In many cases this zealousness is the inevitable result of the competition between paradigms for legitimation within a field (*à la* Kuhn, 1970). In other cases it bespeaks the need for persons to legitimate a political ideology, a social class, an ethnicity, a reference group, or a combination thereof. Whatever the case, part of the zealousness can probably be attributed to the attempt by its possessor to advance herself in the profession.

But I would suggest that most social theorists and researchers forcefully believe their 'discoveries' for another reason as well: these apparent truths struck the investigators forcefully. They stood out among a variety of possibilities and amid great confusion. Regardless how much of this process we care to explain via social, psychological, and physiological mechanisms, one point must remain. Persons who allow themselves initial confusion, experimentation and critical inquiry believe their major theoretical positions because these positions make understandable for them previously disparate and murky aspects of social works. The 'ah-hah!' experience so frequently noted by Gestaltists cannot be adequately reduced. Those moments at which the various parts come together to form something distinctly different are moments at which a theorist or researcher solidifies his position.

Theoretical positions tend to have integrity, then, even amid equally serious criticisms. Consequently when I turn to the functionalists for some understanding of the instrumental nature of prejudice and thereby open myself to the accusation that functionalism has been rejected as inadequate social theory, I can offer only one reply. I agree that 'the trouble with functionalism is that it is committed to the present society, with all its dilemmas, contradictions, tension, and indeed, with all its immorality' (Gouldner, 1970: 281), that it is functionalism's blindness to rationalize what is and to neglect what society can become, and how it should be changed (Lee, 1975) and that the organic analogy is inappropriate. Indeed, I recently presented a critique of functionalism (Glassner and Freedman, 1979). But in the face of these arguments I refuse to neglect the valuable insights functionalists offer and prefer instead to use functionalist sites *in light of* the comments of their critics.

To assist in the fieldwork at the functionalist sites we add a new key informant. Jack Levin has made a recent elaborate tour of the sites where the functionalist position is supported, in a book titled *The Functions of Prejudice* (1975). I have read this report on the sites and interpretations from them and revisited almost all of these sites.

Our continuing goal is to uncover essential interactions among a variety of manifestations. This was attempted in the present case through first looking as closely as possible at the ways in which prejudice was used as an instrument at the sites (which include various historical periods and physical locations). These uses were constantly compared between sites (including non-functionalist sites) to answer a single major question: What are the essential parameters of the potential for this instrument? The question is also answered through phantasy variations of possible uses for the tool and an analysis of the essence 'instrument' in general.

A social psychological instrument: why?

On the social-psychological level, prejudice appears to be an instrument which assists (1) in the release of aggression; or (2) in simplifying the task of defining situations. We first look at why people use prejudice to accomplish these tasks.

Aggression

A variety of sites concern prejudice as the product of frustration leading to aggression leading to displacement. The most famous of these sites is Dollard *et al.*, *Frustration and Aggression*, where the conclusion is that aggression is the inevitable consequence of frustration. This inevitability is difficult to support. Woodworth (1921) and Allport *et al.* (1941), found that the commonest reaction to frustration is not aggression, but a direct attempt to surmount the source of frustration. Phenomena such as planning, avoiding, and reasoning often can be found in adults as substitutions for the allegedly immediate reaction of the infant to become angry.

Frustration-aggression-displacement syndrome when applied to prejudice has still more problems. Many individuals are capable of detaching themselves from their frustrations to the point that they may be described as impunitive, while others take *in* their aggressions rather than taking them out (Rosenzweig, 1945). Sherif (1966), found that the children at his summer camp did not exhibit aggression following frustrations when the norms of their own groups prohibited such behavior.

Berkowitz (1962) looked at a variety of frustration-aggression sites and concluded that 'every frustration increases the instigation of aggression.' That such instigation is present can be demonstrated via numerous sites. Most often cited at other sites is Hovland and Sears (1940), who computed the correlation (-0.60) between the annual per-acre value of cotton in the South and the number of lynchings per year for the period 1882 and 1930. Similarly, the depression of the 1930s saw the birth of 114 organizations concerned with increasing anti-Semitism (Rose, 1958). During this same period a substantial number of nativist organizations worked to exclude potential immigrants and to deport recent arrivals, blaming these people for America's economic difficulties (LaGumina, 1973).

Other indications derive from Bettleheim and Janowitz's (1950), study of relative deprivation among new army veterans in Chicago. They report aggressive attitudes most highly concentrated in the downwardly mobile group, while the pattern was significantly reversed for those who had advanced in social status since the period of their previous employment. Those who had experienced no change were somewhat in the middle.

Mobility-frustration is not limited to the downwardly mobile, however, as seen at the Greenblum and Pearlin (1953), site. Both downwardly mobile and upwardly mobile persons of those studied were more willing to accept anti-Semitic statements than those in stationary positions. That frustration seems significantly involved in these studies was illustrated by Silberstein and Seeman (1959), who conducted similar research, but distinguished persons according to degree of motivation for changing their social position. Those who were mobility-oriented and downwardly mobile or stationary were more often accepting of anti-Semitism than those who were not mobility-oriented or were upwardly mobile.

A number of laboratory studies also indicate that aggression via prejudice frequently follows frustration. These studies put people in frustrating situations, ranging from incarceration to testing, then ask their feelings about minority groups (e.g. Miller and Bugelski, 1948; Cowen *et al.*, 1959; and Holmes, 1972). But other sites point out that this aggression may be long-standing and itching for release upon a variety of targets, including those against whom the person is not prejudiced and regardless of whether frustration elicits this aggression. One part of a study by Frenkel-Brunswick and Sanford (1945), points this out clearly. The prejudiced persons were shown pictures of persons representing a variety of types. Some were intended as parents of the same ethnicity and social class as the prejudiced person, others were persons of two races interacting, others were public servants, etc. Even in the cases of photographs of parent-types, the high-prejudice persons much more often than the low-prejudice persons offered explanations of the pictures which included very aggressive themes for the participants.

We can see from these site-comparisons that one way in which prejudice serves as a social psychological instrument is in the accomplishment of displacing aggression arising amid frustration. We also see that it is not inevitable amid frustration or aggression that prejudice will occur. Hence, this is not an essence of prejudice but rather a possible indicator of the parameters or structures of essences. For our immediate concerns, we can see that one reason why people use prejudice is that they feel a need to release aggression.

Simplification

The sites reveal several ways in which persons employ prejudice to simplify. These consist of issues surrounding (1) authoritarian personality research, (2) stereotyping, (3) social and personal distancing, and (4) the affective responses of prejudiced persons to their targets.

In classifying the prejudice-literature sites by theory within my fieldnotes, it became very obvious midway through the process that the largest group would be those sites related to authoritarian personality theory. This neo-Freudian theory began with the 1950 publication of *The Authoritarian Personality* by Adorno, Frenkel-Brunswick, Levinson, and Sanford. The proposition that prejudice is rooted in socialized character structure dates back at least to the 1930s, however (Horkheimer, 1936; Stagner, 1936; Maslow, 1943; Hartley, 1946).

Vertical comparisons among these sites suggest that *Authoritarian Personality* marks a turning point in value-commitments within the research on prejudice. Organizers of the work had suffered Nazism and by the mid-1940s they were actively conducting questionnaire and laboratory research in California with prejudiced college students (e.g. Frenkel-Brunswick, 1945). Throughout this early work, and especially in *Authoritarian Personality*, the emphasis is on anti-Semitism. More questions concern Jewish targets and more discussion concerns anti-Semitic findings than any other topic, although Blacks, foreigners, Puerto Ricans, and Catholics are also included as targets. The value commitment was not only to the reduction of anti-Semitism and other prejudices, however. Unlike most prejudice researchers to that point, Adorno and colleagues dedicated themseles to investigating what they perceived to be a generalized personality type. The researchers thought they had seen a pattern in their everyday interactions with a large group of persons; that these persons were ethnocentric, economically and politically conservative, and 'implicitly antidemocratic' (fascistic). This was exemplified for the researchers by remarks heard during their early studies grouping ethnic, economic and political hates within a single phrase, such as 'nigger-loving bureaucrats' or 'Jewish international bankers,' or 'the Jew is the dictator of democracy' (Allport, 1958: 67). The researchers set out to demonstrate the existence of this personality type, to describe it more precisely, and to indicate its persistence among varied groups and throughout the life cycle. The researchers set up their research with the goal of finding intercorrelations between the dimensions of this alleged personality.

Self-reports, clinical interviews and projective techniques were employed. The main written tests were the anti-Semitism (A–S) scale, the Ethnocentrism (E) scale, the Political and Economic Conservatism scale (PEC) and the Implicit Anti-democratic Trends (F) scale. Adorno *et al.* administered the scales to 2000 persons: college students, union members, and members of civic and service groups. As expected, the replies indicated high correlations between anti-Semitism, general ethnocentrism, ideological conservatism, and authoritarianism. The researchers conclude that the prejudiced person uses clear-cut attitudes to maintain a rigid defense against his or her own unacceptable impulses and moral uncertainties. This conclusion is in accord with the other neo-Freudian sites. The researchers make several leaps in order to come to this conclusion, and we must tear apart their decision making process, both vertically, through a look at how it occurred within the study, and through horizontal comparisons with other studies.

Of the high correlations, one must look closely at the scale items. The F, E, and PEC scales included some items of similar content. The items 'The artist and professor are of just as much value to society as the businessman and manufacturer' and 'The businessman and the manufacturer are much more important to society than the artist and professor' are from the PEC scale and the F scale, but are identical except in direction of scoring. A person who agrees with one should agree with the other and will spuriously increase the degree of correlation among the scales.

The scales contain items considered high, or low prejudice by the researchers rather than by the 'subjects' or other groups within the society. Simpson and Yinger (1972: 80) note:

> If a person high on a scale of prejudice (ethnocentricism) admires generals and political figures and one low in prejudice admires scientists and writers, this is not necessarily evidence of a different outlook on life. If a prejudice scale is negatively

correlated with education (as many studies have shown), the difference in selection of admired persons may be a function of the educational differences, not of the attitudes toward minorities.

More generally, we could suggest that such admiration disparaties result from differential reference groups.

Other sites have criticized Adorno *et al.* on the basis that they ignore the tendency of some people to answer 'yes' to any questionnaire statement (Bass, 1955; Christie, 1958; Peabody, 1961; A. Campbell, 1960). Jackman (1973), looked for separate indications of working-class authoritarianism, this time from a series of random public opinion polls. On the basis of path models, she concluded that 'the theory of working class authoritarianism has depended heavily for support on the use of items phrased as positively-worded agree-disagree statements that yield an education-related acquiescence response-bias that has very little to do with the respondent's true attitudes.'

From a more qualitative viewpoint, a serious difficulty is the forced-response questionnaire format itself. Persons who neither agree precisely nor disagree precisely were given no way to indicate their true feelings. As Shils (1954) suggested, the operationalized framework describes political issues in a simple continuum from liberal to conservative. Such a continuum has the consequences of obscuring the ideological components of all sides. This would seem to be the case for feelings about role-holders as well. Where elaborated responses *were* offered, we are not told the rationale for coding them. One respondent said: 'Very, very fine man – intelligent, an understanding, excellent father, in every way.' Is this to be coded as 'conventional idealization' or 'positive affect' (Christie and Jahoda, 1954)?

Additionally, ethnicity of the investigator can influence the response patterns (Summers and Hammonds, 1966), and questionnaire research about attitudes produces one answer from a person at one time and another later. Kendall (1954), twice administered to 219 persons the F-scale item, 'Prison is too good for sex criminals; they should be publicly whipped or worse.' Twenty-seven per cent gave different responses after six months, which would suggest that these specific attitudes are not as deeply rooted as Adorno *et al.* want to argue.

Nor can we determine whether some of the scales measure what they purport to measure. Ethnocentrism is usually conceived as a group-centered, ethnicity-centered, or nation-centered attitude cluster. The Sullivan and Adelson (1954), site would question the ability for traditional scales to measure ethnocentrism. These researchers took twenty-nine items from the ethnocentrism scales and rewrote them to refer to 'people' or 'most people', instead of Jews, blacks, or other specific groups. 'Jews seem to prefer the most luxurious, extravagant, and sensual way of living' becomes 'People seem to prefer the most luxurious, extravagant, and sensual way of living.' The revised scale was administered to 221 mid-western college students, along with a 20-item E scale. The correlation between the two was 0.53. The students in general would attribute these characteristics to most people, not only to the target groups.

At a still more basic level, we must question how the researchers can tell anything related to general personality or prejudice structure with items such as: 'Some day it will probably be shown that astrology can explain a lot of things.' This depends upon whether one has experienced astrology, whether it seemed to 'work,' and similar questions for one's reference group members, as well as one's degree of superstition, which was what Adorno *et al.* attempted to measure with the question.

The other part of the conclusion noted above – that prejudice is used as a defense against one's own unacceptable impulses and moral uncertainties – depends in large part upon 70 in-depth interviews. Adorno *et al.* coded these responses to reveal five categories of personality traits: repression versus awareness, externalization versus internalization, conventionalism versus genuineness, power versus love orientation, and rigidity versus flexibility. The highly-prejudiced persons cluster on the left side of each pair, tolerant persons on the right. A look at the responses between the groups does reveal striking differences in orientations toward social worlds, although their differences would be characterized in different terms by different groups (e.g., the prejudiced's peers might speak of 'repression' as 'appropriate thoughts').

But to make the leap that prejudice results from unacceptable impulses and moral uncertainties may be unwarranted. 'Aware' or 'flexible' persons also have unacceptable impulses and moral uncertainties, just of different varieties. Projective tests (and simple phantasy variations) indicate that such 'love-oriented' persons in many cases repress their feelings of violence. Any committed person has unacceptable impulses (and therefore moral uncertainties on some level). Yet we do not find all persons employing prejudices to deal with these conditions.

These vertical and horizontal comparisons indicate that we cannot conclude that a predictable set of beliefs or a single personality type is an essence of prejudice, nor *vice versa*, that prejudice is an essence of a personality type. The *Authoritarian Personality* sites do suggest, however, that prejudicing is one of several phenomena available to persons for simplifying social worlds. These sites indicate additional interaction possibilities for prejudice. A major reason that prejudice is used as an instrument appears to be the perceived need of groups and persons to simplify. Hence, prejudice is likely to be employed along with other simplification tools.

Why people stereotype

Anti-Semitism and Ethnocentrism scales in the *Authoritarian Personality* research ask persons to agree or disagree with various common stereotypes about targets. In the previous chapter we noted that stereotyping is not an essence of prejudice. Now we look at sterotyping in order to learn more about the suggested instrument essence of prejudice; i.e. one activity persons often do when prejudicing seems to be stereotyping.

Walter Lippman (1922), is credited with coining the term 'stereotype' and defining it as 'pictures in our heads.' Lippman did not distinguish between stereotypes and categories, however. A necessary distinction between the two is that a category may take on many varied descriptions and shadings, whereas a stereotype specifies the category and limits it (Allport, 1958: 187):

> A stereotype, then, is not a category, but often exists as a fixed mark upon the category. If I say, "All lawyers are crooked," I am expressing a stereotyped generalization about a category. The stereotype is not in itself the core of the concept. It operates, however, in such a way as to prevent differentiated thinking about the concept.

Levin's (1975), review of the sites concerned with stereotyping led him to a same conclusion as did our consideration of these sites: Stereotyping is performed by the prejudiced person in order to reduce cognitive uncertainties about targets and to produce order and clarity about these targets. It is used to 'define the situation.' As Katz (1975), and McHugh (1968), have noted, a person tends to give adequate structure to his universe. McHugh found that people try to restore a definition to situations in which they find themselves, nearly as soon as former definitions are broken down.

Culturally supported prejudices provide instant definitions of others based upon alleged characteristics of the groups to which they belong. This permits the prejudiced person to limit his cognitive interactions with these groups to a relatively small number of items. Katz (1960), offers the example of a prospective employer who uses a stereotype of blacks in order to form a conclusion regarding the applicant's abilities, rather than using a variety of life-

ELABORATION OF ESSENCES: I

and work-histories, interviews, etc. Although all prospective employers must simplify their applicants on the basis of a relatively small number of information bits, this can be accomplished in a variety of ways. A prejudiced strategy is via limiting cognitive responses to stereotypes of 'this sort of person.'

This discussion forces us to confront another proposed essence from the definitions at the sites (noted in the previous chapter). In these definitions appear a conflict between whether the targets of prejudice are individuals, groups, or individuals on the basis of group membership. The Katz site and others suggest that the third target type may be essential. Stereotyping asserts that individuals must be like an alleged characteristic of their group.

The assertion which stereotyping makes is, 'All A are B.' As is readily apparent, this assertion is of the form of an induction. If we consider an induction adequately defended, then we can be reasonably certain that, 'This particular A is B.'

Here we have a case in which a way of prejudicing looks like a way of logical and scientific thinking. We will see throughout our inquiry that indeed the line between prejudicing and 'normal' social-mental phenomena is either very thin or non-existent. In their review of some of the sites we have considered, Hogan and Emler (1978) conclude that individuals who stereotype are not appropriately characterized as persons who make faulty inferences. The inferences are often correct. How do scientists distinguish these phenomena?

The frequently offered distinction between 'adequate' and 'inadequate' inductions offered by Hempelian scientists and philosophers of science is that, 'An inductive inference from an observed association of attributes $(A_n - B_n)$ can justify inference to another case $(A_{n+1} - B_{n+1})$ or inference to the corresponding generalization (All A are B) only if the association is somehow known to be lawlike, not merely accidental' (Black, 1967). But upon what do laws rest? As Pierce, Hume and Hanson have noted in various ways, the laws cannot rest upon immediate experience or *a priori* knowledge, since people disagree about these. In social sciences (and perhaps inevitably in other sciences) the laws tend to be accepted or rejected according to their competitive advantage at predicting better than competing theories. New laws and models are argued in terms of their capacity for more or better predictions than their competitors.

Goodman (1955: 91), remarks on the absurdity of the view that 'truth and significance of a hypothesis lie in the accuracy of its predictions.' He offers what he calls the 'new riddle of induction' to illustrate this point. Suppose all emeralds examined before a certain time t have been green; use the label 'grue' for the property of being

85

FIRST ILLUSTRATION OF A METHOD

green up to the time *t* and blue thereafter. Then all the evidence supports equally well the competing laws 'All emeralds are green' and 'All emeralds are grue.' If laws are to be accepted or rejected on the basis of predictive ability, then the already violated statement 'All emeralds are grue' would be true if all emeralds not examined before time *t* are blue.

Prejudiced persons do in fact offer Goodman's riddle, though in much less sophisticated forms. A question asked by researchers at some sites is of the variety, 'How do you know that the next Mexican you hire will be lazy?' It is not uncommon for the response to be, 'The last four have been good workers, so this one will be lazy.' We must note that this reply is not unreasonable. It is in the form of the 'grue' emeralds. All of the evidence is equally good that Mexicans are energetic or that they are 'lazigetic,' once we recognize Hume's point that prediction on the basis of past experience has no ultimate justification, but is justified only by tradition.

In the case of contemporary social worlds 'grue inductions' can be especially well defended. The experiences of everyday life are frequently that what was commonplace last week has been replaced today. (A couple of years ago it had happened that for several years I could drive my car rapidly to and from work each morning without stopping along the way more than once a week. Then one morning 'gas crises' had occurred, and I was forced to drive more slowly and to wait frequently in long lines at gas stations for my allotment of gasoline.)

Several escape routes have been suggested from the abyss in which we have placed induction. Goodman's own proposal has been to consider as adequate inductions those with 'entrenched' predicates. He works out the solution in detail, but it translates roughly to accepting *B*s which have been frequently employed in previous inductive judgments. Of course, this is what the prejudiced person does, usually on the basis of his reference groups' usages, and again we lose the distinction between prejudiced induction (stereotyping) and other sorts.

A popular solution is that suggested by Popper, which builds into the situations the possibility for falsification. Popperians would convert statements of 'All *A* are *B*' to make them as potentially falsifiable as possible. We noted in Chapter 4 the general difficulties with the Popperian method. In the case of induction, Popperians simply turn the original difficulties upside down, but this does not make them go away. Why should one have greater assurances of the appropriateness of the conclusion by being unable to refute it than one has by being unable to demonstrate it? Neither strategy demonstrates that all A *are* B. And stereotyping certainly does not disappear once falsification is demonstrated. This is well illustrated by the Karlins *et al.* (1969), site. These researchers compared the stereotypes accepted by Princeton students during Gilbert's (1951), site and Katz and Braly's (1933), site. At all three times the students accepted stereotypes, but over the years some disappeared and were replaced by others. In our present terms, some were falsified by reference group experiences, media and social science debunking, etc. Hence, blacks in 1933 were considered lazy by 75 per cent of the students, but by only 26 per cent in 1967. Yet in 1933 only 26 per cent of the students considered blacks to be musical, while in 1967 47 per cent stereotyped blacks as musical. A similar shift is noted by Bayton *et al.* (1956). When they asked white students their stereotypes about blacks, but specified that the blacks were upper-class, none of the usual stereotypes for blacks were offered, perhaps because superstitious, lazy, ignorant, etc. are considered impossible characteristics for upper-class persons to possess. But the same students did assign other sets of stereotypes to the 'new' blacks, and assigned many of the usual stereotypes against blacks to lower-class persons when asked about this group. Apparently we can falsify inductions repeatedly with the result that new inductions will be used to replace them.

In light of these problems some thinkers have suggested that inductions are necessarily inadequate or unjust. It appears, in fact, to be difficult to distinguish stereotype-inductions from other inductions. The numerous attempts by philosophers to adequately defend their inductive leaps (e.g. via *a priori* defenses, searches for supreme inductive principles, etc.) have all been shown incapable of answering (1) the Humean critique that the leaps are finally based on tradition and (2) Goodman's demonstrations of the possible difficulties which can result. The most generally accepted response at present among both philosophers and social scientists is a recourse to probability (Black, 1967).

Contemporary social science inductions are expected to be reworded into probability language; 'B has probability relative to A,' or 'All A have probability of being B.' The probability conclusion still extends beyond the premises by disguised reference to sets of events not covered by the given premises (usually future events). We can avoid these difficulties by turning the inductive statements into deductive statements, and many scientists and philosophers of science are demanding this, notably through variations on Carnap's call for limiting oneself to 'state descriptions,' within which one can describe rather fully in simplified languages the items in one's propositions and the ways one is weighting these propositions. But we thereby lose the possibility of inductions in the process, because the very idea of this sort of induction is that on the basis of an adequate limited sample, we can make leaps to almost the entire universe.

Stereotyping appears then, as a form of everyday induction which people may use to reduce cognitive uncertainties about targets and to permit predictable reactions to these targets.

This is not to argue that inductions can never be justified. Rather, I wish to illustrate the great difficulty with which scientists and social scientists justify their inductions, to indicate that prejudicing persons are not necessarily simply 'sloppy' or 'unscientific' in their everyday inductions. Nor do they exhibit behavior which is universally proscribed in other activities. Inductions are sought in a variety of inquiries and are highly valued. Indeed, in our essential interactionist research we seek statements of the form 'All A are B' (e.g. 'All prejudice is instrumental'). We attempt to avoid some of the noted problems by showing not only probability within a sample but also necessity within as many manifestations and variations as are necessary to reveal the existing perspectives on the phenomenon and the logic of its structures. This differs from prejudicing techniques for induction in that the prejudiced do not seek perspectives of their target groups, nor are they concerned with possible variations. The goal among stereotyping persons is to construct inductions in order to simplify targets, while our goal is to construct inductions in order to elaborate the necessary properties of targets.

Why people social distance

Researcher Richard LaPiere traveled across the United States with a Chinese couple in the early 1930s. Ever since his journey the study of prejudice has been obligated to consider the *conative* dimension.

Only once in ten thousand miles of motor travel were LaPiere and the Chinese couple met with rejection from hotels, restaurants or camping establishments. They traveled across the United States twice, and up and down the Pacific Coast. LaPiere (1934: 232), reported his group was received at 66 hotels, auto camps, and 'Tourist Homes', served at 184 restaurants and cafes and treated with more than ordinary consideration in 72 of them.

When LaPiere returned home he sent questionnaires to all of these businesses, asking, 'Will you accept members of the Chinese race as guests in your establishment?' Replies came from 81 restaurants and 47 hotels. Of these, 92 per cent checked 'No,' and the remainder checked 'uncertain, depend upon circumstances.' His control group, consisting of establishments not visited, responded similarly. Other sites are replication studies (e.g. Kutner, Wilkins, Yarrow, 1952), and others offer tales of prejudiced nondiscriminators and non-prejudiced discriminators (e.g. Pilcher, 1972).

These suggest an essence underlying our note in the previous chapter that discrimination is distinct from prejudice. We can now see that the prejudicing person may be one who assigns simplified behavioral intentions to himself with regard to target groups, even if he does not carry out these intentions under certain circumstances.

This point became especially clear to me in light of a report by an executive of a large American corporation. The executive's job was to implement 'affirmative action' guidelines from the federal government for the hiring of minority workers. He reported his surprise at visiting corporate officers in Alabama and in New Jersey. The personnel executives at the Alabama office apparently complained bitterly about 'having to hire coloreds,' while the personnel executives at the New Jersey office apparently complained that they 'sure would like to hire some blacks.' Yet the Alabama office had quickly reached its federally-determined percentage quota for black employees, while the New Jersey office had hired only a small percentage of the number of blacks required by law. The New Jersey office explained that they could not find qualified black job applicants.

One would have to research both offices to determine how these contrasting outcomes resulted, but clearly the conative reactions of these employees were inversely related to their hiring behavior.

The conative dimension of the tool of prejudice is usually described in terms of social distance, a scale for which was devised first in 1925 by Emory Bogardus. The scale offers persons a list of statements indicating varying degrees of desired social intimacy, together with a list of names of social groups. In the first Bogardus scale, persons were asked (1925):

> According to my first feeling reaction, I would willingly admit members of each race (as a class and not the best I have known, nor the worst members) to the classifications which I have marked.

Bogardus asked a panel of judges in 1932 to rate 60 statements about degrees of distance. From their rating, these seven statements were selected as roughly equidistant along a scale of increasing social distance:

1 Would marry
2 Would have as a regular friend
3 Would work beside in an office
4 Would have several families in my neighborhood
5 Would have merely as speaking acquaintances

6 Would have live outside my neighborhood
7 Would have live outside my country

Bogardus administered the test to a large number of subjects in 1926, 1946 and 1956 and found a basic consistency in attitudes. After considerable testing of scaleability, the final version of the Bogardus scale was:

1 Would marry into group
2 Would have as close friends
3 Would have as nextdoor neighbors
4 Would work in the same office
5 Would have as speaking acquaintance only
6 Would have as visitors only to my nation
7 Would debar from my nation (Bogardus, 1959; Baton, 1967).

At other sites one finds considerable criticism of the social distance scaling procedures. Poole (1927: 116) argues that social distance relates to the intimacy which group norms allow between any two persons and should not be confused with personal distance, those degrees of intimacy which persons construct independent of the dictates of social norms:

> The relations between social distance and personal distance show the often observed difference between the individual and the group, the part and the whole. As the group exists only in the individuals who make it, so social distance exists only in the degree of personal distance which it requires. As a result there can be no social distance where there is no personal distance.

On the basis of Poole's site we can suggest that the reasons why persons use prejudice conatively may be from: (1) value orientations (right and wrong); (2) manifest norms (actual practices in the groups around them); (3) social norms (social acceptability); (4) personal norms (what the individual would do regardless of other normative demands); (5) possession of stereotypes (concurrent simplifications held about the target); and (6) possession of affective responses (concurrent feelings about the suggested behavior or about the target).

These specifications suggest the complexity of social distance and of any reading of social distance research. Modification of any of these six possibilities can change a person's distance ranking. This is illustrated at Brooks's (1936), site, where persons were asked to complete a modified Bogardus scale indicating their distance for twelve ethnic groups. Brooks added some information about the groups, however. Some were to be considered as having sixth grade education and others as having a college education. Six of the twelve groups changed their distance rank as a result of this modification, and two groups shifted one scale point on the six-point scale of distance.

Rokeach, Smith and Evans (1960) gave white college students descriptions of a pair of target persons. The students judged how likely they were to become friendly with each of the persons. The target pairs were presented as follows:

1. Race varied-belief constant (e.g. a white person who believes in God vs a black who believes in God).
2. Belief varied-race constant (e.g. a white person who believes in God vs a white person who is an atheist).
3. Race and belief varied (e.g. a white person who believes in God vs a black who is an atheist).

The students were asked to indicate their own feelings about each of the eight belief statements, so that they could compare their own beliefs with those given for the targets. The students indicated preferences for whites to blacks when beliefs were held constant, and for people with whom they agreed to people with whom they disagreed when race was held constant. Of the third pairing, the students tended to choose persons with their own beliefs, rather than those of their same race. This site suggests that social distance tests cannot in their usual form discriminate which types of target (e.g. belief or race) the prejudiced persons wish to avoid. It also suggests that the conative aspect of prejudice appears to be directed more on the basis of targets' beliefs than on targets' races. As Triandis (1960), and others note, however, one cannot predict (and certainly not make essence statements about) the relative importance of beliefs and race among prejudiced persons in general on the basis of the Rokeach site. Belief-congruence may be more consequential only for the conative response of 'friendship.' For other distances – neighbor, co-worker, fellow citizen – race may be more important than belief. Or the relative importance of these items may be situationally determined.

This discussion points out several difficulties for researchers who investigate prejudice by using social distance scales to determine who is prejudiced and how strongly. But our own concern is with utilizing these specifications of the conative aspect of prejudice to describe essences of prejudice. An essence which appears to emerge from the foregoing is simplification. We saw in the discussion of why people stereotype that they do so in large part to simplify their definitions of targets. We can see from the present section that people use prejudice in other cases as a conative instrument for purposes of simplifying their behavior intentions towards targets. The targets they choose may be belief-holders, ethnic groups, or other types. Going beyond the sites with a variation we can suggest the possibility of a person simplifying her conative responses to *herself*, as in the following self-dialogues: 'I wouldn't want to work with someone like myself' or 'I would not want to be *my* next door neighbor.'

Why people simplify affect

In addition to, or instead of, stereotyping and social distancing, prejudiced persons may have affective relationships with their targets. One's interactions with others may be simplified not only by simplifying the other or simplifying one's behavior intentions toward the other, but also by how one feels about the other. The need for affective simplification can arise from a variety of social interactions. A commonly recognized source is the requirement to compete economically, which may end up with some persons limiting their responses to a competing group by a variety of dislikes, in order that their possible positive affective responses not interfere with successful competition. Another source is within political ideology. In order to avoid the many complex issues underlying our own and others' ideological positions, we can simplify these others in our affective responses to help ourselves avoid confronting the persons and the complexities of the issues. This can be seen, for instance, in those who are hostile to or aggravated by 'commies' or 'damned capitalists.'

Affective simplification can also aid one in dealing with restrictive or confusing sexual norms. It is almost a commonplace to recognize this as operating with regard to the treatment of women as sexual objects. Restricting one's affect toward women to interactions with the genitalia helps to exclude them from economic, political and other roles. Where interethnic sexual confusion exists, simplified affective responses can be employed to many ends. Lillian Smith points this out in her novel, *Strange Fruit* (noted in Allport, 1954), which describes the emotional sterility of a small southern town. Affective simplification accomplishes not only the apparent sterility, however, but also escapes from its own prison. Religious orgies and racial conflicts are also regular features of the town.

Similarly, blacks have been depicted throughout American history as lusty, facilitating simplification in the 'justice' system. During the years 1938–48, thirteen southern states convicted 15 whites and 187 blacks and executed them for rape. Blacks made up only 23.8 per cent of the population and there is no evidence that they committed 53 times as many rapes as did whites. One can reasonably conclude that judges and juries were simplifying their task of publically controlling this type of sexual behavior via their responses (affective and cognitive) to race (Dombrowski, 1950). On the other side, Cleaver (1968), was capable of similar affective simplification in justifying a program of mass raping of white women on the grounds that the correct response of a black militant to white women is hate and punishment.

From the foregoing we can suggest, along with Ehrlich (1973), that the potential ways that prejudice can be used as an instrument are at least three: stereotyping (the cognitive dimension), social distancing (the conative dimension), and affect. These three possibilities are apparently used for purposes of simplifying social worlds relative to target groups.

A social psychological instrument: how?

The sites exemplify a common aspect of social science literature sites: the questions being asked at the sites are almost always of the variety, 'Why are people prejudiced?' One reason is that most of the literature was produced by persons who think in causal terms, and 'why' questions are varieties of causal questions eliciting 'because' replies.

The instrumental nature of prejudice suggests that another type of question may be more appropriate, namely, 'How do people use prejudice?,' or a possible variation, 'How do people prejudice?' This can be seen if we compare to material instruments. We may well ask questions such as, 'Why does she use a hammer to accomplish job X?' In response, we expect causal answers: 'because that is the tool people use for job X most of the time,' 'because she is constrained by social or physical circumstances to use a hammer for job X,' 'because she perceives a hammer as uniquely suited for accomplishing job X owing to its properties A, B, and C.' As essential interactionists we seek the third sort of answer, except where elements of the first two answers prove to be essential to the phenomenon of hammers or hammer-use. And this chapter thus far has dealt with answering this sort of question.

We may also ask 'How do people use hammers,' or 'How can people use hammers?', or 'How does one hammer?' The first two questions seek descriptions, the last seeks prescription. I would argue with Fritz Perls (1969), that in general *how* questions lead to more informative and more essential answers than do *why* questions. The latter lead to explanatoriness, probably due to their implied causality. I have suggested that such questions can be answered with interactionistic replies rather than causal replies, but at that point they are very close to having been re-thought as *how* questions.

We can see within the literature on prejudice as a tool some answers to 'How does one prejudice,' and 'How do persons use prejudice,' and such answers give important understandings of the instrument essence.

How people stereotype

Indo-European language facilitates prejudicing through three of its structural characteristics. (1) Words used to describe individuals also may be used to describe groups. (2) Collective nouns without qualification can be unambiguously employed to encompass collectivities. The statement, 'Socialists are radicals' tends to be transliterated 'All socialists are radicals.' (3) Qualification of collective terms requires a great deal of work to be precise. It is 'natural' to talk of groups with the words we use to speak of persons (Ehrlich, 1973: 21).

The actual process of using linguistic tags to simplify persons or groups exemplifies that properties of both the observers and the objects determine the state of social worlds. Prejudiced persons tend to depend upon cues as to the target's group affiliations in order to determine how to simplify the target. This can be seen at Razran's (1950), site, in which he displayed photographs of 30 'attractive and ethnically nonspecific white girls' faces' to 150 students. The students were then asked to rate the pictures in terms of liking, beauty, intelligence, character, ambition, and entertainingness. Two months later the students were shown the same pictures, but with ethnic surnames attached. Five were assigned Jewish names (e.g. Goldberg), five Italian names (e.g. D'Angelo), five Irish names (e.g. Kelly), and the remaining Anglo-Saxon names (e.g. Clark). Few changes occurred in judgments of those with Anglo-Saxon names. Judgments of *liking* and *character* significantly decreased for the Italian and Jewish labeled photographs, and the rating of ambition significantly increased with the Jewish labels.

Secord (1959), demonstrates even more dramatically the importance of labeling for the accomplishment of prejudicing via stereotypes. He presented a variety of people with ten photographs of persons with a range of Negro and Caucasian features. The researcher identified the photographs as either blacks or whites at random, and the persons looking at the photographs attached common stereotypes according to the race named by the researcher. The categorical response weakened when the photographs was so Caucasoid that they could not be spontaneously identified as Negro. Even then, highly-prejudiced persons accepted the researcher's labeling and responded categorically.

A suggestion of how persons are able apparently to defy their own eyes is offered by the Katz (1972 and 1975), sites, which show persons attributing to deviants a set of inherent and unchangeable characteristics which do not demand visible proof. Just as witches have been considered 'possessed' and the mentally ill are said to 'have a problem,' so it is possible for a variety of types of targets to be considered possessors of something invisible which makes them necessarily members of a group. Persons at the Secord site apparently considered blackness and whiteness to be items which people possess, regardless of whether others can see these items with their eyes. The voluminous evidence reviewed by Montagu (1974), also supports the suggestion, through case studies of groups at various historical periods attributing race to persons on the basis of evidence which these same persons would have considered inadequate for supporting other attributions. He further notes that prior to the sixteenth century, the concept of race did not exist. Montagu offers case after case in which the attribution of race cannot be justified empirically, but is accepted.

These sites and others suggest an explanation of stereotyping much in accord with that of labeling theory (Lemert, 1951 and Becker, 1963). This bespeaks of the relative nature of social worlds, including the present feature of stereotyping.

But amid this relativity, there seems to be some object determinism. Films of a subnormal ten-year-old girl and boy were shown to 42 college students by Guskin (1962). Half of the students were told that both children were retarded, the other half were told only that they were school-children. The filmed boy displayed obvious physical symptoms; the girl had none. After viewing the films, the students rated the children on scaled items such as confident-timid, strange-normal, capable-helpless, unintelligent-bright, and clumsy-skillful. Whether labeled subnormal or not, the girl's ratings on these adjective lists remained about the same. Hence, the site suggests that the labeling of subnormality had an effect only when the target's characteristics were in some sense perceived as relevant and validating.

My visits to the prejudice sites overall reveal that part of *how* people simplify target groups is by picking up some objective feature about the group and using it to replace several features. In his survey of popular anti-Semitic writings, Selzer (1972), illustrates this point. In small-town America at various historical points, it was not far from accurate to say that Jews owned the major businesses, that they were shrewd businessmen, or that they were mercenary. Yinger (1964), summarizes the dialectic at work here:

> However one may explain the origin of tendencies of minority-group members, to the contemporary generation – few of whom

can be counted on to be moral philosophers – these tendencies are simply there, as facts of his environment. Thus prejudice and discrimination can be sustained in part by their consequences.

Yinger's case can be analogized to our hammer in order to note a similarity among instruments. The more we use hammers the more we find we 'need' them rather than being content to use rocks. (Is it merely coincidental that one end of the hammer is for putting nails into things, and the other end is for removing them?)

From a more macro perspective, we can see that people stereotype in large part by picking up simplified media images. Larrick (1965) performed a content analysis of all children's trade books published during 1962, 1963 and 1964. Of the 5206 books published, only 6.7 per cent contained one or more blacks. The majority of the books portraying blacks placed them outside of the United States. Thus these children's media simplify minority groups by excluding them (discrimination).

Stereotyping is often employed as a method of conveying a character without spending many words. Berelson and Salter (1946) noted this in their study of portrayals of minority characters in short stories. O'Hara (1961) found that stereotyping is widely used by mass communicators as a technique for framing messages with the least amount of effort, and thereby also enabling the reader to receive and employ the message with minimum effort. O'Hara found that scenes and character types are repeated in various types of mass communication.

Until the 1970s, it was not uncommon for television and film actors to portray ethnic groups simply by changing pronunciation of a few letters. Blacks were simplified in this manner by substituting the 'd' sound for 'th' (e.g. 'lift dat bale'). Mexicans were characterized as using double 'e' sounds (e.g. 'theenk'). American Indians were played as devoid of any English and a linguistic ability generally limited to 'ugh', 'kemo sabe' or other monosyllabic grunts (Levin, 1975; Deloria, 1970). These are blatant simplifications, but more subtle ones are also frequently employed, as Elson (1964: 340), found in documenting ethnic stereotypes in educational media:

> Each race and its subdivisions – nationalities – are defined by inherent mental and personal characteristics which the child must memorize . . . And these traits are used to determine the rank of each race and nation . . . The American, as the ideal man, is of the white race, of Northern European background, Protestant, self-made, and if not a farmer at least retaining the virtues of his yeoman ancestors.

How people social distance

We noted above that the conative way of prejudicing can be used to simplify groups 'as needed,' be they ethnic groups or belief holders. This can be expanded as an introduction to how people prejudice conatively by including a few additional sites.

Shim and Dole (1967), questioned Hawaiian college students and their parents concerning preferred personal distances from persons who are missing one or two legs, and from blacks. The physical disability turned out to be a stronger determinant of personal distance than did race, but in further questioning, the attribution of incompetence or lack of empathy brought greater rejection than did either disability or race.

Especially interesting is the innovative site by E. L. Hartley (1946), in which college students were asked their attitudes, using a Bogardus Social Distance Scale, concerning thirty-five nations and races. Three of the ethnicities listed were fictitious – the 'Daniereans,' 'Pireneans,' and the 'Wallonians.' The result was that the students who desired high social distance from the actual ethnic groups also preferred high distance from the nonexistent groups. The correlation between social distance scores for the real and nonexistent groups was around +0.80. When one looks at the answers written in longhand, given in addition to the forced choice responses, an interesting insight emerges. One student wrote of the nonexistent peoples, 'I don't know anything about them; therefore I would exclude them from my country.' Another student, low on social distance against real groups, wrote, 'I don't know anything about them; therefore I have no prejudices against them.'

We can see, then, that one answer to how people social distance is that they simplify their behavioral intentions either toward or away from groups who appear to be threatening. How do persons determine which groups are threatening? Three answers emerge from the sites.

First, persons are socialized by their own groups concerning who to exclude. Spoerl (1951: 76), administered the Bogardus Social Distance Scale to 900 freshmen students in an eastern college. Among her findings:

> Jewish students stood highest in their rejection of Canadians, English, Finnish, French, German, Irish, Norwegian, Scottish, and Swedish (a rejection of the 'majority' or 'favored' groups in our country). Catholic students stood highest in rejection of Chinese, Hindus, Japanese, Negroes, and Filipinos (a rejection of the colored groups – possibly associated with the idea of 'heathen'). Protestant students stood highest in rejecting

FIRST ILLUSTRATION OF A METHOD

Armenians, Greeks, Italians, Jews, Mexicans, Polish, and Syrians (a rejection of familiar 'minority' groups in our culture).

Whether or not Spoerl is correct about the associations these persons make concerning the target groups, she has pointed out that groups differ in their selection of targets for high social distancing. This must not be carried too far, however, as evidenced by another site. Americans appear to provide a reference group for one another, despite the subdivisions of ethnicities within America. Americans of diverse ethnic backgrounds and socioeconomic positions exhibit high social distance preferences concerning blacks, Japanese, Chinese, Hindus and Turks, and widespread preference for English, German and Spanish persons (Derbyshire and Brody, 1964).

Second, persons turn to the mass media to make their social distancing choices, as we saw they did for stereotypes. Berelson and Salter (1946) studied popular short stories and found that American characters – i.e. white Protestants with no distinguishable ancestry of foreignness – were rarely depicted as loving and marrying minority and foreign characters. Barcus and Levin (1966), reported more intimate social relations between characters of like ethnic backgrounds than between characters differing ethnically. And the preference for intragroup relations was found in both black and white magazine fiction.

Third, persons can derive or maintain their social distancing toward specific targets through the supporting technique of physical distancing. This was well described at Brewer's (1969), site in Kenya, Uganda, and Tanzania. Four levels of physical distance (adjacent border, separation by one tribe, separation by two tribes, more remote) were compared with persons' answers to an abridged social distance questionnaire. Fifty members in each of ten tribes were questioned. Adjacent outgroups were responded to with significantly lower social distance. (The average intratribe correlation between physical and social distance was 0.54.)

Of course, in industrialized urban areas the support of physical distancing for conative prejudicing is often via residential segregation. These residential and ecological physical barriers facilitate protection of social distance norms within groups by obviating the opportunity for persons to actually interact with the targets of their behavior intentions and possibly discover that their behavior intention does not match their actual behavior.

How people simplify affect

A review of 15 factor analyses of checklists of words denoting affect reported the possibility of twelve categories of affect:

1. aggression: defiant, rebellious, angry, furious, ready to fight.
2. fatigue: drowsy, dull, sleepy, tired, sluggish.
3. concentration: careful, contemplative, attentive, serious, efficient
4. surgency: carefree, playful, witty, lively, talkative
5. social: affectionate, forgiving, kindly, warm-hearted, sociable
6. anxiety: clutched up, fearful, jittery, tense, nervous
7. skepticism: skeptical, suspicious, dubious
8. egotism: egotistic, self-centered, boastful, aloof
9. sadness: sad, blue, lonely, down-hearted, sorry
10. vigor, general activation: active, energetic, vigorous, bold, strong
11. elation: overjoyed, elated, pleased
12. nonchalance: bored, leisurely (Nowlis, 1965)

Other sites offer different lists. For example, Davitz (1969), offers such categories as:

activation: admiration, amusement, awe, cheerfulness, delight
moving toward: affection, love
hypoactivation: boredom, depression, anger, fear, panic
inadequacy: anxiety

We can expect affective responses to groups to change over time, since they are developed within intra- and inter-group interactions, and these interactions change in type, magnitude, meaning, etc. Persons at the sites restrict their 'subjects' responses through forced-response and numerical-response demands, of course, and through the simplifying nature of questionnaires as a medium. Probably prejudicing persons could name other affective interactions with their targets as well. But it does appear that some prejudicing persons can identify their repertoire of affects to simplify interactions with targets.

That these sorts of affective reactions can effectively simplify on a large scale – and that they are distinguished from the other ways of prejudicing – are pointed out by two sites: Myrdal (1944), and the novel *Invisible Man*. Both portray the attitudes of Northern whites as involving a convenient ignorance of blacks. Blacks were hardly noticed, and if noticed are avoided. Myrdal notes that this type of reaction to blacks permits them to be further simplified, into the equally invisible (to middle and upper classes) lower classes.

A similar strategy for affective simplification can be seen in Kitsuse's (1964), site concerning reactions to homosexuals. The modal reaction to persons suspected of homosexuality 'is disapproval, implicity rather than explicitly communicated, and a restriction of interaction through partial withdrawal and avoidance.'

Interactions

The preceding discussion offers details concerning prejudice as an instrument for simplification. Three techniques employed for this process are stereotyping, behavior intentions, and affect. Now we look briefly at the interactions among these techniques (the internal structure of the essence).

The only sites I have been able to locate which consider these relationships are those reported in Ehrlich (1973). The first is a questionnaire checklist study Ewens (1969) administered to college students. He narrowed the most often given checklist items by whites concerning blacks to 60 words, as follows:

Stereotypes	Behavioral Intentions	Affect
1 Alert	1 Accept help from	1 Affectionate
2 Ambitious	2 Admire ideas of	2 Aggravated
3 Athletic	3 Approve of	3 Agreeable
4 Boastful	4 Ask opinion of	4 Alarmed
5 Conceited	5 Avoid	5 Angry
6 Courteous	6 Be an enemy of	6 Annoyed
7 Honest	7 Be friendly to	7 Antagonistic
8 Industrious	8 Be loyal to	8 Confident
9 Intelligent	9 Be on first-name basis	9 Contemptuous
10 Intolerant	10 Be prejudiced against	10 Disagreeable
11 Kind	11 Be proud of	11 Friendly
12 Lazy	12 Be unfriendly to	12 Hostile
13 Loud	13 Dislike	13 Indignant
14 Musical	14 Fear	14 Intimate
15 Quarrelsome	15 Feel superior to	15 Intolerant
16 Quick-tempered	16 Hate	16 Jovial
17 Radical	17 Help	17 Loving
18 Revengeful	18 Look down upon	18 Outgoing
19 Rude	19 Respect	19 Sympathetic
20 Sportmanlike	20 Treat as subordinate	20 Tolerant

Ewens used *tau* as his measure of association and reported that scores on the affect scale correlated 0.46 with stereotyping and 0.43 with personal distance. Stereotypes and personal distance scales correlated at 0.29. All coefficients were significant beyond the 0.05 level, illustrating that all three are positively correlated.

A study by Morse and Allport (1952) concluded the highest correlation between stereotype and conative at $r = 0.72$; with affect and stereotype correlated at 0.42 and affect and behavior intention at 0.64. Campbell and McCandless (1951), reported correlations (r) between affect and personal distance as 0.87 and affect and stereotype as 0.77. Ostrom (1969), found the average intercorrelation of each component with the other two was 0.59. In this study Ostrom was looking at attitudes about church, rather than those about the usual targets of such studies.

Here we have a case of important constant conjunctions within an essence. These conjunctions reveal that the three techniques for simplifying tend to be found intermingling. But we must look at the sites critically. In all cases the prejudiced persons were forced to respond to the words given to them, rather than to devise their own prejudicing. What these sites reveal is that many prejudiced people tend to be capable and willing to use all three techniques for simplifying; not that prejudiced persons necessarily use all three. Indeed, Kramer's (1950), site is similar to several which make this point clear. Whites were shown papers containing 'distance zones' from an area where blacks were moving. Zone 1 was the closest to this area of expanding black residency. Zone 5 was the most remote, being three miles away. There was a general tendency among whites living in these regions to exclude blacks from their neighborhoods. Kramer checked further, however, to seek relationships between these desires and the stereotyping the residents were doing. In Zone 1, where the white residents had the closest contact with the blacks, only five per cent offered stereotypes as reasons for exclusion; as against 25 per cent of the residents in Zone 5. In contrast, the intensity of hostile feelings or behavior intentions in Zone 1 was higher than in Zone 5. In Zone 1, 64 per cent of the residents made spontaneous expressions of hostility, whereas only four per cent in Zone 5 offered hostile reactions. Apparently hostility and stereotypes were not conjoined for most of these persons.

These studies suggest an important (though apparently nonessential) interaction which helps to determine which technique(s) individuals will employ. The prejudicing person interacts with the target of his prejudice and on the basis of this interaction selects techniques for simplifying. In other words, the target is influential in determining the choice of simplification techniques. The Ewens and Ostrom studies note, for instance, that the affective technique was stronger for the subjects in prejudicing towards blacks, but the behavior intention technique was stronger for prejudicing toward the church. This helps to make some sense of the reports at many of the sites for the empirical basis for stereotypes. Jews are regularly stereotyped as aggressive capitalists (Selzer, 1972), Americans as spoiled brats (Lederer, 1958), drunks as skid row bums (Pittman,

1967), etc., each of which is based in part upon tendencies of the members of these groups with whom the prejudiced person has been acquainted either in everyday interactions or in media depictions.

This empirical basis for prejudicing will be discussed from other angles throughout the remainder of the book. An important initial point can be made on the basis of the foregoing, however. Prejudicing persons do base their prejudices on empirical data, on observations, at least in terms of which techniques they choose to accomplish their prejudicing. Hence, some liberal proposals to diminish prejudice by exposing prejudiced persons to their targets tend not to work (Collins, 1970), partly owing to the ability for prejudicing persons to incorporate new information into their simplifications.[1] Even more fundamental is the prejudiced person's ability to employ the same data to different convenient ends. A site by Saenger and Flowerman (1954), consists of questions to 450 college students concerning characteristics which made them like or dislike certain groups. Thirty-one per cent stated that Jews were mercenary, 24 per cent said that Americans were mercenary, and 38 per cent said that businessmen were mercenary. But of these three groups, only Jews were disliked for this quality.

Indeed, Merton's (1949) site exposes the possibility for prejudiced persons to choose without fear of contradiction to simplify one group according to their refusal of in-group attributes while simplifying another group according to acceptance of in-group attributes. Blacks have received prejudice on the basis of their alleged rejection of in-group values such as cleanliness and achievement orientations, while Jews have been rejected on the basis of accepting these values. The same observational data is used by the prejudicing person in 'opposite ways.' Merton notes an apparent irony which grows out of this possibility (1949: 432):

> In a society which ordinarily looks upon wealth as a warrant of ability, an out-group is compelled by the inverted attitudes of the dominant in-group to deny that many men of wealth are among its members. 'Among the 200 largest non-banking corporations . . . only ten have a Jew as president or chairman of the board.' Is this an observation of an anti-Semite, intent on proving the incapacity and inferiority of Jews who have done so little 'to build the corporations which have built America?' No, it is a retort of the Anti-Defamation League of B'nai B'rith to anti-Semitic propaganda.

Merton further offers a list of Jewish authors including Heine, Borne, and Kafka; composers Mendelssohn, Offenbach, and Mahler; scientists Mayerhof, Michelson, and Einstein; and mathematicians Kronecker, Minkowski and Jacobi. Asks Merton (1949: 434):

> And who is thus busily engaged in singing the praises of the Jews? Who has so assiduously compiled the list of many hundreds of distinguished Jews who contributed so notably to science, literature and the arts – a list from which these few cases were excerpted? A philo-Semite, eager to demonstrate that his people have contributed their due share to world culture? No, by now we should know better than that. The complete list will be found in the thirty-sixth edition of the anti-Semitic handbook by the racist Fritsch. In accord with the alchemical formula for transmuting in-group virtues into out-group vices, he presents this as a roll call of sinister spirits who have usurped the accomplishments properly owing the Aryan in-group.

The material at the Merton site suggests an additional note about the structure of the simplification-essence. The simplifying apparently need not be of a consistent nature, and 'empirical cues' are made to fit the need of accomplishing the prejudicing.

Where can prejudicing persons turn to determine how to prejudice in those cases in which interactions with the target are not definitive? Tumin's (1958) site, as reanalyzed by Blalock (1967: 131), offers an answer. Tumin administered a questionnaire to 287 Greensboro, North Carolina white male adults. He found virtually no difference between high socio-economic status persons and low status persons with respect to their stereotypes of blacks. This remained true even when differential educational, income, and occupational groups were considered. Tumin inferred that underlying prejudice levels were basically unrelated to class differences. But Blalock notes that significant differences occurred with respect to questions such as what the prejudiced expected of their own and blacks' behavior in hypothetical situations, of what they would do about blacks, and their feelings about blacks. In our terms, class differences in this community did exist. Apparently various classes were using different techniques for prejudicing, or at least using the techniques in varied strengths.

Even within an individual technique for prejudicing it appears that groups utilize their ability to manipulate the instrument to satisfy the needs of the group members. Bettleheim and Janowitz (1964), argue that stereotypes of Jews help prejudiced persons deal with superego concerns, while stereotypes toward blacks concern the id. Adjectives typically applied to Jews by anti-Semites include: ambitious, striving, crafty, clannish, shrewd, hyper-intelligent, sly, and dishonest. Compare these with adjectives typically applied to blacks by white racists: unambitious, lazy, happy-go-lucky, irresponsible, stupid, dirty, smelly, uninhibited, and oversexed. Whether or not we accept the psychoanalytic theories in full, they do point in this case to a distinction in tool-use which helps make sense out of apparently reciprocal stereotype assignments. We will see in the next chapter that the contents and techniques of prejudicing are determined by groups with more in mind than simply serving individuals' psychological needs, or even the group's collective social psychological needs.

Summary

Examination of the possible instrumental essence of prejudice begins in this chapter. Through first visits to the sites we propose that prejudice may be (1) a social psychological instrument or (2) a social instrument. The remainder of the chapter investigates prejudice as a possible social-psychological instrument.

The sites concerning frustration-aggression are first examined, and through horizontal comparisons the argument is made that frustration does not necessarily result in aggression, and where it does so result, the aggression need not be exhibited as prejudice. Of greater interest to our essentialist analysis is the use of prejudice in simplifications, which concerned issues of authoritarian personality research, stereotyping, social and personal distancing, and simplified affect.

The classic *Authoritarian Personality* site was investigated through vertical comparisons of how and why it was constructed. The argument was made that the researchers had built into the design of their research the conclusions they derived. This was further detailed through horizontal comparisons with other sites, which indicated that (1) items on three of the scales were often similar in content, (2) researchers' reference groups were used without regard to subjects' concerning meanings of the scale items, (3) response patterns were ignored and 'yeah' saying may have resulted, (4) a simple continuum from liberal to conservative may have obscured the thickness of persons' attitudes, (5) race and ethnicity of the 'subjects' was neglected, and (6) the coding ignored important qualitative concerns. Our conclusions from these vertical and horizontal comparisons was that a predictable set of beliefs or a single personality type is not essential to prejudicing.

The next question concerned why people stereotype. At the most basic level the sites revealed that persons use stereotyping to reduce cognitive uncertainty about targets and that prejudicing is a strategy for simplifying, through culturally supported instant definitions of target persons. Stereotypes are verbalized as 'all A are B,' which is the classical form of an induction. This insight led to a discussion of works by philosophers of science to determine whether distinctions exist between prejudicing inductions and scientific or logical inductions. The brief survey suggested the difficulty for any induction to support its reliance upon tradition in choosing predicates or its future predictions. Several comparisons were made between social scientists' methods for inductive reasoning and prejudicing persons' methods, to demonstrate both the close relationship and the distinctions between prejudicing and 'normal' behavior.

Social distancing was investigated next, beginning with vertical comparisons to reveal the birth of this concept with LaPiere's (1934), site and the Bogardus scales. Sites were offered which revealed that behavior intentions do not necessarily predict actual behavior, and it is suggested that social distancing appears to be a way of prejudicing which is distinct from stereotyping.

The possibility of simplification as an essence of prejudice then began to emerge as we recognized that both stereotyping and social distancing were ways in which prejudice was brought to be an instrument for simplification of targets. To this list was added a final way of prejudicing, namely, simplified affect. A variety of uses for simplified affect were noted through horizontal comparisons of sites dealing with several historical periods.

The three methods for prejudicing (stereotyping, social distancing and simplified affect) were next investigated by replacing 'why' questions with 'how' questions. How persons stereotype is related to features of language, and the acceptability of attributing inherent features to persons. The object-dependent nature of stereotyping was elaborated through comparisons of similar sites at different historical periods, which showed the partial dependence of stereotyping persons upon characteristics of their targets. A final source of stereotypes was shown to be media depictions of groups.

Persons were seen to social distance on the basis of threat, which appears to be determined by the prejudicing person's reference groups, the mass media, and physical distance from the targets. Persons apparently affectively simplify by narrowing their possible reactions to targets to a relatively small list which is applied by habit when the target persons are confronted.

The tendency for more than one method of prejudicing to be employed by prejudicing persons was uncovered at some sites. But an essential insight emerged from noting that (1) no cases were found in which persons did not accomplish prejudice by at least one of the three methods (stereotyping, social distancing or simplified affect), and (2) some persons prejudiced through use of only one of these methods. Hence, a suggested essence is the presence of at least one of these three methods.

7 Elaboration of essences: II

The many sites visited in the previous chapter have specified ways in which prejudice is instrumental. The visits included psychoanalytic, interactionist, experimental, functionalist and other sites. Never was a case found in which prejudice was not instrumental. In the present chapter, we keep instrument as an essence 'in brackets,' and continue to look for why and how prejudice is instrumental. This time we look for why and how prejudice is a social instrument. Necessarily this search will take us to additional sites, including Marxist, conflict theorist, and descriptive-historical sites. We also search for information about the simplification essence which emerged in the previous chapter.

A social instrument: why?

Intergroup competition

Sherif's (1953 and 1966), sites are among the most frequently discussed at the other prejudice sites. Through a type of vertical comparison, or reconstruction, we can examine this site, on the basis of Sherif's reports.

Sherif set out to conduct a sociological experiment which would examine in-group friendships, intergroup conflict, prejudice and conflict reduction via situations constructed and controlled by the experimenter. In 1953 he took twenty-four eleven- and twelve-year-old white Protestant boys from similar middle class neighborhoods in New Haven to a three-week summer camp in Robber's Cave, Oklahoma. During Phase One, for three days, the boys all stayed in one bunkhouse and engaged in camp-wide activities, choosing friends according to any criteria the boys themselves devised. Sherif concluded that the friendship choices were based upon personal attractions and upon common interests and abilities. Activities were arranged by adults, but the boys decided upon team mates, seats at meals, and buddies for free time play. During these three days, friendship clusters emerged and leadership structures were apparent within the boys' groups.

Sherif's presentation of material from these three days is minimal, but there is indication of the effective natural ordering the boys began during this period. The following is from a summary by an adult participant observer of a two-hour hike (1953: 245):

> The hikers did not proceed according to plan up the river toward New Boston. Along the highway, the boys saw a dirt trail veering off to the left, and with the assent of the lead counselor, they took it. The trail ended abruptly and the hikers decided to climb the mountain. About half way up it was decided to have a race to the top. The three boys who won the race were Hall, Miller, and Crane. Hall told (staff member) that they all walked to the top abreast by mutual agreement, so that no one of them would arrive before the other two.
>
> After this incident the three boys called themselves 'The Three Musketeers.' The next morning they went out to catch salamanders while the other boys were playing softball. Upon their return, they talked to Mr. Mussee and a participant observer telling them of plans to build a wire basin to hold salamanders. When asked why they had not been swimming with the others, Crane replied, 'When one of us doesn't do something, then none of us do it'.

Later in the study, under adult-constructed conditions, these boys assumed leadership positions again, but in competing teams consisting of prejudiced and violent members. An important point is that the three apparently got along very well with one another and with other groups when they were in their self-constructed group during this early phase of the experiment. Sherif apparently recognized the importance and strength of self-organized groups, because prior to his next step he 'anticipated that the split into two groups might not be taken easily by some of the boys' (1953: 247).

Sherif then separated the boys into two groups and placed the groups in separate cabins for Phase Two of the experiment. The campers were divided such that for each boy two-thirds of his initial friends were in the other bunkhouse. To ease the pain of this adult-determined division, the two groups were taken on 'activities which had first preference with most of the boys' (e.g. cook-outs with steaks broiled over open fires). Still, some were distressed by the adults' action (247):

FIRST ILLUSTRATION OF A METHOD

> One boy, Thomas, had cried for ten minutes after the announcement of the split, which meant his separation from another camper with whom he had struck up a friendship in camp.

For the next few days the two groups were physically separated, with all activities away from the immediate vicinity of the other group. They also ate at separate tables and served on 'K.P.' duty on alternate days.

As soon as intergroup organization and self definitions developed, Sherif organized highly competitive games between the groups, including football, baseball, tug-of-war, and a treasure hunt. Within a few days the boys ceased to socialize with their former friends from the competing group and took on new 'best friends' from their own group. Although the games had begun in a spirit of friendly rivalry, soon the teams were taunting one another physically and verbally. And the performance of the members of one's own group was consistently judged to be superior to the performance of members of the other group. Sherif contends (1966: 81):

> When members of two groups come into contact with one another and a series of activities that embody goals which each urgently desires, but which can be attained by one group only at the expense of the other, competitive activity toward the goal changes, over time, to hostility between the groups and their members.

Indeed, when Sherif attempted to decrease the conflict between the groups, he found it difficult to do so. Simply providing contact situations for groups, regardless of how pleasant these situations were for both groups, did not decrease conflict. Going to movies, eating together, and shooting off fireworks simply ended with new conflicts between the groups (e.g. shoving contests in the dining hall, in which one group shouted 'ladies first' at the other).

The Sherif study is regularly summarized at other sites (e.g. Jones, 1972 and Jack Levin, 1975) as demonstrating that prejudice arises out of intergroup conflict. This is certainly a reasonable conclusion. But if we look at the decisions and actions of Sherif himself, an understanding on another level becomes possible. Sherif set up not only a summer camp, but a summer camp in which the participants were under social control by a university professor and his assistants. The *boys* did not set up their own competition or their own groups. Rather, these were forced upon them from the outside. What the boys knew was that they were going to a camp to play in various groupings set up after a short period of time by some adults. At the beginning of the three weeks they did *not* fight or prejudice among the groups which they themselves had constructed, although at times they played competitive games.

The Sherif site is comparable in important respects to the Asch (1952), experiments, which sought to demonstrate the negative influence of peer groups upon individuals. As is well known, Asch placed a group of college students in a room and projected upon a screen black lines of varied lengths. One of the lines was physically the shorter. Asch then asked each person which of the lines was the shorter, and consistently the students would name the line which was physically longer. Asch had hired 'confederates,' in order to determine whether or not the experimental student invited in each session would also verbalize the incorrect response. These experiments have been criticized, however, on the ground that a real peer group situation did not exist, but rather a peer group invaded by two authority-figures (the experimenters-professors), and that two thirds of the non-confederate students were *not* negatively influenced by the peer group (Embree, 1975; Orne, 1969).

The same sort of note applies to the Sherif site. Consider the situation: Summer camps are generally defined as places where games are played and skills are learned; one is invited to a summer camp; one is placed in groups in reverse of one's own friendship choices; one is told to compete and to win. Why would one *not* play the role assigned? It's all a game anyhow, and one came to the camp to play in the scripts set up by the adults (allegedly for one's own enjoyment). The kids were playing the parts assigned to them in the various plays set up by the adults. Perhaps they were following the scripts they perceived that the adults desired to have them act out. When the adults play the competition-games script, they do so complete with name calling, high energy desires to win, and so forth.

In contrast, consider a site (Glassner, 1976a), in which kids are not given scripts by adults, but only a stage upon which to build their own performances (as at the beginning of Sherif's study). This site was an elementary school playground, in which about 100 kids, mostly ages eight through ten, played unsupervised twice daily. Approximately half of the students were whites, half were blacks, half males and half females. They were from a variety of religious, socio-economic and neighborhood backgrounds. The kids divided each day into competing groups according to their skills, friendships, and the games they wanted to play. Frequently the groups would compete, but very seldom did name-calling or serious fighting occur. Rather, the kids worked off their needs or desires to fight through play fighting. Most of the time a group of kids was engaged in play fighting, but this was distinguished from real fighting in three ways: (1) no one was going to consider himself or herself badly hurt during the fight; (2) the fighting partners were either ambivalent towards one another or were friends – never were the partners enemies; and (3) though the outcome (i.e. who will win) may have been considered extremely important, this outcome settled nothing more than who was the best fighter. Real fights were just the opposite. It was expected that someone might be injured in such a way that he would consider himself badly hurt, the fight partners defined themselves as enemies, and the outcome determined something besides fighting abilities (e.g. 'you're going to leave me alone').

Further, the kids were found over a period of several weeks to leave the larger societies' prejudices out of their own 'kid society.' Their self-formed play groups were integrated for sex, race or both in two-thirds of the cases. Even racially segregated groups were never observed to resort to prejudicing to achieve their intergroup competitive successes.

Similarly, Moreno (1953) and Criswell (1937), sites found no sociometric evidence of segregative friendship choices before ages eight to ten. In both sites, the kids played on their own and were then asked by the researchers for their sociometric choices.

In short, the low prejudice found at the beginning of Sherif's study, the reanalysis of the Asch site, and the Glassner, Moreno, and Criswell sites, provide good reasons to revise Sherif's proposal of the inevitability of prejudice amid intergroup conflict.

One answer we cannot give to our 'why' question, then, is that prejudice is an essence of intergroup conflict. It certainly has been employed in numerous intergroup conflicts, however. By looking at several of these perhaps we can understand why prejudice is so used (and in the following section how it is used, and how it comes to be used).

Economic competition

Prejudice seems most consistently used at the sites in intergroup conflicts to achieve economic advantages. We have already noted cases in which persons could have used prejudice to their economic advantage but chose not to do so. In addition, sometimes persons and groups have been interested in promoting their advantages in other areas than economic concerns. At times entire nations have been dominated by non-economic values, such as Japan during the rule of Buddhist Prince Shotoku around 609 A.D. (deBary, 1969). Likewise, prejudice has been used in many sorts of conflicts which were not chiefly concerned with economics. Quakers and Mormons in the United States were the targets of intense prejudice and persecution, primarily on the basis of intergroup religious conflicts.

The social science sites do not deal very often with such societies or groups. The uses of prejudice in intergroup conflict at the sites have sprung most often from economic competition. Our search for essential interactions of prejudice within intergroup conflicts will therefore concentrate upon the uses of prejudice in economic conflicts, but we will also bring out some uses in political, sexual, and religious conflicts.

Two related economic uses appear historically, as noted by key informant Jack Levin (1975): (1) for the maintenance of social class and status, and (2) for distribution of tasks considered unpleasant.

Maintenance of class Weber noted that status groups hold onto their prestige by allowing only their own offspring to adopt distinctive values and credentials. An effective way to maintain this system has been to justify exclusion of other groups via prejudicing. Several correlational sites suggest that this need not be limited to activity by a small elite. Simpson and Yinger (1972), note that a direct relationship appears between the occurrence of anti-immigration nativist activity and the incidence of economic depression. The Native American Party in the 1930s, the Know-Nothing Order in the 1950s, the American Protective Association in the 1880s and 1890s, and 'one-hundred per cent American' groups in the 1930s all argued prejudice against recent immigrant groups to improve a shaky capitalistic economy. LaGumina (1973) reviewed the history of Italian-Americans and concluded that opposition to further immigration from Italy solidified during the depressions of 1893 and 1907. Dollard (1939), reported that white Southerns became more hostile toward Germans moving into their town as economic conditions worsened and competition for jobs increased.

When such prejudicing is felt to be needed it is constructed on bases similar to those Weber found elites using for their purposes of exclusion (Simpson and Yinger, 1972: 115):

> Racial differences or supposed differences, national, religious, cultural differences, or simply a general "inferiority" are the reasons ordinarily given to explain opposition to immigrants.

Sung (1961), reviewed stereotypes of Chinese-Americans during various periods of American history. Chinese immigrants in the 1800s tended to be regarded as honest, industrious, and peaceful. But when the job market tightened and the Chinese began to seek work in mines, farming, domestic services, and factories, new images emerged. They quickly became stereotyped as dangerous, deceitful, vicious, and clannish.

FIRST ILLUSTRATION OF A METHOD

We can also explain the long-standing prejudice against blacks in the general white population of the South in large part via economics. During slavery many whites profited directly by turning black persons into objects; slave labor was cheaper than paid labor (including white indentured servants). But what about the thousands of Southern whites who did not own plantations? Stampp (1956), found that three-fourths of these other whites also profited. Slavery was a method of limiting competition from blacks and providing whites with caste superiority over at least one group at all times.

The impression should not be given that prejudice arises as a natural reaction to economic competition. It is one instrument among several which have been employed. The point is that as a readily available instrument, prejudice is 'on the shelf' when needed. A ramification of this is the potential for powerful groups to manipulate other groups to use prejudice to facilitate the powerful groups' ends. Hence, the insight at Marxist sites is warranted, that one class can divide another class and thereby divert its revolutionary potential by encouraging prejudices among the proletariat. An illustration is at the McWilliams (1948), and Simpson and Yinger (1972), sites, which look at prejudices against the Japanese. Trade unions and small landowners in California in the early 1900s often participated in prejudice and discrimination against the Japanese. But organized and continuous opposition to the Japanese stemmed directly from the owners of huge estates in California. These men did not fear competition with Japanese farmers, however. What they did fear was (1) a battle with small-scale, white American landowners who found it difficult to compete with the big estates, (2) union organizing by their poorly paid field hands, and (3) federal legislation against monopoly farming. They diverted attention from their own control of the land by stereotyping the Japanese farmer as the cause of everyone's problems. Out of such opposition came the 1913 and 1920 Alien Land Acts in California. Groups of politicians also recognized the value of these scapegoats and attacked the Japanese in order to obtain votes. The Japanese Americans were small and unorganized, and thereby a safe target. Even Woodrow Wilson declared in 1912: 'The whole question is one of assimilation of diverse races. We cannot make a homogeneous population of a people who do not blend with the Caucasian race.'

Distribution of tasks The use of prejudice in the second way noted above – for the distribution of unpleasant work – also has been common. Robert Park (1939), found that strangers may perform better than in-group members in market situations requiring objectivity and impersonal dealings, and a certain amount of buyer-seller conflict. Park's example is the Metics in Athens. Other cases include Jews in the Middle Ages in Europe, East Indians in Burma, and several immigrant groups in the United States. These groups could be called directly exploited, whereas Japanese farmers mentioned in the last section were indirectly exploited. Park's work suggests that essential characteristics of directly exploited minorities may be their identifiability and powerlessness. Further research would be preferred before concluding that these features are essential, but our rounds to sites dealing with several of these minorities does recommend the possibility, as follows:

Indentifiability results from a property of the group (such as dialect or skin color) and from labeling by the majority groups. Powerlessness has tended to result from the numerically small size of the group. Numerical size certainly is not essential, however, as can easily be illustrated by the exploitation of female labor.

There is obviously a thin line between directly and indirectly exploited groups. Both must be identifiable and relatively powerless. Whether such groups become directly exploited or indirectly exploited seems to depend upon the needs of the exploiters, and these needs have varied results for the exploited. Jewish money-lenders in medieval Europe were thrust into the middle class, but Jews in Nazi Germany were murdered.

Why are groups used in one way or another? (What are the possible social uses for prejudices?)

The medieval Christian church viewed the lending of money for interest as sinful. Dimont (1962), argues that the dominant economic organizations necessitated the existence of money lenders, and rather than write off Christians from heaven, another strike against Jews' already impossible salvation was produced, by placing them in money-lending positions.

Especially telling is Dollard's (1939), suggestion that these groups are placed in between masses and elites, and thereby receive the frustration-aggression of both groups. We can go beyond the psychological to see that such groups effectively inhibit social change which threatens elites. Massing (1949) documents the opportunistic policies of Bismarck and his elite during the late 1800s and early 1900s. When the elite's power was secure they disclaimed anti-Semitism and even referred to it as 'a tool of the opposition.' But when worker groups began organizing, Bismarck and his colleagues employed anti-Semitism to divert the energies of the proletariat.

Numerous other cases could be described of using prejudice to help achieve role ascriptions to undesirable work positions. In each case the pattern is the same. An identifiable and powerless group is exploited to meet the perceived needs of dominant groups. As these needs shift, so do the uses to which the target is put and the methods of prejudicing used. This is well illustrated by the seemingly contradictory treatment of Japanese Americans. For several decades beginning in 1882, the Japanese were exploited as a major source of farm labor in California. After 1910, two factors resulted in the exclusion of Japanese from this exploited position. Anti-Japanese prejudices were employed by politicians and monopoly farmers (as noted above), and at the same time a revolution in Mexico persuaded many thousands of rural Mexicans to flee to the United States. London and Anderson (1970), found that clearly defined prejudicing methods (notably stereotyping) against the Mexicans began almost immediately and continue to this day, as does the exploitation of their cheap labor in California.

Economic uses of prejudice are unsuccessful when essential conditions are not met, however. Stampp (1956), narrates cases of American Indians enslaved on American plantations and the pronounced prejudicing accompanying each exploitation. But several factors precluded the successful use of Indians as plantation slaves. First, Indians often escaped and were protected by their own tribes within walking distance of the plantation. Second, the whites needed Indian knowledge of the land, which was not forthcoming under slavery. To this list the Wagley and Harris site (1958), adds other conditions. Third, semi-nomadic tribes cannot be subjugated for their labor because they can pack up and move further into the forest. Fourth, treaties with one tribe cannot be enforced for others. And fifth, such people are generally unaccustomed to the hard, day-to-day agriculture which plantation life demands. The crucial point for us is that the Indians were not powerless. The early use of Indians as slaves is an example of the inadequate application of the prejudice-instrument. Some sites (e.g. Blalock, 1967), offer models of prejudice-use which are entirely rational and system-supporting. From our perspective we can see that persons sometimes attempt to use prejudice, like any other instrument, in ways which violate its essential possibilities and thereby fail. Prejudice appears to be essentially limited to application upon relatively powerless groups.

Another cheap labor possibility attempted by Colonial Americans did not work because it violated the essential demand that target groups be identifiable. At least half of the white European immigrants to Colonial America paid their passage by agreeing to indentured servitude of periods from two to seven years (Stampp, 1956). Soon vast numbers of these person gained their freedom, and newer arrivals of whites frequently paid their way in cash. Given the similar religious, racial and language characteristics of plantation owners and the potential indentured servants, the indentifiability criterion could not be adequately met.

A societal tool: how?

General entrenchment

We saw in the previous chapter that psychoanalytic sites such as Bettleheim and Janowitz (1964) attribute the often conflicting stereotypes in groups and societies to needs of ids, egos, and superegos. Hence, stereotypes such as sly, ambitious, and hyper-intelligent relate to superego projections, while those such as lazy, dirty, and over-sexed relate to the id projections. We noted that this type of response to Merton's puzzle concerning conflicting stereotypes points us in some social-psychological directions for an answer (even if we rejet psychoanalytic theory *per se*). Of course, stereotypes are more than projections of a prejudiced person's impulses. The impulses, targets, and attributes are significantly socially constructed and socially maintained. Examining how this is so will give us further understanding of the possibilities for prejudice's instrument-essence.

Prejudicing is intricately woven into society. We can understand this concretely by looking closely at case examples from key informant Jones (1972), of contemporary American institutions and the historical entrenchments from which prejudicing has emerged.

We discussed in the previous pages the entanglement of prejudice and economic competition. We can now specify how this entanglement leaves residual prejudice in social institutions, even years after the direct and prejudicing competition. Consider several examples.
1 Relatively few black families have been able to buy homes in the United States. They are discriminated against additionally by the tax structure, because home owners are permitted to deduct the interest payments on their mortgages from their taxable income. But even those blacks who are able to buy homes remain at a disadvantage. In Boston, for instance, the value assessment of houses in black neighborhoods was proportionately higher than in other areas. The average assessed property in black neighborhoods was declared to be approximately 56 per cent of the market value, in contrast to other areas of the city, where the assessed value averaged 28 per cent. Property taxes in Boston were $160 per thousand dollars of assessed value.
2 Targets who have been locked into the lower classes also receive discriminatory interest rates. Banks will seldom give loans to persons who cannot demonstrate membership in the middle class.

FIRST ILLUSTRATION OF A METHOD

Lower-class persons must go to loan companies and retailers' monthly payment plans to obtain loans. Both sources charge higher interest rates than do banks. And by borrowing from these sources the poor as a group unavoidably support their continuing entrenchment, because these companies borrow money from the same banks which will not provide loans to lower class persons. They are also forced to support the continuing entrenchment during high unemployment times by fighting to get jobs they would not want if given a choice. Again, the big losers in this battle are the traditional targets of prejudice. As unemployment rises, black unemployment rises proportionately faster and higher than does white. And blacks are pushed out of even menial jobs, such as garbage collecting, which Jones notes in the 1970s has become dominated by whites in Boston. The net result: the median black family's income is approximately 60 per cent as large as the median white family's.

3 Many minority targets are forced to pay more for the items they buy. Most ghetto businesses are owned by whites, and prices in ghetto stores tend to be higher than at other stores throughout the cities. An item selling wholesale at $100 retails at an average price of $165 in a general merchandise store but $250 in a low-income specialty store.

4 Some persons attribute black economic discrimination to inferior education. We will see in a moment that this simply shifts the responsibility to another major institution, where prejudice is just as deeply entrenched. But the education argument is inaccurate even at face value. A black man with a college education can expect a yearly salary comparable to that of a white man with one to three years of high school.

What about the educational institutions? It is common knowledge that Southern states passed laws against teaching slaves to read, and Northern abolitionists argued for segregated schooling on the basis of black inferiority. By the time 'integration' occurred, prejudice had entrenched segregation so deeply that the results in many places have been 'white flight' from integrated schools, voluntary segregation within the schools by the students, and gross inequalities in expenditures between inner city and suburban schools.

The classic study by Rosenthal and Jacobson (1968), shows another way in which prejudicing is entrenched in education, namely, in teachers' expectations. These social psychologists told teachers at a South San Francisco school that certain children (randomly selected) were 'potential spurters.' On the basis of tests administered on several occasions over the next two years, 'children from whom teachers expected greater intellectual gains showed such gains' (22). The average gain of these children was over 27 IQ points. And their teachers perceived them as having a better chance of being successful later in life, as being happier, more curious, and more interesting than other children. Of course, expectations of target groups such as blacks, Chicanos, Puerto Ricans, and women have frequently been low.

5   The legal institutions exhibit the entrenchment of prejudice as well. In major American cities the white population averages 65 per cent but produces 95 per cent of the police population. Conversely, the percentage of jail populations that are blacks is roughly ten times the percentage of blacks in the American population generally. A single story from Jones (1972: 142), based on *Boston Globe* accounts, offers some qualitative dimensions resulting within these statistics.

A 12-year-old black girl from Boston left at about 4.30 one afternoon to buy her mother a pie at the corner store. When she did not return by 5.30 her mother began looking for her in the neighborhood. At 8.30 p.m. she called the police. The police advised the mother that the daughter was probably visiting friends, to which the mother responded that her daughter never stayed away without permission.

The police never searched for the girl. A week and a half later they finally filed an official missing-person bulletin. The newspaper published a notice about the girl, but with a picture of the wrong girl. A tap was promised for the home telephone, in case a ransom call was received. The girl did call home at 7 a.m. one morning, sounding dazed and asking if her mother loved her, then hanging up. The mother immediately asked for a trace and was informed that no tap had been put on the telephone and no trace was possible. Two and a half weeks after she disappeared, the girl's body was found with a bullet in the head.

'Let's face it,' a telephone company official is quoted as saying, 'the wheel turned damned slowly in this case. It's not just the police. It's the double standard of our whole society. If a 12-year-old girl disappears on her way to buy a pie and she's white, the presumption is she's met foul play. If a little girl disappears on her way to buy a pie and she's black, everyone assumes she's just run away.'

Entrenchment in the justice institutions can also be seen in the ways some target persons come to spend their time behind bars. Black defendants raise bail money 38 per cent of the time, compared to white defendants' 57 per cent. This is due not only to social class differences, but also from consistently higher bail prices in predominantly minority-processing courts.

The Sherman (1972), site notes institutional interconnections. White sharecroppers in the South are the most oppressed and poverty-stricken group in the region, except for black sharecroppers. But the white sharecropper has regularly supported the wealthy white Southerners' candidates in political elections, while consistently fighting blacks and refusing to unionize with them. Indeed, effective unionization of sharecroppers has been impossible in large part because whites serve as strikebreakers during blacks' strikes, and vice versa. This results in perpetual entrenchment in the political, economic, educational and family institutions.

Target characteristics

Anti-Semitism and anti-black prejudice refract the social position and values of Jews and blacks, brought about by the general entrenchment of prejudice and discrimination. Anti-Semitism in the United States derives in part from the image of the Jews as middlemen or 'economic man,' a stigma developed in Europe. Quite separately, anti-black prejudice stems from the stigma created and maintained by slavery and later by poverty (Elkins, 1959). These stereotypes are perpetuated at present through the fairly stagnant and separate positions of Jews and blacks in American society. Jews are overwhelmingly middle-class, and disproportionately large numbers of Jews engage in professions and white-collar occupations, resulting in median family income for Jews surpassing the national median. Blacks are overwhelmingly lower-class and found disproportionately in the service and blue-collar occupations, resulting in median family income of barely three-fifths of the national median (Pettigrew, 1971). As we have seen, they are disproportionately represented in jails and education drop-out statistics as well.

As one would predict, these different histories, perpetual separateness, and different class backgrounds result in different values held by Jews and blacks. As the Kluckholn (1953), site reveals, Jews share with Protestant Americans such values as 'man-over-nature,' 'doing,' 'individualistic,' and 'future-time orientation.' This is pointed out most dramatically by Rosen (1959), whose site indicates that the Jews he interviewed more often accepted the 'Protestant ethic' than did Protestants. On the other hand, blacks' exclusion from dominant social worlds in America has resulted in value-sets often at odds with those of whites.

I do not bring up this discussion of the roots of stereotypes in actual culture to indicate that prejudicing is empirically justified. As Simpson and Yinger (1972: 160) inform us:

1 The minority groups are not inferior in any absolute sense, but only relative to the standards of the dominant group. The

'proof' that the prejudice is justified, therefore, is convincing only to a person who accepts the values of the dominant group as absolutely valid.
2   Reality is taken *as is* by the prejudiced person. He is scarcely interested in *why* minority groups are 'inferior'; or his explanation is likely to be very simple – it is their nature.

MacIver (1948: 65), explains:

> Its peculiar property is that it takes the existence of one link in the circle as independently given, as a fact of nature or even as ordained by God, and concludes from the premise that the next link, the behavior predicted on the earlier link, is not prejudicial or discriminatory but a rational and proper response to the inferior capacities or qualities of the group subjected to it. Those who put forward the argument wilfully or blindly ignore the sector of the circle that lies on the other side to recognize that the conditions on which they base their argument arise out of, or are themselves sustained by, a prior process of discrimination.

Blaming the victim is unjustified. But it does indicate that entrenchment of prejudice in cultures results in observables for prejudiced persons to use. Knowledge of this permits us to move beyond the psychology or social psychology of prejudicing to search for where and how it is rooted in social worlds. Our discussion above indicates that prejudice and discrimination create some differences in target groups' own values and behaviors. These vary from high levels of individual achievement to self-doubt and frustration-aggression. They can also create intragroup conflict or in-group separatism. These creations appear to the prejudiced person to be the very reasons for his prejudice, and to be good, empirical reasons at that. Prejudiced persons exaggerate the differences and simplify the situations, permitting papers in journals with titles such as 'Abnormal and Social Psychology.' But such concerns are secondary to the processes of entrenchment of prejudice in societies in the first place. As far as the prejudiced person is concerned, the attributes he chooses of his targets in order to construct his prejudicing are simply out there, in objective reality. As we have seen, in some senses he is right. Some of our earlier discussions have suggested that identifiability may be essential to prejudicing. We may now add that this possibility may involve histories of the target characteristics by which the person or group is identified. We will consider identifiability again later in this chapter.

FIRST ILLUSTRATION OF A METHOD

Entrenchment assistance by scientists and philosophers

By lumping a group of people together and calling them 'prejudiced' or 'abnormal' or 'subjects', social scientists have been able to do comparisons of 'them' and 'us.' In addition to being a prejudicing strategy itself, this permits us to ignore the intellectual community's support for prejudicing. A brief historical survey of this support provides yet another perspective on how prejudice is entrenched in societies.

Since most of the social science literature deals with American prejudice, and in light of space and time limitations, I will limit this discussion of intellectual roots of modern prejudice to influences within and upon the United States. (The roots of this prejudicing will be traced to Europe, however.) Our key informant on these questions is Richard H. Popkin (1974), who has spent much of his adult life editing *The Journal of the History of Philosophy* and bases his report primarily upon primary sources (the writings of the intellectuals themselves or the reports of those directly influenced by these writings).

We begin with the Spaniards and Portuguese, who before they came to America had employed prejudice theories to account for injustices against Jews in Europe. These theories relied upon Biblical explanations of who the targets were. But ready made theories about the Indians were unavailable. Most of the theorizing up to the eighteenth century proposed that Indians came from migrations of some Biblical people. Popular theories claimed that the Indians were the Lost Tribes of Israel in a degenerate state, that they were of Phoenician or Arabic origins, that they were Asians, even that they were Norwegians who had arrived with Leif Erickson's expedition. One major claim ran counter to the Bible-based explanations, however. This held that the Indians were not descendants of Adam and Eve, but were pre-Adamites.

The early reports of the explorers varied. One extreme held that Indians could not have abstract ideas, were incapable of morality (given their practices of sodomy and human sacrifices), and that therefore the Europeans had to take control of Indians' lives. An opposition movement began in the early 1500s, when the Bishop of Chiapos argued the humanity of Indians. He was debated by several Spanish theorists, notably Sepulveda, who theorized that to be human a creature must (1) have understanding and volition, (2) have five exterior senses and four interior senses, (3) be moved by these senses, and (4) take satisfaction in goodness and abhor evil.

Sepulveda's arguments were grounded, he contended, in Aristotle. Sepulveda had edited the leading Renaissance edition of Aristotle's *Politics* and contended that the Indians were the people Aristotle had described as being by nature slaves. Oviedo, a fellow theoretician, argued that Indians lack rationality and morality and therefore must be controlled for everyone's good. When these theorists were answered by Alonzo de la Vera Cruz at the University of Mexico, the response was deportation of de la Vera Cruz to lower Yucatan.

These sixteenth century theories about Indians were only the ground work for the next two centuries of prejudice theories, which have become intricately woven into scientific and everyday thought. These culminated in Hume's probability theories, which provided an empirical ground for prejudice.

The sixteenth century theorists had depended upon Biblical explanations, which proved inadequate amid growing American "show-me" pragmatism requiring reliance upon current states, not upon distant and invisible pasts. The Europeans in America were encountering immediate problems staying alive and conquering one region after another. They needed their best European thinkers to provide immediate but well-defended theories to meet these needs.

The English invaders of the seventeenth century turned to John Locke. Locke had contended that everyone was created equal, and endowed with the natural rights of life, liberty and property. He had no difficulty, however, in dealing with the American Indians and Africans. He said the Indians and Africans were not properly using their land, and they had been captured in 'just wars,' and so could be enslaved. Locke drafted the Constitution for the Carolinas and was very influential in the emerging Degeneracy Theory.

During the eighteenth century a vast literature appeared on why blacks are black, why people speak different languages, and similar concerns. Montesquieu offered his climate theory in *De l'esprit des lois*. Linnaeus (1806), a founder of modern biology, divided men into 'wild men,' 'Indians,' 'Europeans,' 'Asiatics,' and 'Africans.' Among his descriptions of Africans are 'crafty,' 'indolent,' and 'negligent,' all of which have remained well entrenched throughout the next century and a half. He contended that the differences between groups was due to climate and social environment.

The climate theory encountered some difficulties. Enough Europeans had lived in Africa and America to discover firsthand that they were not changing as the result of climate. But biologist Buffon (1785) was already at work developing a more complete explanation. Buffon argued that 'white, then appears to be the primitive color of Nature,' and that climate, food, diseases, and modes of living changed some groups' color. He offered detailed comparisons of various groups. Among his descriptions which have remained entrenched in modern stereotyping are the Chinese as 'superstitious,' 'ceremonious,' and 'parasticial'; blacks as 'indolent' and 'stupid'; and American Indians as 'savage' and 'ignorant and destitute of industry.' (He also claimed: 'The most temperate climate lies between the 40th and 50th degree of latitude, and it produces the most handsome and beautiful men. It is from this climate that the ideas of the genuine colour of mankind, and of the various degrees of beauty ought to be derived.') For all of his statements he offered what was considered the best empirical evidence of his time. Also noteworthy for our earlier discussions of the distinctions between prejudice and discrimination is that Buffon was against slavery.

We can derive an even clearer insight into the nature of the entrenchment of prejudice by viewing how prejudice theories are answered. Perhaps the leading antiracist at the turn of the nineteenth century was Abbé Gregoire, who was himself arguing from a degeneracy theory. He argued that Jews of his day had degenerated from their former state but could be improved and eventually maybe even become Christians. He held similar contentions about Africans, and about both groups argued that it was not their fault, but rather resulted from oppression and lack of opportunity. He noted that proofs of suppressed qualities were that some Africans had written books and were scientists and artists. These groups performed less well than they could because of adverse environmental factors. He saw the solution to prejudice and racist oppression in making everybody an equal participant in European culture. The parallels to contemporary 'affirmative action' and assimilation theories by American intellectuals seem obvious. In both cases the way critics of prejudice combat prejudice involves similar prejudicing.

Concurrent with these theories was another variety, the polygenetic theory, which also remains well entrenched. Paracelsus and Bruno argued in the sixteenth century that groups such as Indians and blacks were not descended from the Biblical Adam. In the mid-1600s La Peyrere argued that the Bible deals only with Jewish history, not world history. Prior to Adam there were millions of Pre-Adamites. La Peyrere was branded a heretic, however, and his books burned, because he contended that only the Jews were descended from Adam.

The polygenetic view did not find its ground until Hume. He claimed in his *Treatise* that human nature can best be studied by observations from human historical behavior, which can be generalized according to the Newtonian method of experimental reasoning, making inductions from observed cases. In his essay 'Of National Character' (1882: 252n.) he replies to the environmental and physical explanation of human differences:

> I am apt to suspect the negroes and in general all other species of

men (for there are four or five different kinds) to be naturally inferior to the whites. There never was a civilized nation of any other complexion than white, not even any individual eminent either in action or speculation . . . In Jamaica indeed they talk of one negroe as a man of parts and learning; but 'tis likely he is admired for very slender accomplishments like a parrot, who speaks a few words plainly.

Hume was applying his method of historical experimental reasoning. First he alleged the historical fact that there never was a nonwhite civilization, while even the least cultured whites have been able to produce some kind of culture. Then the historical law governing the situation is offered: 'Such a uniform and constant difference could not happen in so many countries and ages, if nature had not made an original distinction betwixt these breeds of men.' (Hume was a good choice to run the English Colonial Office in 1766.)

One might expect that someone would accuse Hume of inadequate sampling. Actually, many of the most careful thinkers of the period lauded Hume's research and reasoning. Kant wrote (as quoted in Popkin, 1974):

Mr Hume challenges anyone to cite an example in which a Negro has shown talents, and asserts that among the hundreds of thousands of blacks who are transported elsewhere from their countries, although many of them have even been set free, still not a single one was ever found who presented anything great in art or science or any other praiseworthy quality, even though among the whites some continually rise aloft from the lowest rabble, and through superior gifts earn respect in the world. So fundamental is the difference between the two races of man, and it appears to be as great in regard to mental capacities as in color.

Hume was answered on methodological and other grounds by James Beattie in his *Essay on the Origin and Immutability of Truth* in 1770. Beattie's work never gained the exposure that Hume's and Kant's did, however, and the latter were by far the more influential.

A generation of careful scientists emerged in the early 1800s to offer other sorts of empirical evidence for the polygenetic theories. Notable among these was Dr Samuel Morton, an ethnologist from Philadelphia. Morton collected skulls and measured their cranial capacity by filling them with pepper-seed, and then weighing the amount that could be fitted into each skull. His followers Gliddon, Nott and Agassiz followed suit. Their conclusions included: (1) that skull measurements and paintings in Egyptian tombs showed that racial characteristics of various groups have been the same throughout recorded history, (2) that the fixed racial characteristics included larger cranial capacities for whites, lower for Asiatics, still lower for Indians, and the lowest for Africans, and (3) that the only reasonable explanation was the separate creation of different species of mankind, each with fixed brain capacities. Agassiz offered reasonable policy implications on the basis of his research (as quoted in Popkin, 1974):

> it seems to us to be mock-philanthropy and mock-philosophy to assume that all races have the same abilities, enjoy the same powers, and show the same dispositions, and that in consequence of this equally are entitled to the same position in human society. History speaks here for itself.

He then suggested that since Africans have never developed regulated societies and have always been slaves, they should remain so, and that it was pointless to try to give Afro-Americans educational opportunities.

The techniques have been modified again, but we can easily find at present basically polygenetic-theories. These are most apparent in the work of Shockley, Hernstein and Jensen. All use Humean probability inference techniques to reach their conclusions about the genetic inferiority of blacks. A few years ago Jensen (1969) cited a significant correlation between race and IQ scores. Citing an average difference of 15 percentage points between blacks and whites in IQ tests, he proposed that different types of education be made available to blacks and whites. He recommended that blacks should be trained for manual trades and whites for professions.

It is perhaps easy for most social scientists to accuse Jensen of inadequate methods. But our sketch of the entrenchment of prejudiced intellectual thinking shows more. We can see that underlying both Jensen's arguments *and* his critics' will likely be deeply entrenched prejudiced thinking. Much as we found Abbé Gregoire two centuries ago replying to degeneracy theories with other degeneracy theories, now we find probability theories answered with other probability theories. Thus, Jensen is criticized for inadequate samples or inadequate IQ tests. Where they are not so answered, another of Gregoire's replies is offered: that when blacks are given a chance within white society (i.e. 'equal opportunities') they regularly learn white values, lifestyles, and so forth. By replying with statistical induction techniques or assimilation arguments, one offers only a reply to immediate manifestations of prejudice, not to prejudicing itself. Such incremental replies are tightly woven into the same fabric of societal consciousness as are the prejudiced statements they attempt to answer.

Identifiability

We may recommend identifiability now in light of the foregoing. In the previous chapter we offered some detail of the possibilities for prejudice inhering in the structure of Indo-European languages. On the basis of the Simpson and Yinger (1972), and Benedict (1940), sites we can now expand that analysis.

Race prejudice is most important in modern societies, but it has not always been, nor will it necessarily continue to be. Just a few centuries ago target groups in Europe were identified by religion in nearly all cases. There was relatively little contact in Europe with members of non-Caucasian races. Religion dominated the way of everyday thought and provided the rationale for considering certain target groups as outsiders. The medieval world considered life on earth as a brief second for those capable of eternal salvation. Prejudice and violence against Antichrists, who led thousands to damnation, were simply acts for the common good. As we would expect from our discussion thus far, such beliefs were entangled with other than religious institutions as well. 'Heresy hunting was profitable, and all those who sought riches and power eagerly took advantage of the opportunity, masking their satisfaction behind the dogma that the heretics were guilty of treason against the Almighty,' Ruth Benedict reminds us.

In a modern world dominated by science in both everyday thought and major institutions, the religious lines of demarcation virtually disappear. Prejudicing persons in relatively recent times have not identified their targets by claiming that they believe the wrong things, but by claiming that they are genetically inferior. This has been the case even for anti-Semitism. As late as 1899 Chamberlain declared in his *Foundations of the Nineteenth Century* that Jews were enemies not because of their special ways of thinking and acting, but because 'one can very soon become a Jew' (as quoted in Popkin, 1974). But with Hitler anti-Semitism became fully biologized. Jews were held to be innately inferior and vicious, and a race to be destroyed.

The shift in prejudice against blacks is also illustrative. Europeans' first contacts with blacks and Orientals occurred at a time when religious differences were still considered most important. Talk was not of these groups' racial differences, but of their status as non-Christians (pagans). MacCrone (1937), found that the earliest practice of Europeans in South Africa was to free slaves who had been baptized. Such practices were inefficient, however, and by the 1670s a series of laws in the American colonies made it acceptable to keep a slave who had converted to Christianity (Elkins, 1959). As we saw above, the prejudicing persons turned to scientists at this point to deliver the needed rationales, which turned out to be measurable physical differences and probability theories of native ability.

It is more than ironic that those who write with hopes of reducing intergroup tensions title their books using the language of prejudicing: Race Relations.

More generally, we can partially specify from this discussion a possible essence that also emerged in several earlier discussions. In every site we have examined, target groups must be identifiable if persons are to accomplish their prejudicing on an ongoing basis (if they are to successfully prejudice). From a macro perspective we have seen that indentifiability is accomplished in each period via arguments within the best respected rationality systems, and consequently dependent upon the type of rationality system which dominates. This suggests that on each micro level, the only groups who can successfully continue their prejudicing are those with the resources to manipulate the justification machinery. This machinery has varied at the sites from the church to local politicians.

Societal control of social psychological ways of prejudicing

The previous chapter noted that persons prejudice through cognitive, conative and affective simplifications. The *how* of these processes can be more completely described through an examination of the ways that prejudicing techniques are entrenched in social processes.

Many sites assume that persons learn prejudice through childhood socialization. Sociology and social psychology generally take for granted that persons acquire social properties through socialization. Through our constant comparisons we can see, however, that the learning of prejudices is not the essential socialization of prejudice which occurs.

Part of the indoctrination of a child into a culture is teaching to the child culturally acceptable prejudices. The Blalock (1967), and Simpson and Yinger (1965), sites point out that both Brazil and South Africa have large black populations, and that color distinctions exist in both countries, but that only South Africa has a strong cultural tradition of color prejudice. Apparently the learning of specific prejudicial attitudes occurs by learning group norms. The agents of this socialization tend to be families, peer groups, schools, and media. Of course, for nuclear family children in most contemporary societies the major agents of socialization are parents. Indeed, at the Mosher and Scodel (1960), site one finds ethnic attitudes expressed by children significantly correlated with those held by their parents.

But the verbalizing of an attitude by a child indicates only that the child knows what he is expected to say on a given subject, not that he believes it or even understands it. No sites I could locate offer longitudinal studies to determine whether or not the specific learned prejudices actually persist. We know from other areas of life that much of what is learned during socialization is later abandoned. Perhaps most importantly, persons learn prejudices in specific contexts, and the sites do not demonstrate whether persons consistently transfer the prejudices into other contexts.

Some sites indicate that the essential learning which occurs in prejudice-socialization is not of specific prejudices. Piaget (1947), demonstrated that children below the age of six or seven have not yet developed a conception of invariance of physical properties. This illustrates that a child's conceptual world is clearly different from that of an adult, and in the process of change. And just as the child has no conception of the invariance of physical objects, that child could be assumed to view people also as being impermanent.

Interviews by Radke, Trager and Davis (1949), reveal the fragility of the meaning of skin color to first and second graders. Among their statements:

> 'Little boys when they get dirty get into a colored boy and when they get clean they get into a white boy.'

> 'When he gets dirty he turns into a colored boy.'

Conversations at the Piaget and Weil (1951), site also reveal the confused status of categories for children. This seven-year-old is typical.

> Have you heard of Switzerland? *Yes.* What is it? *A canton.* And what is Geneva? *A town.* Where is Geneva? *In Switzerland.* (But the child draws two circles side by side.) Are you Swiss? *No, I'm Genevese.*

Many socializing agents take over by the time a child reaches age seven, and in contemporary societies these groups are not likely to present a single, consistent set of prejudices. Havinghurst (1975), notes that only about one-fourth of American children attend schools at which most of the other children are of the same social class. Peer groups tend to be quite important soon after children attend school, and these groups create their own norms and socialization priorities. Piaget (1965), reveals that the last half of elementary school is for most children a time when their own societies attain their maximum organization and codification. The several children's societies he studied were found to contain children who no longer saw rules as external laws from adults, but as outcomes of free decision and mutual consent by members of the society. As noted above, the children's groups at the Glassner (1976), site were highly integrated and few prejudices were expressed.

These weaknesses imply that more important than the specific prejudices learned through socialization may be that some children *learn how to prejudice.*

One site gives some interesting detail on this learning. Porter (1971) presented dolls to 185 white Boston area children. The children were asked which of the two dolls is 'lazy and stupid.' Their choices:

	Three years	Four years	Five years
chooses white doll	50%	33%	30%
chooses black doll	50%	67%	70%

The children learned stereotyping between the ages of three and five. They also learned social distancing (behavior intentions). Porter asked them to choose the doll they would invite home to lunch. For the 107 who selected the white doll, she asked if they would also invite the black. At three years 13% said they would not, at four years 36% would not, at five years 42% would not.

Our comparisons above with other sites suggested that these specific prejudices may be unclear to the child and subject to change depending upon setting (including reference group). What need not vary among settings is that once the ways of prejudicing are learned, they may be applied to a variety of targets.

These sites also offer the possibility for a phantasy variation which provides further detail for our inquiry into the instrumental-essence. Although the children noted above may eventually give up specific stereotypes, behavior intentions or simplified affective responses at age five they did seem to be prejudicing. Those 70% of the five-year olds who attached 'lazy and stupid' to the black doll would seem to be prejudicing. Was their prejudicing instrumental? And if not, how can instrumentality be an essence of prejudice? Apparently it was instrumental for their parents, who wished to simplify their children's encounters with blacks. But suppose we extend the example to those children who retain their tendencies after their parents die. Can we then consider it instrumental for anyone?

If these offspring are not prejudicing to any ends, I would suggest that they are not in fact prejudicing. Among the most potentially important uses of essential interactionist analysis stems from its ability to name not only essences but also relationships among essences. As Psathas (1968: 506), put it, 'The necessity for apprehending essential relationships among the elements of the phenomena... remains important. It is not enough to discover and describe the components: rules regarding their possible combinations must also be defined.' The difficulty with considering our imagined offspring as prejudiced can be seen by looking beyond single essences. Even on the basis of our initial essential analyses we can note this difficulty. The offspring are stereotyping, but they apparently are not simplifying, nor are their actions apparently socially instrumental. Essential interactionist analyses can be especially useful in distinguishing between phenomena. Apparently what the offspring is doing is some sort of habitual reacting, rather than prejudicing. We would expect that other essences of prejudice also are missing within the actions of these offspring (though we have yet to uncover additional essences of prejudice).

Summary

Some central questions in this chapter are, 'Why is prejudice a social instrument,' and 'How is prejudice a social instrument.' Answers were offered by the sites in terms of (1) intergroup competition, (2) economic competition, (3) entrenchment in institutions, and (4) target characteristics.

An initial investigation concerned vertical and horizontal comparisons to the Sherif (1953 and 1961), sites. Sherif's suggestion that prejudice necessarily results from intergroup competition is not supported during such comparisons. This emerges in vertical comparisons in which low-prejudice was found in the early stages of Sherif's research (at which time the persons were permitted to form their own competitive groups) and horizontal comparisons to Asch, Glassner, Moreno and Criswell sites, each of which demonstrated that prejudice does not emerge from all intergroup conflict situations.

Most of the sociological sites deal with economic competition, and these are compared. The sites reveal that (1) use of prejudice within economic competition is not limited to elites; (2) powerful groups have the greatest opportunity to deploy prejudice as an instrument for simplifying economic competition; (3) frequent uses of prejudice in economic competition are for distribution of unpleasant work and the maintenance of social class and status; and (4) target groups selected must be identifiable.

The entrenchment of prejudice in societies was elaborated first through numerous sites which reveal the self-perpetuating nature of the chain: discrimination-support of stereotypes – justification for prejudice – further discrimination. This process is noted within economic, educational, and justice institutions.

FIRST ILLUSTRATION OF A METHOD

The assistance which scientists, philosophers and other intellectuals offer for such entrenchment of prejudice in societies is described historically via informant Popkin's tours of historical sites from the 1600s to present. A revealing pattern is uncovered, demonstrating the tendency for persons attempting to combat prejudice to reply to immediate manifestations of the phenomenon, rather than to the phenomenon itself. Such incremental replies appear to result only in new justifications for prejudicing.

Identifiability as a possible essence is suggested and partially elaborated. Justification for criteria of identifiability (e.g. race, class, belief) depends upon the dominant rationality systems of the time and needs of powerful groups to separate certain groups from other groups.

The chapter concludes with a discussion of how persons come to learn prejudice. Horizontal comparisons indicate that teaching specific prejudices is not the crucial process which occurs in socialization of prejudice. Rather, persons are socialized in the methods of prejudicing, and they tend to retain their abilities to use these methods even as they lose specific stereotypes, behavior intentions or simplified affective responses. The chapter thereby indicates some social control of social-psychological processes.

8 Possible applications

I have suggested and partially elaborated four essences: instrumentality; simplification; identifiability; and that prejudicing must occur either by stereotyping, social distancing, simplified affect or a combination of these. The numerous rounds throughout the sites to elaborate these essences found no cases in which they were not present in some form. Hence, we are able to increase our confidence in the possibility that these are essences of prejudice. In Chapter 9 we will discuss further research necessary concerning these essences, but at least at this point we have established through a series of constant comparisons reasons to believe that these features are essential.

Now we begin to make use of our initial essences, even as we further elaborate them, through the critiques they suggest of other theories and researches, additional phantasy variations, and discussions of theoretical possibilities they may permit. These discussions and applications center around (1) a critique of functionalist claims that prejudice is 'functional for the minority group,' (2) the possibility for prejudice in classless societies, (3) the normality of prejudice, (4) whether or not our suggested essences distinguish prejudice from other phenomena, and (5) possibilities for new configurations of essences of prejudice.

Critiques of a functionalist proposal

It should be clear by now that several functionalists' sites have been very useful in our inquiry. I would present an incomplete report of our first experiment were I to neglect problematic aspects of functionalist sites, however. These problems stem from functionalism's organic analogy (critiqued in Glassner and Freedman, 1979), which in one group of sites is so deeply interwoven in the research that the sites become almost useless. Cases of this sort concern themselves with what key informant Levin calls 'functions of prejudice for the minority group.'

Prejudice is a tool available within societies and may be used by those who can and wish to operate it, regardless of their status as targets. Hence we would expect targets to try to use prejudice in the ways Levin suggests: to reduce competition, maintain solidarity, and reduce uncertainty. For instance, the Marx (1969), site illustrates that blacks know how to accomplish stereotyping and use it to simplify whites. Marx interviewed more than 1000 blacks in various parts of the United States. Seventy-three per cent of the respondents agreed with the statement, 'Most whites want to keep Negroes down as much as they can.' Such research illustrates a further entrenchment of prejudicing – within target groups' communities.

But statements such as Frazier's (1951), concerning 'the Negro's vested interest in segregation' provide apologies for the entrenchments of prejudice in society, with very little understanding of that entrenchment. Frazier claims that middle-class blacks have profited from segregation because they were protected from competing with whites in the marketplace (335):

> Thus, Negro physicians may advocate separate hospitals on the grounds that in them they would have more opportunities to develop their skill and to serve their 'own people.' But this, too, is only a rationalization because there is abundant evidence that the standard of medical care in segregated hospitals, where Negro physicians are supposed to have every professional opportunity, is lower than in unsegregated institutions. It is scarcely necessary to point out that to abolish segregation would create technological unemployment for Negroes who secure a living from the existence of segregation.

This type of assertion is among the most vicious objectivism, and the fallacies are easy to see. Frazier neglects that it was whites who entrenched prejudice so firmly within American institutions. The hypothetical black physician is reacting, at least in part, to prejudice he anticipates were he to practice with white colleagues and patients. In 1951 his fear was not unfounded. White patients who could afford white doctors regularly sought white doctors, and white physicians regularly underestimated the competence of black physicians. This resulted in large part from another type of prejudice entrenchment by whites. Prior to Affirmative Action legislation medical schools tended to be as segregated as did the rest of academia, including the inferior secondary schools most blacks were forced to attend. Educational institutions continue to assume life histories of white students and to gear instructional material and IQ and other tracking materials to whites (e.g., Blauner, 1972 and Jones, 1972).

To support conclusions such as Frazier's, Howard (1966) interviewed 100 black physicians, dentists, lawyers, and teachers regarding their attitudes toward competition with whites. He sought their agreement or disagreement with hypothetical situations such as the following (1966: 23):

> Dr J., who is a white physician, opened an office in an all-Negro neighborhood about 6 months ago. Recently, he advised a white physician friend to open an office in the same neighborhood. The white friend decided to open the office. Negro physicians in the neighborhood heard about the decision of Dr J's friend and urged him not to open the office. They advised him on several desirable locations in all-white neighborhoods. How do you feel about the advice of the Negro physicians?

On the basis of responses Howard concludes that black professionals are only in slight agreement with competition with whites. Howard calls this 'the Negro dilemma': a commitment to the goal of free competition and concurrently a social interest in segregation which inhibits their approval of such competition.

We require only a simple phantasy variation to see that such inductions by social scientists reveal more about the potential blindness of functionalism than about prejudices or ethnic relations. Which group of doctors *does* support competition? Attempts to lift the ban on physician advertising, or to radically increase the number of positions in medical schools, have consistently been defeated. For Howard's research to become meaningful the same question would have to be asked of physicians generally. Or to be more accurate – white physicians should be given a scenario such as the following:

> Dr J., a well respected physician, opened an office in a neighborhood about 6 months ago. Recently, he advised another well respected physician to open an office in the same neighborhood. The friend decided to open the office. Less famous physicians in the neighborhood heard about the decision of Dr J's friend and urged him not to open the office. They advised him on several desirable locations in other neighborhoods. How do you feel about the advice of these less prominent physicians?

Until the advent of black pride campaigns in some black communities, the white physician probably would have been better respected than the black physician and for good reason. More money was likely spent on the white physician's education from childhood through medical school than upon the black physician's; the white physician probably obtained internships and residencies in better equipped and better respected hospitals; and so forth.

That competitive economic structures such as capitalism encourage persons to seek to eliminate some of their better-endowed competitors does not indicate 'the Negro's vested interest in segregation.' If anything it suggests capitalism's vested interest in segregation. Or more accurately, that segregation is vested in capitalism.

The functionalist fails to see that the ways in which instruments are used are determined by (1) properties of the instrument, (2) intentions of the user, and (3) societal interactions delimiting the lists of possible users and targets. Let us consider a suggested 'function of prejudice for the minority group' which is better supported than are the above examples.

Simmel (1955), proposed that an external threat could reduce the tensions and strengthen the solidarity within a group. Target groups have frequently strengthened their group cohesion in order to resist the external threat of prejudice. This phenomenon is perhaps best illustrated by Theodor Herzl's declaration for Jews: 'We are a people – the enemy makes us a people.' At some sites it is even argued that Jews' group definitions are determined by their enemies. Lazarwitz (1970), contends that American Jews continue to define their common bonds through the religion, while Israeli Jews are less concerned about religion but quite unified about the State of Israel. Hofman (1970), sees this as a transfer of identity from the religion, which used to be attacked, to the State, which presently is attacked.

The difficulty with viewing group cohesion as caused by prejudice (an external threat) is that if we compare at other sites we can easily find examples in which cohesion does not result. Jack Levin notes (1975: 196) that 'in the collective experience of black America prejudice has contributed to a diminution of group solidarity, leading to rejection and escape more than to any sense of group spirit.'

These various examples suggest that target groups can employ prejudice only under certain circumstances to increase group solidarity. Much more of our ongoing essential interactionist analysis is needed before we can give an adequate theoretical statement of the essential possibilities for prejudice use by targets. But even on the basis of our insights thus far we can indicate in a more propositional manner some underlying fallacies of these functionalist arguments. For individual targets or target groups to use prejudice to their advantage via discrimination against other individual targets or against the original prejudicing groups they must be able to meet the following conditions which apply to any prejudiced person's or group's (A) profitable use of prejudice against any target (B): (1) A must be more powerful than B in the areas of social life to which prejudice will be applied; (2) A must intentionally simplify this area of social life; (3) A must have ability in at least one method of prejudicing; and (4) B must be identifiable by A.

These are our first essential conditions, and they arise from internal determiners of prejudice noted thus far – its instrumental and simplification essences. In order for a person or group successfully to use an instrument, they must be able to identify that upon which the instrument will be used, they must be more powerful than their target, and they must know how to use the instrument. Since prejudice is an instrument for simplification, it must be used to that end in some sense.

These points require a few additional comments. It might be argued that just as a hammer can be used either for driving a nail into a wall or for killing a cat, is it not the case that prejudice can be used to ends other than simplification? Our reply is that the two uses of the hammer are two separate possibilities within the range of possibilities for its striking-instrument essence. Comparably, prejudice may be used to simplify a range of possible groups or phenomena. It must be recalled that we are speaking of essential conditions for successful use of prejudice. A hammer cannot be deployed as a hammer without striking it against another object (e.g. hammers cannot be successfully deployed for sawing wood, but can be used to similar ends by breaking the wood).

Similar questions could be raised about the other conditions. Cannot one use a hammer without knowing how to use it? Are not such instruments sometimes used successfully by weak persons against strong persons or objects? In all cases our reply must be of the same order as the above. One need not have had specific instruction in the use of hammers in order to successfully use a hammer, but one must have ability at striking one object with another. And the second question can be interpreted only to describe apparent, not actual, strength. The strongest of two entities in any given battle is the one which is actually capable of winning. Although A may have fewer weapons that B, it is the stronger if what is consequential for winning is creative use of weapons, effective vehicles for transportation, or some other criteria in addition to number of weapons.

These objections notwithstanding, we can apply the above to the functionalist claim. American blacks do not command greater resources than do dominant white groups. Blacks are divided among factions concerning what they want to simplify (ranging from black capitalism to American socialism and from 'melting pot' values to African values), and there is little agreement about target. Some groups of blacks wish to identify targets simply by skin color (e.g. Cleaver, 1968), while others (e.g. socialists and feminists) advocate that some whites are not to be included as targets.

An important endeavor which would help to specify the four conditions is for mathematical sociologists to determine the minimum and maximum degrees to which each of these (and any combination) must be met for successful prejudicing to occur.

Classlessness and prejudice

We can apply our essential insights thus far in another direction. At several points in the preceding discussion we have seen how deeply entrenched prejudice is within economic competition, and a question arises about the possibility for prejudice in non-capitalist societies. Since there are no large-scale societies operating from a Marxist socialism, the possibility for adequate sites is difficult to imagine. I could locate no social science sites dealing with self-described Marxist societies such as the Soviet Union, the People's Republic of China or Cuba.

Our essential analyses do provide some ground for phantasy variations, however. Economically entrenched prejudice would seem to be impossible within a truly classless society. The condition of identifiability of targets could be met through ethnic, gender or other means, but relative powerlessness is ruled out, unless the democratically organized collectives Marx envisioned become competitors in some extra-economic sense.

Prejudice entrenchment primarily in non-economic areas of life seems quite possible, however, at least in the short run. Several self-described Marxist countries reveal prejudice and discrimination against alcoholics, gays, and Jews. Even in nearly ideal imagined classless societies such prejudices are not obviated. To apply our four conditions to the case of gays: (1) heterosexuals in such a society may command critical social resources; (2) heterosexuals may continue to feel in such a society that it is efficient to simplify sexual relations to opposite-sex partners, or that the threat to existing sex roles presented by gays must be destroyed; (3) if prejudicing does continue against homosexuals, then children likely will be socialized in the ways of prejudicing; and (4) heterosexuals and gays have regularly made gays identifiable. Identifiability has been accomplished in various ways at various times and locations, ranging from the perceived need by gays for gay political organizations, to distinctive mannerisms attributed to gays, to genetic determinisms argued by heterosexuals.

My argument might be answered by the phantasy variation of some Marxists along the lines that once economic classlessness entrenched itself in the society, other distinctions would also disappear or at least become incapable of providing greater social resources to one group than to another. I would welcome such a variation, but I have been unable to build one which demonstrates the essential possibility of each step in the change. For instance, the logic of a single social class would certainly not obviate a logic of singular sexual orientation, which could be encouraged through prejudicing against bisexuals or homosexuals.

Normality of prejudice

The discussion in Chapters 6 and 7 permits a potentially significant theoretical insight concerning the essential possibilities for prejudice interrelating with other phenomena of social consciousness or personality.

Authoritarian personality research and frustration-aggression research in a general way, want to hold that prejudice is part of a configuration of interrelated personality characteristics. We have concluded on the basis of vertical comparisons within the *Authoritarian Personality* site and horizontal comparisons with other sites that the personality type described by Adorno *et al.* is not essential for prejudicing. A phantasy variation further suggests that it may even be improbable under certain conditions. This variation is of the several sites noted by Simpson and Yinger (1972: Chapter 5), which suggests that the overall level of negative stereotypes about minority groups has been steadily decreasing in the United States over the last five decades. Various reasons are offered, ranging from the spread of social science to a simple change in verbal conventions. The point is that *Authoritarian Personality* employs agreement with stereotypes as its chief measure of prejudice and correlates this with political, moralistic, and other belief-agreements. When persons consider it unattractive, economically unwise, etc. to express stereotypes, they can stop such acceptance. The same can be imagined for items from the fascism scale such as, 'Some people are born with an urge to jump from high places.' Or we can imagine persons who find it to their advantage to accept stereotypes about minorities while rejecting the 'fascism' items. More concretely, sites such as Rokeach (1960), have demonstrated that anti-Semitism and fascism can be found among radicals and liberals, as well as among conservatives such as those Adorno *et al.* questioned. Persons' prejudicing does not seem to depend upon (though it may be related to) persons' gestalts of beliefs or ways of believing.

Our discussion of stereotypes-as-inductions does suggest the beginning of a holistic theory of prejudice, however. This theory finds prejudice necessarily dependent upon societies' major ways of thinking.

The distinction between our essential interactionist theoretical perspective and that of the correlational (and functionalist-Freudian) perspective exemplified by *Authoritarian Personality* and similar sites should be obvious: (1) Rather than a dependence primarily upon persons' beliefs (truth statements or opinions), prejudiced stereotyping appears to depend upon persons' ways of thinking; and (2) although persons' beliefs may derive primarily from their immediate reference groups, persons' ways of thinking derive from their fuller cultural environment.

Should the first statement need any further support from the field we can reiterate the Saenger and Flowerman (1954), site. Here 450 college students were asked their feeling of dislike for a number of groups. They were also asked to indicate the characteristics which they believed marked these groups. Students who disliked Jews ascribed to them characteristics which they also ascribed to other groups whom they did not dislike. For instance, 31 per cent complained that Jews were mercenary, but 24 per cent complained that Americans were mercenary and 38 per cent that businessmen were mercenary. Further, we can repeat the conclusion at sites such as Piaget (1965), Radke-Yarrow *et al.* (1949), and Porter (1971), that persons easily lose the specific prejudices learned through socialization, but retain the ability to stereotype, simplify behavior intentions, and simplify affect.

These points help to explain why it is that prejudicing persons span the range of political ideologies, socioeconomic positions, etc., but accomplish their prejudicing via the same methods. South Bostonites may be prejudiced against blacks, express this prejudice when they respond to questionnaires, and also score high on 'fascism' scales. Their Cambridge neighbors may not be prejudiced against blacks, but rather against Appalachian whites, and they may hide this prejudice and score low on 'fascism' scales. But all will be prejudicing via: (1) stereotyping (simplified inductions); (2) social distancing (simplified behavior intentions); or (3) affective simplification. We have seen that stereotyping is not easily distinguished from inductions in 'more acceptable' phenomena of social thinking, and the same can be said of simplified behavior intentions and affect. No one wants to condemn a person for simplifying his behavior intentions toward his car at red lights to putting his foot on the brake of his car nor for having few affective responses to clerks at grocery stores. Nor would we criticize someone for the stereotypes that 'All red lights mean stop' or 'All check-out clerks deal with money.'

A picture begins to emerge, then, of the normalcy of ways of prejudicing within the larger structures of social consciousness. Similarly, we have seen that the suggested essences 'instrumental' and 'simplification' are properties of other social phenomena as well as of prejudice.

Essences of prejudice as general essences

Our discussion above, along with several others concerning entrenchment of prejudice and social control of the social-psychology of prejudicing, have placed prejudice back in its societal context (from which it is frequently removed by those who wish to study it in itself).

As noted in the Preface, my goal is not simply to understand prejudice as a social phenomenon, but to be able to change social interactions in ways which diminish the undesirable products of prejudiced interactions. To accomplish this one must be able to distinguish prejudice from other social phenomena, while still recognizing its entrenchment in societies. To the limited extent possible on the basis of our first experiment with the method, I begin now to distinguish prejudice as a phenomenon by examining for which ends it can be instrumental.

We suggested at several points in Chapters 3 and 4 that separate social phenomena often share common essences, and that an essence can be investigated by looking at how it exists in other phenomena. We can step back now from the prejudice sites and see simplification in other situations. Such a search leads to an essential insight which is an important corrective to several sites' proposals for reducing prejudice by reducing simplification. Those who suggest that greater education or more scientific thinking in everyday life will reduce prejudice ignore that simplification is a positively valued goal of many endeavors. Simplification itself is not something that we would want to universally proscribe.

Two proposed prejudice-reduction agencies, education and science, themselves strive for simplification. A general goal of education is to place experience into simplified categories ('to make sense out of' nature, art, human behavior, etc.) Simplification is a goal of science as well, though not necessarily an essence thereof. Simplicity is frequently said to be a desirable characteristic of concepts, laws and theories in science (Rudner, 1966).

It is not the case that we want to deal with the social problem of prejudice by finding ways to reduce persons' simplifying, or even to reduce their simplifying of other persons and groups. Of the latter, we need only recall the Garfinkel (1967), experiments in which supermarket shoppers argue about the price of standard priced items. If many people involved themselves in such elaborating, grocery shopping would become an all-day affair.

Confusion regarding this issue can be seen in informant Levin's reports. After explaining that a social psychological function of prejudice is simplification, he throws out (58):

> Undoubtedly, there are times when interpersonal attitudes must be formed in the absence of detailed information about another person. For instance, a prospective employer might have to form a judgment of the abilities of a job applicant after having interviewed him for only a short period.

How can he distinguish this case from prejudicing?

Similarly, Allport (1958) talks of stereotyping and notes, 'It costs the Anglo employer less effort to guide his daily behavior by the generalization "Mexicans are lazy," than to individualize his workmen and learn the real reasons for their conduct.' But would Allport consider it prejudiced to say, 'It costs the Anglo employer less effort to guide his daily behavior by the generalization "Mexicans want to be paid," than to individualize his workmen and learn their real desires'? It seems inadequate to reply that the laziness statement is inaccurate and the payment statement is accurate. One socio-physical state among many is being lazy, and one socio-physical desire among many is to be paid.

A distinction between these two statements might be the implicit parts of each. One might argue that the first statement leaves out the implied hyphenated insertion 'the few Mexicans I have bothered to consider,' and that we can invalidate the statement on the grounds of poor sampling (inadequate data); whereas the latter statement omits 'because he needs to eat like any other worker.' What these suggest is a continuum of prejudicing and along with each point on the continuum are criteria of acceptability. The continuum probably ranges in statements from 'All Mexicans are from Mexico' to 'All Mexicans are lazy.' The statement concerned with workers being paid on time is near the left hand side, because a crucial criterion for this side is the logic that if the first half of the sentence can be considered true the second half necessarily can be considered true.

An instance of a simplification continuum has been noted by Robb (1954), during his ethnographic survey of anti-Semitism in a London working-class suburb (98–100):

There are some interesting changes in stereotypes as one progresses from the more to the less anti-Semitic. Those who are rated [highest] for anti-Semitism are most inclined to accuse Jews of the more heinous crimes, of being firebugs, swindlers, warmongers, and traitors. They also state that Jews have too much political and economic power, occupy the best houses, are lazy, cowardly, selfish, and (surprisingly) great lovers of poultry . . .

[Less anti-Semitic persons] are reasonable in the sense that some people (both Jewish and gentile) could easily be found to whom many of these descriptions would apply. Taken individually they are well within the range of experience of the ordinary man and they lack the air of extravagant phantasy typical of the plottings and high life described [above].

Several difficulties present themselves from Robb's analysis, despite its 'grain of truth.' Is it not also true that 'some people (both Jewish and Gentile) could be found . . . who are selfish, lazy, and warmongers?' What makes these more serious accusations than those of the 'less anti-Semitic' statements?

Difficulties with any continuum solution to the simplification problem appear to be the relative nature of continua themselves, and dealing with middle grounds on any continuum. Although the words may be the same, a stereotype in one time, place, and group may be strong and elsewhere it may be weak. Calling a group of persons by any stereotype can be a compliment or an insult, depending upon the group members' self perceptions and definitions, the use to which this stereotyping is being put by the prejudiced, the social events during which the stereotyping occurs, and so forth.

Another possibility for distinguishing simplification in prejudice from other sorts of simplification appears in Hesse's (1967) work reviewing philosophers' of science attempts to define what would constitute adequate simplification. Currently posited as the most nearly adequate is Goodman's proposal that complexity depends on the principle that if every set of predicates of one kind is replaceable by some set of predicates of another kind, then the first cannot be more complex than the second. In short, a set of predicates which is always replaceable is simpler than that by which it is replaced.

Viewed from this perspective, our example above might be seen as a case in which attempted simplification actually results in greater complexity. Stereotyping Mexicans as lazy may initially simplify reactions to Mexicans. But since Mexicans exist who are not lazy, it could be argued that 'Mexicans are lazy' results in greater complexity, rather than in simplification. When the prejudiced meets active Mexicans she will have to find ways to fit these persons into the laziness assumption, and these will necessarily entail increasing complexity. This helps us to understand behavior such as excluding others on the basis of race from athletics even when these athletes would increase the probability of the prejudiced person's team winning. To admit such persons after stereotyping them as lazy, inferior, etc. would obligate the prejudiced person to complicate his simplifications (e.g. with 'except for a few,' or 'but they sure can throw a football').

A distinction between scientific simplification and prejudicing simplification on the basis of Goodman's definition does not hold up from a sociological perspective because criteria of replaceability vary among reference groups. The scientists turn to scientific reference groups to determine the universe of predicates for replacement, the ways of seeking and examining predicates, etc. Likewise, the prejudiced turns to prejudiced reference groups for norms about predicates. Both groups choose as their universes of predicates a sample which is manageable with the resources they perceive as appropriate for them.

Which distinctions *can* we find between instrumentality and simplification in various phenomena?

One which we can note right off is the distinction between these items as essences of a phenomenon and as frequently occurring features. Prejudice apparently cannot exist without instrumentality and simplification as features. On the other hand, science regularly chooses concepts and theories which are not perceived to be the simplest of those which work or are considered true or verified. Several philosophers of science and several scientists have argued that the most acceptable criterion for a good theory in science is whether or not it is more aesthetically pleasing than its competitors (Siu, 1957). Similarly, education frequently teaches students more complex explanations and techniques than do everyday peers.

Music is an especially illustrative case of a social phenomenon which does not necessarily include simplification or instrumentality.

Music is a social phenomenon regularly produced in groups. Although a single person may write a piece, others will perform, publish, distribute, or critique it. The musician works within a historical period and musical conventions, and usually with instruments invented by others (Becker, 1976).

It is not unusual for a musical convention to exist which specifies that good music is complicated music. Certainly there have been types of music within which a convention has been to perform simple pieces, but much of classical music and jazz attempts not at all to simplify.

Similarly, music has frequently been composed for ends which were not socially instrumental. Musicians emerge who compose music 'for its own sake' or for their own pleasure, rather than to facilitate social relations. This is not to deny that jazz was born out of the social interactions of status-anxious blacks in New Orleans (as Walton, 1972 notes), nor that most music is intended at the least as an instrument for group entertainment. But clearly we cannot include either simplification or instrumental as essences of music.

Where one of the essences of prejudice apparently *is* shared by another social phenomenon, it may still be possible to distinguish that phenomenon in its current state from prejudice. Both sciences and education do seem to share the instrumental essence with prejudice. An important point here is one we noted in the methodology section, of the necessity to examine relationships between essences as well as essences themselves if we are to understand a social phenomenon. On the basis of what we know from our initial investigations we can see that prejudice is an instrument for simplification. On the other hand, science, education, and music are not necessarily instruments for simplification, but may be instruments for deriving beauty, for increasing understanding, 'for their own sake,' etc. – none of which appear to be possibilities for uses of prejudice. Furthermore, even in cases where one of these social phenomena is being used as an instrument for simplification, it can be distinguished from prejudice if its ways of accomplishing the simplification do not rely upon stereotyping, simplified behavior intentions, or simplified affect.

Another major distinction is between the goals of persons who construct social phenomena. Thus, Frank (1957: 356) noted of contemporary scientists:

> This metaphysical concept of a true theory as a "replica of physical reality" is not prevalent in the scientific philosophy of today. A theory is now rather regarded as an instrument that serves some definite purpose. It must be helpful in predicting future observable facts on the basis of facts that have been observed in the past and in the present. The theory should also be helpful in the contribution of devices which can save us time and labor. The scientific theory is, in a way, a tool that produces other tools according to a practical scheme. Scientific theories are also accepted, however, because they give us a simple and beautiful world picture and support a philosophy which, in turn, supports a desirable way of life.

A criticism of our argument must be considered as well, however. It might be that instrumentality and simplification are essences of any language usage. Language is said to be necessarily simplifying, instrumental, and instrumental for simplification.

FIRST ILLUSTRATION OF A METHOD

Although it may well be the case that most uses of language include instrumentality and simplification, again examples from the arts provide cases in which these features need not be present. A novelist may use language not to simplify events, characters, or other creations, but rather to elaborate them. And again, novels are sometimes written 'for their own sake.' Indeed, only about three per cent of the novels written in the United States are published (Bessie, 1958). The low probability of publication is well known to many fiction writers, who thereby hold little or no expectation to facilitate social life (or even their own ego needs) by writing novels.

Concerning solutions

We have seen that some frequent solutions offered at the sites for reducing prejudice do not withstand our essential analysis thus far. Many of these solutions suggest that persons be educated about social scientific investigations concerning prejudice and target groups. Various correlational sites answer this by noting that education does not reduce prejudice. Jackman (1975), showed through path analyses of previous researches that response sets contributed more to the fewer prejudice-verbalizations of persons at several other sites than did education. Selznick and Steinberg (1969), found an inverse relationship between anti-Semitism and amount of formal education (a relationship that could not be accounted for by social class). Stember (1961), argued that the educated persons he researched expressed their prejudices in subtle, more sophisticated ways, especially in the context of the paper-and-pencil questionnaires generally used by social science researchers. Freedman's (1962), work with Bennington College graduates indicated that soon after graduation the persons were less prejudiced, but that after twenty-five years they were not in general lower in prejudice than other Americans.

We can propose essential interactionist theoretical statements to account for the inability to reduce prejudice through exposure. Prejudice is not an abnormality. Rather it is a configuration of essences, each of which are conidered normal and appropriate in other phenomena.

A thorough appreciation of this position about prejudice permits a reply as well to the seeming difficulties with prejudice-as-simplification and stereotyping-as-induction. It might be supposed that to reduce prejudice we must reduce instances of simplification and induction. Now we can see that reduction is not the appropriate goal. These essences *themselves* must be changed, notably within institutions which house the phenomena. We have noted that the changes possible for essences are coming into being, passing away,

POSSIBLE APPLICATIONS

joining together with other essences, and disjoining from other essences. We have excluded on practical grounds the passing away option. Hence any solutions for reducing prejudice which would make sense within our essential interactionist theory must concern new configurations of essences.

Considerations of induction offer examples of possibilities for new essence configurations. This is precisely the attempt which is being made by those philosophers who are most successfully tackling the difficulties of induction. Their arguments are beyond the scope of the present work, but a cursory introduction to a couple of the major works should illustrate the point. Both Goodman and Pierce have suggested ways in which induction can be brought into new configurations with other essences to accomplish science.

Goodman's (especially 1955), greatly elaborated theory attempts to solve his 'new riddle of induction' by arguing that the better-entrenched predicates are to be preferred over less-entrenched predicates. Degree of entrenchment of predicates for Goodman is basically determined by whether or not the predicate has been employed successfully many, few or no times in the past. Although in his emerald example noted in Chapter 6 there is equal evidence for 'grue' as for 'green', 'grue' has been much less frequently employed than other predicates in the cases of correct predictions. Entrenchment also depends upon how important in light of the rest of one's system of thought the predicate turns out to be. A variation of this type of induction strategy might preclude stereotyping as induction. The specific stereotype may be important to the prejudicing person or group, who may have used it frequently in the past. But it seems doubtful that prejudiced persons would use this variety of predicates in same-order situations from other parts of their lives. For example, rules for inductions used for stereotyping a target probably are not used for conducting inductions concerning friends, sales persons, business associates, etc. Whatever justifications make it possible for 'all A to be B' when one is prejudicing are unlikely to be the same justifications which make B's of A's in other areas of one's life.

Summary

The purpose of this chapter was to provide a very general idea of the possibilities for theory construction and application were a full elaboration achieved of an essential interactionist theory of prejudice.

Treating our suggested essences as if they were in fact essences of prejudice we critiqued the functionalist notion of 'functions of prejudice for the minority group' and indicated that the ways in which an instrument is used depend upon properties of the instrument, intentions of the user, and societal interactions delimiting the lists of possible users and uses. More specifically, it was recommended that for a person or group (A) to use prejudice against a target (B) to the advantage of A, the following conditions must be met: (1) A must be more powerful than B in the areas of social life to which the prejudice will be applied; (2) A must intentionally simplify this area of social life; (3) A must have ability in at least one method of prejudicing; and (4) B must be identifiable by A. Some target groups can meet these conditions and thereby use prejudice to their own advantage, others cannot.

A discussion followed which proposed that an essential interactionist theory of prejudice would find prejudice dependent upon societies' major ways of thinking, rather than upon the presence of any particular personality type. Indeed, essences of prejudice are frequently found as features of other "respectable" phenomena, such as simplification and instrumentality within many applications of education, science, and everyday activities such as driving a car.

Distinguishing among phenomena by the degree to which these essences are present was found to be unenlightening. Rather, the distinctions which exist between a feature in two phenomena seem to depend upon whether the feature is essential or simply frequently occurring; and upon configurations of essences within phenomena.

The last section of the chapter discusses the apparent inability of education to reduce prejudice. This suggests that reduction of prejudice in societies requires a thorough understanding of the configurations of essences which constitute prejudice, and social movements to bring about new configurations.

Discussions in this chapter are necessarily cursory and open to revision, due to the limited research upon which they are based. They were successful if they indicate that a thorough essential interactionist inquiry may permit social planners and activists to decide upon their own goals and means to these goals more adequately. Past theories of prejudice have generally dealt only with manifestations of prejudice and thereby offered agents of social change with maps or theories primarily of incidents, not of phenomena.

The next chapter will assess the method in order to suggest how it must be filled out to provide the means for a comprehensive elaboration of essences and understanding of configurations of essences of large social phenomena.

9 Assessment and further development

The preceding chapters have presented an initial illustration of one methodological strategy for essential interactionist research into large social phenomena which have been widely researched from other perspectives. A major goal has been to uncover some of the strengths and limitations of the method.

Much potential for developing a method exists within analysis of the incompleteness and inadequacies revealed by its early applications. This concluding chapter assesses the method in light of the fieldwork and the analysis it permitted. The assessment is in two parts: first, a listing of points noted during the illustration, which further specify what was said in Part II; and second, a series of recommendations for changes and additions which seem needed if the method is to permit thorough application.

Methodological notes from the first illustration

1 The literature sites proved to be rich sources of material for (a) suggesting essences, (b) elaborating these, and (c) critiquing previous research and theorizing. Each of these provide higher levels of generality about the phenomenon.

(a) The capacity for suggesting essences was anticipated in our discussion in Part II and is demonstrated both in the initial work with definitions from the sites and in the additional essences which were suggested during rounds through the sites.

(b) The elaboration of suggested essences illustrates an unique potential for the method and also an inadequacy. Unlike survey research or traditional participant observation, the literature sites *en masse* provided tremendous detail about the phenomenon as seen in a variety of historical periods, distinct settings, and a variety of methodological and theoretical lenses. The point is exemplified by such thick descriptions and theoretical detail as our discussions of stereotyping-as-induction and of entrenchments of prejudice. On the other hand, during these elaborations it was found that the strategy of sticking to social scientific literature sites was inadequate. Very quickly it became necessary to employ philosophical and novelist sites to accomplish the elaborations.

(c) The capability for critiquing previous research and theorizing was seen in horizontal comparisons which revealed the inability of concepts such as 'functional' or 'dysfunctional' to explain prejudice. Similar instances were our critiques of the Sherif conclusions and of functionalists' declarations of 'functions of prejudice for minority groups.'

2 An advantage of the literature sites which was not fully anticipated during Part II is the possibility for other researchers to visit the sites employed here, for their own conceptual decisions and theory-building. Traditional fieldwork sites usually cannot be visited by other researchers because they change or vanish. Thus, a trip to Cornerville would hardly offer another researcher the same material which awaited Whyte.

Literature sites permit replication, the chance for others to develop their own essential interactionist theorizing about the phenomenon, and comparing of notes for collective development. The context of validation was underemphasized in our discussions in Part II, in favor of much consideration of the context of discovery. Now we see the great potential for the essential interactionist research strategies in contexts of validation – both for the validation of other theories (through analysis of sites groups) and for validation of essential interactionist research.

3 A few procedures emphasized in Part II and in the first chapter of Part III proved less consequential than had been expected; namely (a) mapping, (b) vertical comparisons, and (c) phantasy variations.

(a) Despite the many hours put into construction of the three maps presented in Chapter 8, they were seldom used in the fieldwork presented in Chapters 9 and 10. The reason is quite simple. Key informants turned out to be more useful than maps for locating sites. The initial maps were organized according to the basic groupings which appeared in the definitions, and my central concerns in the field undercut these. For example, material concerning the suggested simplification essence was found at sites listed under a variety of headings in the initial maps, whereas reports from the key informants included references specifically to simplification and to sites dealing with this issue.

(b) Under-utilization of the second strategy, vertical comparisons, is regrettable. The great potential for this technique was illustrated in vertical comparisons of the Sherif site and of *Authoritarian Personality*. But in general, these literature sites do not contain enough information about how they were constructed to permit vertical comparisons. One needs tremendous detail about the decision-making processes by those who wrote the site and about actions at every step in the research process.

(c) Under-utilization of phantasy variations is also regrettable. This technique permits direct examination of the logic inherent in suggesting the essences which we propose or their configurations, and possible validation of discoveries. Phantasy variations are especially important for elaborating one sort of essence, the metaphorical. Quite clearly instrumentality is a metaphor.

Metaphors have offered much to the arts and sciences for understanding phenomena. Many apparently discrete entities share features in common, and the metaphor helps us to make these connections. Rashevsky (1961) notes examples of the use of analogies between the heart and vascular system and pumps and systems of pipes, with resulting discoveries of expressions between the mass of the heart, the heart frequency, and total mass of the animal. The relative power of various metaphors depends upon the degree of isomorphism between the items. An excellent way to further elaborate a metaphor is through determining which items within a group serve best for the analogy.

In our case, elaboration of the instrumental essence requires determination through systematic variations of which tool is most nearly isomorphic with prejudicing. Once this is determined a great specificity about instrumentality within prejudice should be possible. (This potential was illustrated even by our inadequate analogies during the first illustration between prejudice-use and hammer-use.)

Greer (1969: 148) noted dangers in the ways we have been using metaphors:

> You are apt to take them for granted and fail even to recognize them as metaphors. Then you adopt the metaphors given by the conventions of thought in your discipline or by common sense. Thus the phrases, 'the political game,' 'the social body,' 'the climate of opinion,' 'the military machine.' These are commonplace shifts of meaning from folk toward technical language. But guiding metaphors are powerful limits and directives for resulting theories. They highlight that which conforms, and they suppress 'irrelevant' aspects; they can lead to a kind of theoretical 'tunnel vision.'

4   A distinction must be spelled out between illustration of the method and definitive results from the method. Only the former has

been accomplished thus far. In Part II it was argued that essential interactionists seek defended possibilities from their research. Such possibilities can be proposed only when one has met three conditions: (a) an understanding of the essences of the phenomenon, (b) knowledge of the essential configurations possible, and (c) the irrevocability of the essences and essential configurations.

(a) We know from Chapter 5 that additional essences of prejudice need to be examined, and as will be seen throughout this assessment Chapter, other sites are needed for filling out the research. Hence, the first condition has not been fulfilled during our initial illustration, although the process got off to a good start.

(b) In order to achieve internal understanding of a phenomenon one needs more information than elaboration of its essences. One needs elaboration of the interactions (configurations) of these essences. But such understanding is impossible prior to thorough elaboration of the essences and, as noted above, we have not yet reached that point.

The need for insight into configurations of essences is clearly visible in the first illustration. For instance:

(i) We noted that persons do not want to stop simplifying altogether, even if they want to decrease prejudice. Through an understanding of the configurations of essences we can consider ways in which single essences can be kept distinct from the configuration of essences which constitute prejudice.

(ii) That our suggested essences interact is apparent at sites where prejudice is instrumental for groups who wish to simplify economic relations with other groups.

(iii) Some parts of our elaboration of the suggested essences offered fascinating descriptions of how prejudice exists but did not make essentialist statements. How do the various forms of entrenchment fit into configurations of essences of prejudice? Apparently this can be answered only in light of much more of our theory development. It is important along the way, however, to describe as completely as possible each entity found within prejudice. It may turn out that entrenchment is of a form similar to that which we concluded stereotyping to be after looking at a variety of ways of prejudicing. At first we noted that stereotyping was not an essence of prejudice. But after elaboration of aspects of prejudicing we were able to suggest a way in which stereotyping seems to play into the essences of prejudice. Our suggested essence turned out to be of the form: 'If A or B or C, then D,' where A is stereotyping, B is social distancing, C is affective simplifying, and D is ways of prejudicing. Of course, another possibility is that an aspect such as entrenchment may turn out to be a frequently conjoined item with prejudice, but not part of the phenomenon's essential configurations.

(c) Goodman's conditions for revocability noted in Chapter 4 can be considered only after the configurations of essences have been suggested. At that point we must ask whether the essences and their configurations as we have proposed them meet the conditions of workability and compatibility. We achieve essential possibilities ('defended results') through our research only when we can argue that our essential interactionist statements work under the variety of manifestations of the phenomenon and are compatible with one another. At this point we have built a qualitative system upon an essential interactionist ontology.

5 Several indications exist for the potential for social policy development on the basis of essential interactionist inquiries and their resulting systems. In the previous chapter we already began to specify the essential conditions for successful prejudicing, and these conditions can be manipulated through policy or social movement work. Our elaboration of the tendency of intellectuals to reply to prejudicing with more prejudicing indicates that one may require an essential analysis to avoid this trap. Finally, combat strategies for target groups can be derived through evaluations of which parts of the essential configurations of prejudicing that targets can change.

Next steps

> There are very many different equally true descriptions of the world, and their truth is the only standard of their faithfulness. And when we say of them that they all involve conventionalizations, we are saying that no one of these different descriptions is *exclusively* true, since the others are also true. None of them tells us *the* way the world is, but each of them tells us *a* way the world is (Goodman, 1972: 31).

Rather than stick to an assessment only of our initial experiment, I wish to conclude with suggestions for the additional research which would be needed to develop a full essential interactionist theory of prejudice.

Obviously, the next steps require first off some elaborations of the other suggested essences revealed in Chapter 8: pre-judging, towards others, and self-other splits. That elaboration of these possible essences is likely to reveal rich material for the theory is already evident:

A phantasy variation in my fieldnotes links the suggested self-other essence with the instrumental essence. This variation looks at a variety of uses of instruments and concludes that they are all used as objects. Even instruments which are applied to persons are applied with the persons objectified. For instance, surgeons do not apply their instruments to persons as subjective entities but rather to their bodies, conceived as objects. Possible connections between this split and simplification are also evident, given that objectifying persons is a way of simplifying them.

The towards others or self-other essences are topics which in their general forms have occupied much philosophical and religious thought throughout recorded history, under titles ranging from 'yen and yang' to 'the revolt against dualism' to 'I-Thou.' They may be social essences which occur in many phenomena, but in a variety of configurations with other essences.

By dealing directly with the necessity for presence of targets we would likely attempt to answer the questions, 'How does an other become an other,' and 'How does an other become a target of prejudice?' Both questions may send us beyond the simple probabilities from the past that targets are selected according to differences in ethnicity. Nearly all of our discussion in the first illustration of the method concentrated upon these types of targets. Some sites indicate that birthright certainly is not essential to becoming a target, however. An example is the Sherif (1961 and 1966), sites, at which boys from very similar backgrounds were brought to prejudice against one another.

Also important as we return to the definitions will be to look again at some of the characteristics suggested by the definitions in Chapter 5 but discounted there through quick visits to the sites. We can now see that some of these items may contribute to an elaboration of our suggested essences, although they are not themselves essential. Thus we noted at some sites that prejudice is positive toward targets and at others it is negative. In our further theorizing we will want to distinguish on the basis of essential interactions between statements such as 'Chinese are regarded as honest, industrious, and peaceful' and 'Chinese are stereotyped as dangerous, deceitful, and clannish.'

Still another group of essences which must be investigated in the next set of comparisons and variations are those which started to emerge during the initial illustration (e.g. identifiability, rationality-dependency, object-dependency, and the various forms of entrenchment).

Missing literature sites

Several indications in the initial illustration of the method recommend the need for literature sites other than those by social psychologists and sociologists when the research resumes:

ASSESSMENT AND FURTHER DEVELOPMENT

1. I frequently moved to other types of literature sites. Sites written by historians were frequently employed; work by philosophers dominated much of the discussion on simplification and on stereotypes-as-inductions; and some novels were noted.
2. Discussion of entrenchment of prejudice in institutions and of prejudice as a social instrument revealed that the sociological literature was limited almost exclusively to sites dealing with economic entrenchment and use. Sites primarily concerned with gender, family, and politics were rare, although some phantasy variations revealed the need for such considerations. As a result, virtually all of the sites dealt with prejudices against ethnic groups, to the exclusion of prejudices against women, gays and others.
3. The need for cross-cultural sites emerges from our discussion of the ways in which Indo-European languages facilitate stereotyping. Does stereotyping exist amid other types of languages? If not, perhaps this major way of prejudicing is replaced by another, which would revise our essentialist statements about ways of prejudicing. The concern about possible economic bases of prejudice also may be better understood via cross-cultural sites.
4. The social science sites typically ask 'why' questions, and we have argued that 'how' questions are also important for understanding of phenomena. Sites by philosophers, ethnographers, and prejudicing persons themselves often address 'how' questions.

Filling out of literature sites is accomplished much the way we sought social science sites in Chapter 5. One begins with card catalogues and abstracting sources, then goes through the references found in the works listed. This creates a spiral of references leading to sites. For literature sites such as novels, diaries and autobiographies this may not work quite as well, however. In such cases it may be necessary to interview persons who are familiar with such sites.

In addition, one may need to manufacture sites. My travels through the literature sites have revealed that three groups construct prejudice in societies: the prejudiced, the targets, and those who study prejudice. By completing the sites lists as specified above, the third group will be thoroughly researched. And as argued in Chapter 4 and illustrated throughout the current Part, much will be gained from these researchers concerning construction of prejudice by the prejudicing and by the targets. A theory derived strictly from these sites would be far better grounded and predictive amid various manifestations of the phenomenon than any previous theory of prejudice I have been able to locate.

Nevertheless, some inadequacies of the sites emerged during the first application and suggest the need for certain additional sites: the nonintentionality of some prejudicing is not discussed adequately at the sites, and sites directly concerned with targets are rare.

A regular feature of prejudicing noted at several sites is that it seems natural to the prejudicing person, who does not even recognize the possibility of other instruments which may be available (Simpson and Yinger, 1972: 129):

> Even the poorest of whites was convinced rather easily that he had more to gain by keeping the Negro down than by uniting with him against the upper-class whites. His own deprivations were made somewhat more bearable by the continuous sight of even more serious deprivations among Negroes. Though he was actually injured by a system that rested upon the exploitation of cheap labor, he was not perceptive enough to recognize the true source of his difficulty.

Only through intersubjective understandings of prejudicing persons can we answer the questions which arise concerning this possible feature of prejudice. Could they be more perceptive? Under what conditions does it seem natural to prejudice? What is it about prejudicing that makes it seem natural? How is it 'naturalized'?

J. Katz (1972 and 1975), notes two attributes generally assigned to deviant targets: violation of rules, and inherent characteristics. Either sort of attribution allows the prejudicing person to keep a distance from the target. The attributions can have very different effects for the prejudiced, however. Rule breakers can always reform, and if they do so it may be difficult for the prejudicing person to maintain the wall between himself and the targets. On the other hand, inherent characteristics are not so easily removed. 'There is actually (or after all or really in fact) a something, a core, a category that the person *is* despite any indication to the contrary' (Lofland, 1969: 128).

Perhaps the most forceful type of inherent-characteristic attribution is genetic attribution. The argument of genetic inferiority of certain 'races' has been especially persistent. Quite popular at present are serious inquiries into genetic bases for alcoholism and homosexuality.

The need for manufactured sites also results from the fact that existing sites seldom deal with targets of prejudice. Since the targets' perspective is one of the three from which prejudice can be experienced (at which it is constructed), the targets' angle is crucial for any complete view of prejudice. Further, we noted at sites such as Guskin (1962), Karlins (1969), Selzer (1972), and Bayton (1956), that answers to 'how people stereotype' must be given in object-dependent terms. A full theory of prejudice must investigate how targets construct their cues, as well as how they construct others' prejudicing.

In addition, we need to answer a question remaining from the previous chapter concerning claims that 'prejudice is functional for minority groups.' Despite the critique noted in that discussion, are there ways in which prejudice becomes instrumental for targets? Or put more generally, in what ways do targets themselves construct their own prejudicing?

In short, any adequate essential interactionist theory of prejudice must make constant comparisons and variations concerning the 'modes of appearing' (Spiegelberg, 1965), of prejudice. On the basis of our research thus far we can see that prejudice exists as my prejudice or another's, and in each case is directed in various degrees and angles toward me, away from me, by me, by others, and in varying grades of visibility and clearness.

By filling out the literature sites in the ways proposed above, we should produce a list of sites that reveal the angles of prejudice needed for an adequate theory. Of the two missing angles noted above, diaries, autobiographies, novels, and ethnographies may well give a rich understanding of the nonintentionality of prejudicing and of constructions by targets. But what can one do if the existing sites do *not* provide a needed perspective?

Let us conclude with general suggestions for a way to manufacture new literature sites, should this become necessary after the existing sites have been employed. At that point, of course, one would have fairly precise notions about the missing angles, and the manufacture of additional sites would be accomplished with these objectives in mind.

The manufacture of additional literature sites can occur in certain cases through the researcher's attempts to accomplish the phenomenon. This is a fundamental goal of ethnomethodologists, who claim that any researcher 'by having to perform in (another's) world, must develop and adopt the perspective that goes with that world' (Psathas, 1968: 519). I would argue that being able to do whatever one is studying is not as instructive as such ethnomethodologists claim. It can be the case that persons who accomplish something accomplish only those aspects of the process which gives the behavioral appearance of 'doing it right,' without necessarily thinking in the ways their 'subjects' think or going through the same decision making steps. And we frequently perform roles in detached manners, without adopting them or even accepting that 'I' am doing the role.

Nevertheless, in one regard accomplishing of the phenomenon may prove profitable for filling in gaps in the literature sites. Inquiry is an undergoing as well as a going over, and a rich source of data can be derived from a search into the essences of one's own prejudicing or being a target. Such introspective research provides another way to 'expand empiricism' and to give the phenomenon a fuller hearing.

In this strategy the researcher places herself at the actual angle which she wishes to investigate, e.g., as a target of certain types of prejudicing, or as one who is prejudicing in specific ways. The researcher must be mindful that her social characteristics will limit where and how she can place herself, and the techniques must not be constructed to create artificial role playing. But most persons can regularly find themselves prejudicing or as targets of prejudice. Sometimes one can enter a setting and become a full-fledged participant, with concurrent responsibilities and risks. A careful evaluation while in such a position permits the creation of new literature sites which can be employed for vertical and horizontal comparisons. Basically, the researcher chooses a location which would be expected to entail construction of the phenomenon from the angle missing in the existing literature sites. Then the researcher takes detailed notes about her own 'hows' and 'whys' of constructing the phenomenon.

Summary

This chapter looks critically at the proposed method for essential interactionist research into large social phenomena which have been widely researched in the past. The first application of the method is assessed and suggested revisions and additions noted.

The first illustration indicated several capabilities of the method: for suggesting and elaborating essences; for critiquing previous works; for replication by others; and for serving social policy and social movements needs. On the other hand, the first illustration revealed limitations: needs for types of sites other than those produced by social scientists; and under-utilization of maps, vertical comparisons, and phantasy variations.

Much of the chapter recommended ways to fill out the list of literature sites. Notably, the literature sites must be expanded to include historical and philosophical research, novels, autobiographies, diaries, and ethnographies. A full hearing must be given to the various angles of the three groups who construct prejudice: observers of prejudice, prejudiced persons, and targets. A technique was indicated for creation of additional sites by the researcher should these be needed to provide perspectives missing from existing literature sites.

The precise form that the method takes will vary according to the phenomenon studied. I have concentrated upon describing the steps which would be used in researching prejudice. But the general methodological strategy should be applicable to research concerning a variety of large social phenomena about which much has been written in the past. In each case one would do well to begin by mapping, comparing and varying literature sites relating to as many groups as one can identify who are involved in constructing the phenomenon, with the goal of suggesting and elaborating essences of the phenomenon. If inadequacies are discovered in such sites, one fills in with additional sites, which are then compared in the same manner. When one is unable to elaborate further the suggested essences of the phenomenon, one compares the sites again to determine the essential configurations of essences within the phenomenon. Once this is accomplished one should be able to talk not only about necessary conditions (as in discussions of individual essences) but also about sufficient conditions for the existence of the phenomenon. The final statements should be of the variety, 'Essences E_1 though E_n in interactions I_1 through I_n permit phenomenon P in any of its manifestations.'

This type of understanding has frequently been missing within sociology and is desperately needed if we are to avoid talking past one another and producing laws about relationships between entities which we do not understand.

Appendix
Sample fieldnotes

Sherif and Sherif studies

Map 1 possibilities – IB (frus-agg), ID (child-rear), II (situation), IIIB (dysfunc) VC (socialization), VF (contact) Map 2 – check generally for ways used, esp. VIIIA&B (soc funcs and dys-economic and comp control), also IX (scapegoat) Map 3 – esp. attitude direction (always negative?) and III (func – advantage for possessor, meet normative demands, reduce group efficiency)

The Sherif "Robbers Cave" experiments are noted throughout the reports of key informants and at other sites, as demonstration of the inevitability of intergroup competition to produce prejudice. Jones (1972: 66):

> Intergroup hostility tends to increase as competition for scarce resources becomes more intense. Sherif and his collabs (1961), demonstrated the link between comp and intergroup host in a series of experiments that took place in an isolated summer camp for 11- and 12-year-old boys. After a period of time together, the boys attending the camp were separated into two groups and placed in different cabins. When each group of boys had developed a strong sense of group spirit and org, Sherif arranged for a number of intergroup encounters – a tournament of competitive games such as football, baseball, tug-of-war, and a treasure hunt – in which one group could fulfill its goals only at the expense of the other group. Though the tournament began in a spirit of friendliness and good-natured rivalry, it soon became apparent that negative intergroup feelings were emerging on a large scale. The members of each group began to name-call their rivals, completely turning against members of the opposing group, even members whom they had selected as 'best friends' upon first arriving at the camp.

APPENDIX: SAMPLE FIELDNOTES

Notes: Stereotyping seems to be the way of prejudicing here. Jones (173) gives similar report, but perhaps from his own black perspective adds that Sherifs' 'subjects' were 'white boys from very similar backgrounds.' This could be important.

Also, this seems to be requiring a vertical comparison: how did Sherif come to do this study? Why set it up as an experiment instead of P–O? (*He* designed the situation, not the boys, or so it sounds.)

Book usually cited by Sherif describing the case is *Groups in Harmony and Tension* (1953). He also summarizes in *Intergroup Conflict and Cooperation* (1961), and in *In Common Predicament* (1966), as well as in some of the general social psych and intergroup conflict books.

From the books generally, a reconstruction:

He set out to conduct 'a sociological experiment' to examine in-group friendships, intergroup conflict, prejudice and conflict reduction via situations constructed and controlled by the experimenters. He notes often his concern that the thing be controlled, that it resemble a lab experiment. Of his major concerns, I note from his earlier books that his previous interest apparently centered on group norms.

In 1953, he took twenty-four 11- and 12-year-old boys to Robber's Cave, Okla. Turns out they were white Protestant boys from similar middle-class neighborhoods in New Haven. (Check later horizontally: any similar studies using other background kids, or using adults?)

Sherif described the experiment in most detail in Chapter 9 of *Harmony and Tension*. He begins by stressing, 'Findings on group formation stress that the content of the individual member's major attitudes toward the group is derived from the social norms of the group. These norms are internalized by the individual members (229).' Talks a lot about importance of the group structure on roles and norms that emerge. Describes the 3 states of the experiment.

1 Informal groupings on basis of personal inclinations and interests. All activities were camp-wide, with freedom of choice and 'mixing'. 'Thus it became possible to single out budding friendship groups and, more or less, to equate the weights of such personal factors in the two experimental groups of State II. (239).' *Note*: for Sherif, the entire purpose of Stage I was to prepare to accomplish Stage 2.

2 Formation of in-groups, with activities planned according to favorites of the boys themselves. This was when the boys were separated into 2 groups opposite of their choices in Stage 1. And 'all rewards given in this period were made on a group-unit basis, not to particular individuals.'

3 To study intergroup relations. Groups brought into competitive games and frustrating situations.

Before continuing, I recall the general conclusion picked up by other sites, but want to find it in Sherif himself. It's p. 81 of *In Common Predicament* (1966);

> 'When members of two groups come into contact with one another and a series of activities that embody goals which each urgently desires, but which can be attained by one group only at the expense of the other, competitive activity toward the goal changes, over time, to hostility between the groups and their members.'

OK – what about this final leap at each stage?

Stage 1 – he gives far less info about this than about the other stages. Why? Says friendship choices were based upon personal attractions, and upon common interests and abilities. (This on basis of his and others' notes from observing.) Activities were arranged by adults, but the boys decided upon teammates, seats at meals, and buddies for free time play. This period lasted only three days. (*Note*: do horizontal later to see if groups of strangers-kids can really emerge and solidify in such an incredibly short time.) Friendship clusters emerged and leadership structures were apparent, he says.

Looks like the natural ordering of the boys during these days was effective. Sherif quotes 'an adult participant observer of a two-hour hike': 'The hikers did not proceed according to plan up the river toward New Boston. Along the highway, the boys saw a dirt trail veering off to the left, and with the assent of the lead counselor, they took it. The trail ended abruptly and the hikers decided to climb the mountain. About half way up, it was decided to have a race to the top. The three boys who won the race were Hall, Miller, and Crane. Hall told (staff member) that they all walked to the top abreast by mutual agreement, so that no one of them would arrive before the others. . . .'

Notes

Chapter 1 Causation and interaction

1 To consider the myriad alternative causal notions of philosophers of science (cf. Ayer, 1951; Collingwood, 1940; Sosa, 1975; and Von Wright, 1974) would not be germane to this discussion, which is preparatory to a particular proposal to sophisticate the vocabulary of determinism in sociology. It may be possible to sophisticate causal sociology as well, notably through nomic linguistic products and through state descriptions of productive systems, but this project I entrust to the sociological causalists themselves.

2 Interactionist positions would explain this example as a case for the position that neural activities interact with other physical activities and with social activities. The 'results' or 'effects' are points within the interaction process at which one group of interactions appears to end.

3 Another way the process of elimination argument is phrased is in terms of necessity and sufficiency. This argument holds that if A is necessary and sufficient for the occurrence of B, then A causes B. The inadequacy of this position is that one can easily imagine constant conjunctions in which both parts are necessary and sufficient for each other, hence, how can one attribute causation to one member and not to the other? The simple example of my current writing activity is one in which the motion of my hand is necessary and sufficient for the motion of the pencil, but the motion of the pencil is also necessary and sufficient for the motion of the hand. Neither the hand nor the pencil can move under the circumstances of my holding the pen in writing position without the other moving with it (R. Taylor, 1967: 65–6).

4 Nothing within this argument for the primacy of action refutes Hume (Von Wright, 1971: 190–1):

> To say that things 'bring about' other things is . . . misleading: this 'bringing about' is nothing but regular sequence. Our knowledge that

161

we can do things, moreover, rests on our assurance that certain states of affairs will stay unchanged (or will change in a certain way), unless we interfere, productively or preventively, with the course of nature. Whence have we got this assurance? Obviously from experience. So, in the last resort the notion of action is rooted in our familiarity with empirical regularities.

Note that Von Wright's statement also answers some critics of interactionism, who hold that interactionism ignores the regularity of life.
5 Weber (1947) declared that action plays a central part as a fundamental concept in sociology. He also noted that a defining characteristic of action is meaningfulness. My argument departs from Weber's (though it is indebted to it) in at least one regard. Weber maintains a causal view of social worlds despite his recognition of action. For instance, one of Weber's classic studies posits ideal-type rational motivations as causing particular effects.
6 My discussion of Hegel and Marx in the preceding passage is from Hegel (1929: Volume II: Chapter III), Von Wright (1971: especially pp. 7–9), and Marx and Engels *Correspondence*, letters 214–29.
7 I am indebted to Professor Manfred Stanley for comments which resulted in this paragraph and the earlier discussion to which it refers.
8 Cf. J. Clyde Mitchell also regarding emergence.

Chapter 2 Symbolic and essential interactionisms

1 I am at work on a paper concerning 'Mead as an Essential Interactionist.'
2 Social interactionism includes both 'variable' interaction and persons interaction. The former I take in the manner of Reuter and Hart (1973: 256): 'The reciprocal influence of the social factors that result in human nature and culture is . . . social interaction.' The latter I take in the Merrill and Eldredge (1952: 486) sense: 'The individual interacts with others through the medium of communication. The result of this activity is the broad and inclusive process of social interaction.' On my view 'social factors' and 'variables' (class, ethnicity, etc.) are, however, elliptical descriptions of the persons form of interaction; usually of routinized webs of such interactions.

Thus, in *purely social* interactionism, the events are persons interacting, the states are the temporal 'structural' conditions created (e.g. 'late capitalism'), the phenomena are the mental and physical tools created (e.g. languages and buildings), and the processes are dynamic and interdependent steps involving the events, states, and phenomena.
3 For a discussion of other social science projects which make use of the position proposed in this paragraph see Stanley (1978: Chapter 3).

Part II Introduction

1 Needs come to mind for essential interactionist methods to investigate

the major substantive areas within sociology *as* phenomena. Medicine, education, deviance, etc. could profit from analyses of the essences of these areas of social worlds. Such analyses could provide grounding for discussions and research in these areas, and might decrease the extent to which researchers and theorists are able to talk past one another. Essential interactionist analyses might also make better sense of the existing disparate literature in the fields (as I hope to do in the following chapters concerning prejudice).

Another important need for essential interactionist methods and inquiries is within existing theories. Such essential interactionist work could investigate the grounding for theoretical positions with the goal of revealing the essential natures of the theories. Or essential interactionist analyses might profitably be conducted on social theory as a phenomenon, to offer necessary and immutable common bases for social theorizing (or to determine whether such bases exist).

Chapter 3 General considerations

1 This paragraph accepts Kockelmans' (1967) analysis.
2 A notable exception is Husserl's 'The Origin of Geometry' in *Crisis*.
3 Among the best general introductions to phenomenology are Kockelmans (1967), Zaner (1970), and Husserl's *Ideas* and *Crisis*.
4 The modern demand is 'observability.' For interesting discussions see Scheffler (1963), Achinstein (1968), Goodman (1951), and Hanson (1971). The positivists' observability demand is better disguised but no less absurd than if they exclaimed: 'We have stopped hearing and smelling for the sake of limiting ourselves to scientific observability.' From another angle the observability demand can be seen as similar to a request that we all become the individuals at the party who stand in the corner watching everyone else but never participate ourselves. A party made up solely of such people would no longer be an activity that merits wakefulness.
5 It is apparent that this conception is similar to Kant's *a prioris* of human reason and to much of Descartes' work, and Husserl admitted as much. I cannot help but wonder whether such similarity is not itself supporting evidence for the thesis.
6 Note also Santayana's (1927: 36), remark: 'Every essence is universal not because there are repeated manifestations of it (for there need be no manifestations at all) but because it is individuated internally by its character, not externally by its position in the flux of nature: and no essence is general for the same reason.' See also Runder's (1966), critique of Weber's ideal types.
7 The following discussion is based upon the interchange between Chisholm (1973 and 1975), and Plantinga (1975).
8 See also Santayana (1927), especially the postscript, for discussions of the inevitability of essence analysis even by those persons who disclaim essentialism.
9 My discussion of operationalism relies upon Strasser (1974: Chapter 2).

Chapter 4 Literature as sites

1. It may be more accurate to say that at such sites many phenomena are present, but a single or few phenomena are essential to each.
2. Notably, it was the phenomenologist Baerwald (1944, 1956), who noted that the social is not simply a psychological experience of other people and our dependency upon them, but that coexistence is the possibility for individuals and groups to overcome the specific limitations of time and space. Through his own methods of phenomenological reduction he arrived first at the individual's time limitation. Through social participation the individual gains a chain of significant past events and makes sense of the future in terms of his relationship to the future existence of the group. Through the group he develops skills, customs, meanings, values, etc. which diminish the limitations time imposes upon him as an isolate. Similarly, Baerwald's reductions led him to elaborate the social as a process in space. The individual's space limitations are widened by participating, contributing to and benefiting or being damaged by transpersonal systems of space. The social involves continuous transformations of time into meaningful pasts, presents, and futures, and the continuous transformations of the geographic habitat into social space.
3. See Glaser and Strauss (1967), on these issues.
4. Note that these strategies are no more or less systematic, rational or intuitive than the 'fishing expeditions' any positivist employs in searching for variables.
5. A useful distinction is between the context of discovery and the context of validation (Rudner, 1966). Constant comparisons are employed within the context of discovery, phantasy variations may be employed within both contexts. For validation we retain in our discussion the similar notion of verification.
6. Most of this section is from Spiegelberg (1965: Chapter IV).
7. Some have found in Husserl a crucial absence of appreciation for the need for meta-analysis. Moreno (1976), concludes his critique of Husserl as follows (29):

> It may be that the notions of "self-evidence" and "purity of consciousness" are steeped in an error which forces us to adopt a more modest attitude toward the truth, as *continually* unfolding and reconstructed rather than apprehendable in some discontinuous sphere of pure consciousness, which if it cannot be gained ought not to be mourned as lost.

8. The discussion of Popper derives from Martin (1972: Chapter 1).
9. Goodman's term is *quale*, and he conceives of *qualia* differently from our conceptions of essences, but his criteria for revocability seem appropriate for our use.

Chapter 6 Elaboration of essences: I

1. We must note that the presence of a physically existing target is not an essence of prejudice. The Hartley (1946) site is a case at which groups which have never existed were the targets of prejudice (see discussion above).

Bibliography

This bibliography contains only those works to which reference was made in the text, not all works which were examined.

ABELSON, RAZIEL (1967), 'Definition,' in *The Encyclopedia of Philosophy*, New York: Macmillan.
ACHINSTEIN, PETER (1968), *Concepts of Science*, Baltimore: Johns Hopkins Press.
ACKERMAN, NATHAN and MARIE JAHODA (1950), *Anti-Semitism and Emotional Disorder: A Psychoanalytic Interpretation*, New York: Harper and Row.
ADORNO, THEODORE, ELSE FRANKEL-BRUNSWICK, *et al.* (1950), *The Authoritarian Personality*, New York: Harper and Row.
AGEE, JAMES and WALKER EVANS (1939), *Let Us Now Praise Famous Men*, New York: Ballantine.
ALLEN, GAY (1970), *William James*, Minneapolis: University of Minnesota Press.
ALLPORT, GORDON (1954), *The Nature of Prejudice*, New York: Addison-Wesley.
ALLPORT, GORDON, J. S. BRUNER and E. M. JANDORF (1941), 'Personality Under Social Catastrophe,' *Character and Personality* (10): 1–22.
ANESAKI, MASAHARU (1916), *Nichiren, the Buddhist Prophet*, Cambridge: Harvard University Press.
ARISTOTLE (1928), *Works*, ed. by W. D. Ross, *Posterior Analytics*. New York: Scribner.
ASCH, S. (1952), *Social Psychology*, Englewood Cliffs: Prentice-Hall.
AYER, A. J. (1951), *Foundations of Empirical Knowledge*, London: Macmillan.
BADURA, A. and R. WALTERS (1963), *Social Learning and Personality Development*, New York: Holt, Rinehart and Winston.
BAERWALD, FRIEDRICH (1944) 'Society as a Process,' *American Catholic Sociologist* (5): 238–43.

BIBLIOGRAPHY

BAERWALD, FRIEDRICH (1956), 'A Sociological View of Despersonalization,' *Thought* (31): 55–75.

BALL, DONALD (1970), 'An Abortion Clinic Ethnography,' in *Qualitative Methodology: Firsthand Involvement with the Social World*, ed. by William Filstead, Chicago: Markham.

BARCUS, F. and J. LEVIN (1966), 'Role Distance in Negro and Majority Fiction,' *Journalism Quarterly* (43): 709–14.

BARKER, S. (1955), 'Authoritarianism or acquiescence?' *Journal of Abnormal and Social Psychology* (47): 778–82.

BAYTON, J., L. McALISTER and K. HAMER (1959), 'Race-Class Stereotypes,' *Journal of Negro Education (25)*: 75–8.

BECKER, GARY (1957), *The Economics of Discrimination*, Chicago: University of Chicago Press.

BECKER, HOWARD S. (1961), *Boys in White: Student Culture in Medical School*, Chicago: University of Chicago Press.

BECKER, HOWARD S. (1963), *Outsiders*, New York: Free Press.

BECKER, HOWARD S. (1976), 'Art as Collective Action', *American Sociological Review* (39): 767–76.

BENEDICT, RUTH (1940), *Race: Science and Politics*, New York: Modern Age.

BERELSON, B. and P. SALTER (1946), 'Majority and Minority Americans: An Analysis of Magazine Fiction,' *Public Opinion Quarterly* (10): 168–97.

BERKOWITZ, LEONARD (1962), *Aggression*, New York: McGraw-Hill.

BERNSTEIN, BASIL (1971), *Primary Socialization, Language and Education*, London: Routledge and Kegan Paul.

BESSIE, SIMON (1958), 'American Writing Today,' *Virginia Quarterly Review* (34): 253–63.

BETTELHEIM, BRUNO and M. JANOWITZ (1950), *Dynamics of Prejudice*, New York: Harper.

BETTELHEIM, BRUNO and M. JANOWITZ (1964), *Social Change and Prejudice*, New York: Free Press.

BIERSTEDT, ROBERT (1950), 'An Analysis of Social Power,' *American Sociological Review* (December): 730–38.

BIERSTEDT, ROBERT (1957), *The Social Order*, New York: McGraw-Hill.

BIRD, CAROLYN *et al.* (1952), 'Infiltration and the Attitudes of White and Negro Parents and Children,' *Journal of Abnormal and Social Psychology* (47): 688–99.

BLACK, MAX (1967), 'Induction,' in *Encyclopedia of Philosophy*, ed. by Paul Edwards, New York: Collier-Macmillan.

BLALOCK, HERBERT (1964), *Causal Inferences in Nonexperimental Research*, Chapel Hill: University of North Carolina Press.

BLALOCK, HERBERT (1967), *Toward a Theory of Minority Group Relations*, New York: John Wiley.

BLAUNER, ROBERT (1972), *Racial Oppression in America*, New York: Harper and Row.

BLEDSOE, JIM (1975), 'Silver Concerns,' *Reflections* Number 1 (October): 1–28.

BIBLIOGRAPHY

BLUMER, HERBERT (1958), 'Race Prejudice as a Sense of Group Position,' *Pacific Sociological Review* (1): 3–7.
BLUMER, HERBERT (1969), *Symbolic Interaction*, Englewood Cliffs: Prentice-Hall.
BOGARDUS, EMORY (1925), 'Measuring Social Distance,' *Journal of Applied Sociology* (9): 299–308.
BOGARDUS, EMORY (1928), *Immigration and Race Relations*, Boston: D. C. Heath.
BOGARDUS, EMORY (1959), *Social Distance*, Los Angeles: The author.
BOGDAN, ROBERT and STEVEN TAYLOR (1975), *Introduction to Qualitative Research Methods*, New York: John Wiley.
BOGUSLAW, ROBERT (1965), *The New Utopians*, Englewood Cliffs: Prentice-Hall.
BREWER, M. (1968), 'Determinants of Social Distance Among East African Tribal Groups,' *Journal of Personality and Social Psychology* (38): 279–89.
BRIDGMAN, P. W. (1954), *The Logic of Modern Physics*, New York: Macmillan.
BUNGE, M. (1959), *Casuality*, Cambridge, Mass.: Harvard University Press.
BURY, R. G. (*trans.*) (1933), *Sextus Empiricus I*, London: Heinemann.
BUSS, A. (1961), *The Psychology of Aggression*, New York: John Wiley.
CAIRNS, DORION (1960), *Husserliana*, Vol. I, The Hague: Nijhoff.
CAMPBELL, A., P. CONVERSE, *et al.* (1960), *The American Voter*, New York: John Wiley.
CARNAP, RUDOLF (1947), *Meaning and Necessity*, Chicago: University of Chicago Press.
CARR, DAVID (1977), 'Kant, Husserl, and the Nonempirical Ego,' *The Journal of Philosophy* (74): 682–90.
CHISHOLM, RODERICK (1973), 'Parts as Essential to Their Wholes,' *Review of Metaphysics*, Vol. 26 Number 4.
CHISHOLM, RODERICK (1975), 'Mereological Essentialism: Some Further Considerations,' *Review of Metaphysics* Vol. 28 Number 3.
CHRISTIE, RICHARD and MARIE JAHODA (*eds.*) (1954), *The Authoritarian Personality*, New York: Free Press.
CHRISTIE, RICHARD, JOAN HAVEL and BERNARD SEIDENBERG (1958) 'Is the F Scale Irreversible?', *Journal of Abnormal and Social Psychology*, (March): 143–59.
CICOUREL, AARON (1964), *Method and Measurement in Sociology*, New York: Free Press.
CLEAVER, ELDRIDGE (1968), *Soul on Ice*, New York: McGraw-Hill.
COLLINGWOOD, R. G. (1940), *An Essay on Metaphysics*, Oxford: Oxford University Press.
COLLINS, BARRY (1970), *Social Psychology*, Reading: Addison Wesley.
COMER, JAMES (1972), *Beyond Black and White*, New York: Quadrangle.
COOPER, J. and M. McGAUGH (1963), *Integrative Principles of Social Psychology*, Cambridge: Schenkman.
COSER, LEWIS A. (1956), *The Functions of Social Conflict*, New York: Free Press.

BIBLIOGRAPHY

COX, OLIVER (1948), *Caste, Class, and Race*, New York: Doubleday.

COWEN, EMORY, JUDITH LANDES, and DONALD SCHAET (1959), 'The Effects of Mild Frustration . . .', *Journal of Abnormal and Social Psychology* (January), 33–8.

CRISTIE, R., J. HAVEL and B. SEIDENBERG (1958), 'Is the F Scale Irreversible?', *Journal of Abnormal and Social Psychology* (56): 143–59.

CRISWELL, JOAN H. (1937), 'Racial Cleavage in Negro-White Groups,' *Sociometry*: 85–9.

DAHRENDORF, RALF (1958), 'Out of Utopia: Toward a Reorientation of Sociological Analysis,' *American Journal of Sociology* (64): 115–27.

DEBARY, W. THEODORE (ed.) (1969), *The Buddhist Tradition*, New York: Modern Library.

DELORIA, VINE (1970), *We Talk, You listen*, New York: Delta.

DERBYSHIRE, R. and E. BRODY (1964), 'Social Distance and Identity Conflict in Negro College Students,' *Sociology and Social Research* (48): 301–14.

DIMONT, MAX (1962), *Jews, God, and History*, New York: Signet.

DOLLARD, JOHN (1938), 'Hostility and Fear in Social Life,' *Social Forces* (October): 15–26.

DOLLARD, JOHN (1939), *Caste and Class in a Southern Town*, New York: Harper.

DOMBROWSKI, J. (1950), 'Execution for Rape is a Race Penalty,' *The Southern Patriot* (8): 1–2.

DOUGLAS, JACK (1970), 'The Impact of the Social Sciences,' in J. Douglas (ed.), *The Impact of Sociology*, New York: Meredith Corporation.

DURKHEIM, EMILE (1954), *The Elementary Forms of Religious Life*, New York: Macmillan.

EASTHOPE, GARY (1974), *History of Social Research*, London: Longman.

EHRLICH, HOWARD (1973), *The Social Psychology of Prejudice*, New York: John Wiley.

ELKINS, STANLEY (1959), *Slavery: A Problem in American Institutions and Intellectual Life*, Chicago: University of Chicago Press.

ELSON, R. (1964), *Guardians of Tradition*, Lincoln: University of Nebraska Press.

EMBREE, SCOTTY (1975), 'Why Do Sociologists Hate Groups?' Unpublished paper presented at the Midwest Sociological Society meetings.

ERIKSON, KAI (1966), *Wayward Puritans*, New York: John Wiley.

EWENS, W. (1969), 'Reference Other Support, Ethnic Attitudes, and Perceived Influence of Others in the Performance of Overt Acts,' Doctoral dissertation at the University of Iowa, Iowa City.

FARBERMAN, HARVEY (1975), 'A Criminogenic Market Structure: the Automobile Industry,' *Sociological Quarterly* 16 (Autumn): 438–57.

FELDSTEIN, STANLEY (1971), *The Poisoned Tongue*, New York: Marrow.

FILSTEAD, WILLIAM (ed.) (1970), *Qualitative Methodology: Firsthand Involvement With the Social World*, Chicago: Markham.

FRANK, PHILIPP (1941), *Modern Science and Its Philosophy*, Cambridge, Mass.: Harvard University Press.

FRANK, PHILIPP (1957), *Philosophy of Science*, Englewood Cliffs: Prentice-Hall.
FRAZIER, E. FRANKLIN (1951), 'The Negro's Vested Interest in Segregation,' in *Race Prejudice and Discrimination*, ed. Arnold Rose, New York: Knopf.
FREEDMAN, MERVIN (1962), 'Studies of College Alumni,' in *The American College*, ed. Sanford. New York: John Wiley.
FRENKEL-BRUNSWICK, ELSE and R. SANFORD (1945), 'Some Social Psychological Factors in Anti-Semitism,' *Journal of Psychology* (20): 271–91.
FRIEDRICHS, ROBERT (1970), 'Choice and Commitment in Social Research,' in *The Impact of Sociology*, ed. Jack Douglas. New York: Meredith.
FROMM, ERICH (1947), *Man for Himself*, New York: Rinehart.
GARFINKEL, HAROLD (1967), *Studies in Ethnomethodology*, Englewood Cliffs: Prentice-Hall.
GASKING, D. (1955), 'Causation and Recipes,' *Mind*, 54.
GEIS, GILBERT (1968), *White Collar Criminal: The Offender in Business and the Professions*, New York: Atherton.
GERASSI, JOHN (1966), *Boys of Boise*, New York: Macmillan.
GILBERT, G. (1951), 'Stereotype Persistence and Change Among College Students,' *Journal of Abnormal and Social Psychology* (April): 245–54.
GLASER, BARNEY and ANSELM STRAUSS (1967), *The Discovery of Grounded Theory*, Chicago: Aldine.
GLASSNER, BARRY (1975), 'Entrance for Novelists,' Paper presented at the Meetings of the American Sociological Association, San Francisco, August.
GLASSNER, BARRY (1976a), 'Kid Society,' *Urban Education* (April): 5–22.
GLASSNER, BARRY (1976b), 'Review Essay,' *Contemporary Sociology* (May): 278–82.
GLASSNER, BARRY and JAY CORZINE (1978), 'Can Labeling Theory Be Saved?' *Symbolic Interaction* (Winter).
GLASSNER, BARRY and JONATHAN FREEDMAN (1979), *Clinical Sociology*, London and New York: Longman.
GLOCK, CHARLES and ELLEN SIEGELMAN (1969), *Prejudice U.S.A.*, New York: Praeger.
GLUECK, SHELDON and ELEANOR GLUECK (1956), *Physique and Delinquency*, New York: Harper and Row.
GOODENOUGH, W. (1957), 'Cultural Anthropology and Linguistics,' in *Languages and Linguistics* No. 9, ed. P. Garvin. Washington: Georgetown University Press.
GOODMAN, M (1964), *Race Awareness in Young Children*, New York: Crowell-Collier.
GOODMAN, NELSON (1951), *The Structure of Appearance*, Cambridge, Mass.: Harvard University Press.
GOODMAN, NELSON (1955), *Fact, Fiction and Forecast*, Cambridge, Mass.: Harvard University Press.

BIBLIOGRAPHY

GOODMAN, NELSON (1972), *Problems and Projects*, New York: Bobbs-Merrill.

GOULDNER, ALVIN (1968), 'The Sociologist as Partisan: Sociology and the Welfare State,' *The American Sociologist* (3), 103–16.

GOULDNER, ALVIN (1970), *The Coming Crisis of Western Sociology*, New York: Basic Books.

GREENBLUM, JOSEPH and LEONARD PEARLIN (1953), 'Vertical Mobility and Prejudice,' in *Class, Status and Power*, ed. by Reinhard Bendix and Seymout Lipset, New York: Free Press.

GREER, SCOTT (1969), *The Logic of Social Inquiry*, Chicago: Aldine.

GUSKIN, S. (1962), 'The Influence of Labeling upon the Perception of Subnormality in Mentally Defective Children,' *American Journal of Mental Deficiency* (67): 402–6.

HADDEN, STUART and MARILYN LESTER (1976), 'Ethnomethodology and Grounded Theory Methodology,' Paper presented at the meetings of the American Sociological Association in New York.

HANSON, NORWOOD (1958), *Patterns of Discovery*, Cambridge: Cambridge University Press.

HANSON, NORWOOD (1971), *Observation and Explanation*, New York: Harper and Row.

HARNISCHFEGER, ANNEGRET and DAVID WILEY (1976), 'Achievement Test Scores Drop. So What?' *Educational Researcher* (March): 5–12.

HARTLEY, E. (1946), *Problems in Prejudice*, New York: King's Crown.

HAVINGHURST, ROBERT (1975), 'Sociology in the Contemporary Educational Crisis,' *Journal of Research and Development in Education*: 13–22.

HEGEL, G. W. F. (1929), *The Science of Logic*, Vol. II, New York: Macmillan.

HEGEL, G. W. F. (1955), *Phenomenology of Mind*, New York: Macmillan.

HEIDEGGER, MARTIN (1962), *Being and Time*, London: SCM Press.

HESSE, MARY (1967), 'Simplification,' in *The Encyclopedia of Philosophy*, New York: Collier-Macmillan.

HIRSCHI, TRAVIS and HANAN SELVIN (1967), *Principles of SurveyAnalysis*, New York: Free Press.

HOFMAN, JOHN (1970), 'The Meaning of Being a Jew in Israel,' *Journal of Personality and Social Psychology* (July): 196–202.

HOGAN, ROBERT T. and NICHOLAS P. EMLER (1978), 'The Biases in Contemporary Social Psychology,' *Social Research* (45): 478–534.

HOLMES, DAVID (1972), 'Aggression, Displacement and Guilt,' *Journal of Personality and Social Psychology* (March): 296–301.

HORKHEIMER M. (1936), *Studien über Authorität und Familie*, Paris: Felix Alcan.

HOVLAND, CARL and ROBERT SEARS (1940), 'Minor Studies of Aggression . . .' *Journal of Psychology* (Winter): 301–10.

HOWARD, DAVID (1966), 'An Exploratory Study of Attitudes of Negro Professionals Toward Competition with Whites,' *Social Forces* (Summer): 20–27.

HUME, DAVID (1888), *A Treatise on Human Nature*, London: Oxford University Press.

BIBLIOGRAPHY

HUSSERL, EDMUND (1962), *Ideas*, New York: Collier.
HUSSERL, EDMUND (1965), *Phenomenology and the Crisis of Philosophy*, New York: Harper Torchbooks.
HUSSERL, EDMUND (1965), 'Philosophy as a Rigorous Science,' in Q. Laver (ed.) *Edmund Husserl: Phenomenology and the Crisis of Philosophy*, New York: Harper and Row.
HUSSERL, EDMUND (1970a), *Cartesian Meditations*, The Hague: Nijhoff.
HUSSERL, EDMUND (1970b), *The Crisis of European Sciences*, Evanston: Northwestern University Press.
HUSSERL, EDMUND (1970c), *Logical Investigations*, trans. by J. N. Findlay. New York: Humanities Press.
HUSSERL, EDMUND (1973), *Experience and Judgment*, Evanston: Northwestern University Press.
HYMAN, HERBERT (1955), *Survey Design and Analysis*, New York: Free Press.
JACKMAN, MARY (1975), 'Education and Prejudice or Education and Response-Set?' *American Sociological Review* (38): 327–339.
JACOBS, PAUL and SAUL LANDAU (1971), *To Serve the Devil*, New York: Vintage.
JENSEN, ARTHUR (1969), 'How Much Can We Boost IQ and Scholastic Achievement?' *Harvard Educational Review* (39): 1–12.
JONES, JAMES (1972), *Prejudice and Racism*, New York: Addison-Wesley.
KARLINS, MARVIN, THOMAS COFFMAN and GARY WALTERS (1969), 'On the Fading of Stereotypes . . .,' *Journal of Personality and Social Psychology* (September): 1–16.
KATZ, DANIEL (1960), 'The Functional Approach to the Study of Attitudes,' *Public Opinion Quarterly* (Summer): 163–204.
KATZ, DAVID and KENNETH BRALY (1933), 'Racial Stereotypes of One Hundred College Students,' *Journal of Abnormal and Social Psychology* (October): 280–90.
KATZ, JACK (1972), 'Deviance, Charisma, and Rule-Defined Behavior,' *Social Problems* (Fall): 186–201.
KATZ, JACK (1975), 'Essences as Moral Identities: Verifiability and Responsibility in Imputations of Deviance and Charisma,' *American Journal of Sociology* (May): 1369–90.
KELSEN, HANS (1943), *Society and Nature*, Chicago: University of Chicago Press.
KENDALL, PATRICIA (1954), *Conflict and Mood*, New York: Free Press.
KITSUSE, JOHN 09(1964), 'Societal Reaction to Deviant Behavior,' pp. 87–102 in *The Other Side*, ed. Howard S. Becker, New York: Free Press.
KLINEBERG, O. (1954), *Social Psychology*, New York: Holt, Rinehart and Winston.
KLINEBERG, O. (1963), 'Life is Fun in a Smiling, Fair-Skinned World,' *Saturday Review* (February 16): 75, 87.
KLUCKHOLN, CLYDE, *et al.* (eds.) (1953), *Personality in Nature, Society, and Culture*, New York: Knopf.
KOCKELMANS, JOSEPH (ed.) (1967), *Phenomenology*, New York: Anchor.

BIBLIOGRAPHY

KOESTENBAUM, PETER (ed.) (1970), *The Paris Lectures of Edmund Husserl*, The Hague: Nijhoff.
KORDIG, CARL (1971), *Justification*, Holland: Reidel.
KRAMER, B. (1950), 'Residential Contact as a Determinant of Attitudes Toward Negroes,' Unpublished doctoral dissertation, Harvard.
KRECH, D., S. CRUTCHFIELD and E. BALLACHEY (1962), *Individual and Society*, New York: McGraw-Hill.
KUHN, THOMAS (1970), *The Structure of Scientific Revolution*, Chicago: University of Chicago Press.
KUTNER, B., C. WILKINS and P. YARROW (1952), 'Verbal Attitudes and Overt Behavior,' *Journal of Abnormal and Social Psychology* (47): 549–652.
LaGUMINA, SALVATORE (1973), *Wop!* San Francisco: Straight Arrow.
LaPIERE, RICHARD (1934), 'Attitudes vs Actions,' *Social Forces* (13): 230–37.
LARRICK, N. (1965), 'The All-White World of Children's Books,' *Saturday Review* (September 11): 63–5, 84–5.
LAVER, QUENTIN (1958), *Triumph of Subjectivity*, New York: Fordham University Press.
LAZARWITZ, LILA (1973), 'Contrasting the Effects of Generation, Class, Sex and Age . . .,' Paper presented to the American Anthropological Association meetings.
LEDERER, WILLIAM (1958), *The Ugly American*, New York: Norton.
LEE, ALFRED M. (1975), 'Humanistic Challenges to Positivisits,' *The Insurgent Sociologist* (6): 41–50.
LEGGETT, JOHN (1968), *Class, Race and Labor*, New York: Oxford.
LEMERT, EDWIN (1951), *Social Pathology*, New York: McGraw-Hill.
LENSKI, GERHARD (1961), *The Religious Factor*, New York: Doubleday.
LEVIN, DAVID (1970), *Reason and Evidence in Husserl's Phenomenology*, Evanston: Northwestern University Press.
LEVIN, DAVID (1975), 'Husserl's Notion of Self-Evidence,' in *Phenomenology and Philosophical Understanding*, ed. by Edo Pivcevic, Cambridge University Press.
LEVIN, JACK (1975), *The Functions of Prejudice*, New York: Harper and Row.
LEVINAS, EMMANUEL (1967), 'Intuition of Essences', in J. Kockelmans (ed.) *Phenomenology*, New York: Anchor.
LIAZOS, ALEXANDER (1972), 'The Poverty of the Sociology of Deviance: Nuts, Sluts and Perverts,' *Social Problems* (20): 103–20.
LINDLEY, WILLIAM (1974), 'Gatekeepers' Avoidance of Group Opinion Sources,' *Journalism Quarterly* (Winter): 724–5.
LINNAEUS, KARL (1806), A General System of Nature Through the Three Grand Kingdoms of Animals, Vegetables, and Minerals, London.
LIPPMANN, WALTER (1922), *Public Opinion*, New York: Harcourt Brace Jovanovich.
LOFLAND, JOHN and L. LOFLAND (1969), *Deviance and Identity*, Englewood Cliffs: Prentice-Hall.
LOHMAN, J. and D. REITZES (1952), 'Note on Race Relations in Mass Society,' *American Journal of Sociology* (November): 240–6.

LONDON, JOAN and HENRY ANDERSON (1970), *So Shall Ye Reap*, New York: Crowell.
LUNDBERG, GEORGE (1954), *Foundations of Sociology*, New York: Macmillan.
McCANDLESS, B. and J. HOYT (1961), 'Sex, Ethnicity, and Play Preferences of School Children,' *Journal of Abnormal and Social Psychology* (62): 683–5.
MacCRONE, I. (1937), *Race Attitudes in South Africa*, New York: Oxford.
McDONAGH, E. and E. RICHARDS (1953), *Ethnic Relations in the United States*, New York: Appleton-Century Crofts.
McHUGH, PETER (1968), *Defining the Situation*, New York: Bobbs-Merrill.
MacIVER, R. M. (1942), *Social Causation*, Boston: Ginn & Co.
MacIVER, R. M. (1948), *The More Perfect Union*, New York: Macmillan.
McLEAN, HELEN (1946), 'Psychodynamic Factors in Racial Relations,' *The Annals of the American Academy of Political and Social Science* (244): 159–66.
McWILLIAMS, CAREY (1948), *A Mast for Privilege: Anti-Semitism in America*, Boston: Little Brown.
MALINOWSKI, B. (1950), *Argonauts of the Western Pacific*, New York: Dutton.
MANNHEIM, KARL (1954), *Ideology and Utopia: An Introduction to the Sociology of Knowledge*, New York: Oxford University Press.
MARCH, ROBERT (1971), *Physics for Poets*, New York: McGraw-Hill.
MARTIN, JAMES (1964), *The Tolerant Personality*, Detroit: Wayne State University Press.
MARTIN, JANE (1970), *Explaining, Understanding and Teaching*, New York: McGraw-Hill.
MARTIN, MARTIN (1972), *Concepts of Science Education*, New York: Scott, Foresman Co.
MARX, GARY (1969), *Protest and Prejudice*, New York: Harper & Row.
MARX, KARL and FRIEDRICH ENGELS *Correspondence*. New York: International Publishers.
MASLOW, A. (1943), 'The Authoritarian Character Structure,' *Journal of Social Psychology* (18): 401–11.
MASSING, PAUL (1949), *Rehearsal for Destruction*, New York: Harper and Row.
MATZA, DAVID (1969), *Becoming Deviant*, New York: Prentice-Hall.
MAYER, FREDERICK (1950), *Essentialism*, London: Hampton Hall Press.
MEAD, GEORGE HERBERT (1934), *Mind, Self, and Society*, Chicago: University of Chicago Press.
MEAD, GEORGE HERBERT (1936), *Movements of Thought in the Nineteenth Century*, Chicago: University of Chicago Press.
MEAD, GEORGE HERBERT (1938), *The Philosophy of the Act*, Chicago: University of Chicago Press.
MENCKEN, H. L. (1958), *Prejudices: A Selection*, New York: Vintage.
MERLEAU-PONTY, M. (1967), 'What is Phenomenology?' in *Phenomenology*, ed. Joseph Kockelmans, Cambridge, Mass.: MIT Press.

BIBLIOGRAPHY

MERRILL, F. E. and H. ELDREDGE (1952), *Culture and Society*, New York: Prentice-Hall.

MERTON, ROBERT (1949), 'Discrimination and the American Creed,' in *Discrimination and National Welfare*, ed. MacIver, New York: Harper.

MERTON, ROBERT (1957), *Social Theory and Social Structure*, New York: Macmillan.

MILLER, NEAL and RICHARD BUGELSKI (1948), 'Minor Studies of Aggression . . .', *Journal of Psychology* (25): 437–42.

MONTAGU, ASHLEY (1974), *Man's Most Dangerous Myth*, New York: Oxford University Press.

MARROW, ALFRED (1962), *Changing Patterns of Prejudice*, New York: Chilton.

MOSHER, D. and A. SCODEL (1960), 'A Study of the Relationship Between Ethnocentrism in Children and the Ethnocentrism and Authoritarian Rearing of Their Mothers,' *Child Development* (31): 369–76.

MORENO, J. L. (1953), *Who Shall Survive?*, Beacon, N. Y.: Beacon House.

MORENO, JONATHAN (1976), 'Adequacy in Husserlian Phenomenology,' Unpublished paper.

MORSE, N. and F. ALLPORT (1952), 'The Causation of Anti-Semitism: An Investigation of Seven Hypotheses,' *Journal of Psychology* (34): 197–233.

MYRDAL, GUNNAR (1944), *An American Dilemma*, New York: Harper.

NOWLIS, V. (1965), 'Research with the Mood Adjective Checklist,' in *Affect, Cognition, and Personality*, ed. by Tompkins and Izard, New York: Springer.

O'HARA, ROBERT (1961), *Media for the Millions*, New York: Random House.

ORNE, M. (1969), 'Demand Characteristics and the Concept of Quasi-Controls,' in *Artifact in Behavior Research*, ed. by Rosenthal and Rosnow, New York: Academic Press.

PARANJPE, ANAND (1970), *Caste, Prejudices and the Individual*, Bombay: Lalvani.

PARK, ROBERT (1939), 'The Nature of Race Relations,' in *Race Relations and the Race Problem*, ed. Edgar Thompson, Durham: Duke U. Press.

PEABODY, D. (1959), 'The Organization of Social Attitudes', Unpublished Doctoral Dissertation, Harvard University.

PEABODY, D. (1961), 'Attitude Content and Agreement Set in Scales of Authoritarianism, Dogmatism, Anti-Semitism, and Economic Conservatism', *Journal of Abnormal and Social Psychology* (63), 1–11.

PERLS, FRITZ (1969), *Gestalt Therapy Verbatim*, Lafayette, Calif.: Real People Press.

PETERSON, W. (1958), 'Prejudice in American Society: A Critique of Some Recent Formulations,' *Commentary* (26): 342–8.

PETTIGREW, THOMAS (1959), 'Desegregation Research in the North and South,' *Journal of Social Issues* (Fourth Quarter).

PETTIGREW, THOMAS (1971), *Racially Separate or Together?*, New York: McGraw-Hill.

PHILLIPS, BERNARD (1976), *Social Research*, New York: Macmillan.

PHILLIPSON, MICHAEL (1972), 'Phenomenological Philosophy and

Sociology,' in *New Directions in Sociological Theory* by Paul Filmer, Michael Phillipson, David Silverman, and David Walsh, Cambridge, Mass.: MIT Press.

PIAGET, J. (1965), *The Moral Judgement of the Child*, New York: Free Press.

PIAGET, J. and A. WEIL (1951), 'The Development in Children of the Idea of the Homeland and of Relations with Other Countries,' *International Social Science Bulletin* (3).

PICCONE, PAUL (1976), Unpublished discussion for Marxist Sociology section at annual meetings of American Sociological Association.

PIERCE, CHARLES (1931), *Collected Papers*, Cambridge, Mass.: Harvard University Press.

PILCHER, WILLIAM (1972), *The Portland Longshoremen*, New York: Holt, Rinehart and Winston.

PITTMAN, DAVID (ed.), (1967), *Alcoholism*, New York: Harper and Row.

PLANCK, MAX (1937), *The Philosophy of Physics*, London: Allen and Unwin.

PLANTINGA, ALVIN (1975), 'On Mereological Essentialism,' *Review of Metaphysics*, Vol. 28, Number 3.

POLANYI, MICHAEL (1958), *Personal Knowledge*, Chicago: University of Chicago Press.

POOLE, W. (1927), 'Social Distance and Personal Distance,' *Journal of Applied Sociology* (11): 114–20.

POPKIN, RICHARD (1974), 'The Philosophical Bases of Modern Racism,' in *Philosophy and the Civilizing Arts*, ed. Craig Walton and John Anton, Columbus: Ohio University Press.

POPKIN, RICHARD (1976), 'Newton, Hartley, and Priestly on Divine Causality,' Unpublished paper.

POPPER, KARL (1969), *The Logic of Scientific Discovery*, New York: Basic Books.

PORTER, J. (1971), *Black Child, White Child: The Development of Racial Attitudes*, Cambridge: Harvard University Press.

PSATHAS, GEORGE (1968), 'Ethnomethods and Phenomenology,' *Social Research* (September): 500–20.

QUINE, WILLARD (1966a), *Elementary Logic*, Cambridge, Mass.: Harvard University Press.

QUINE, WILLARD (1966b), *The Ways of Paradox*, Cambridge, Mass.: Harvard University Press.

QUINE, WILLARD and J. ULLIAN (1970), *Web of Belief*, New York: Random House.

QUINN, O. (1954), 'The Transmission of Racial Attitudes in the Deep South,' *Social Forces* (33): 41–7.

RAAB, EARL (1969), *Prejudice and Society*, New York: Freedom Books.

RADKE-YARROW, M., H. TRAGER and H. DAVIS (1949), 'Social Perception and Attitudes of Children,' *Genetic Psychology Monographs* (40): 327–447.

RASHEVSKY, N. (1961), 'Is the Concept of an Organism as a Machine a Useful One?' in P. Frank (ed.), *Validation of Scientific Theories*, New York: Collier.

BIBLIOGRAPHY

RAZRAN, G. (1950), 'Ethnic Dislike and Stereotypes,' *Journal of Abnormal and Social Psychology* (45): 7–27.
REID, THOMAS (1788), *Essays on the Active Powers of Man*, London.
REUTER, E. B. and C. HART (1937), *Introduction to Sociology*, New York: McGraw-Hill.
RICOUER, PAUL (1954), 'Sympathie et respect,' *Revue de metaphysique et de morale*, 380–97.
ROBB, J. (1954), *Working-Class Anti-Semite: A Psychological Study in a London Bar*, London: Tavistock.
ROKEACH, MILTON, P. SMITH, and R. EVANS (1960), 'Two Kinds of Prejudice or One?' in *The Open and Closed Mind*, ed. Milton Rokeach.
ROSE, ARNOLD (1948), *Studies in Reduction of Prejudice*, Chicago: Council on Race Relations.
ROSE, ARNOLD (1951), *Race Prejudice and Discrimination*, New York: Knopf.
ROSE, ARNOLD (1958), *The Roots of Prejudice*, New York: UNESCO.
ROSE, ARNOLD (1965), *Sociology*, New York: Knopf.
ROSEN, BERNARD (1959), 'Race, Ethnicity, and the Achievement Syndrome,' *American Sociological Review* (February): 47–60.
ROSENTHAL, R. and L. JACOBSON (1968), 'Teacher Expectations for the Disadvantaged,' *Scientific American* (218).
ROSENZWEIG, S. (1945), 'The Picture-Association Method . . .,' *Journal of Personality* (14): 3–23.
RUDNER, RICHARD (1961), 'Value Judgments in Acceptance of Theories,' in P. Frank (ed.), *Validation of Scientific Theories*, New York: Collier.
RUDNER, RICHARD (1966), *Philosophy of Social Science*, Englewood Cliffs: Prentice-Hall.
SAENGER, GERHART and SAMUEL FLOWERMAN (1954), 'Stereotypes and Prejudicial Attitudes,' *Human Relations* (7): 217–38.
SANTAYANA, GEORGE (1927), *The Realm of Essence*, New York: Charles Scribner's Sons.
SARTRE, JEAN-PAUL (1965), *Anti-Semite and Jew*, New York: Schocken Books.
SAXTON, S. (1968), 'Words which Measure Affect Toward Negroes,' unpublished.
SCHEFFLER, ISRAEL (1963), *The Anatomy of Inquiry*, New York: Knopf.
SCHLESINGER, GEORGE (1963), *Method in the Physical Sciences*, London: Humanities Press.
SCHUR, EDWIN (1969), *Our Criminal Society: The Social and Legal Sources of Crime in America*, Englewood Cliffs: Prentice-Hall.
SCHUR, EDWIN (1973), *Radical Non-Intervention*, Englewood Cliffs: Prentice-Hall.
SCHUTZ, ALFRED (1964), 'The Problem of Rationality in the Social World,' in *Collected Papers*, Vol. II, The Hague: Nijhoff.
SECORD, P. F. (1959), 'Stereotyping and Favorableness in the Perception of Negro Faces,' *Journal of Abnormal and Social Psychology*, (59): 309–14.
SELZER, MICHAEL (1972), *Kike!*, New York: World Publishing Co.

BIBLIOGRAPHY

SELZNICK, GERTRUDE and STEPHEN STEINBERG (1969), *The Tenacity of Prejudice: Anti-Semitism in Contemporary America*, New York: Harper and Row.

SHERIF, M. (1966), *In Common Predicament*, Boston: Houghton Mifflin.

SHERIF, MUZAFER and CAROLYN SHERIF (1953), *Groups in Harmony and Tension*, New York: Harper and Row.

SHERIF, MUZAFER and CAROLYN SHERIF (1961), *Intergroup Conflict and Cooperation*, Norman, Oklahoma: University Book Exchange.

SHERMAN, HOWARD (1972), *Radical Political Economy*, New York: Basic Books.

SHILS, EDWARD (1954), 'Authoritarianism: "Right" and "Left",' in *The Authoritarian Personality*, ed. Christie and Jahoda, New York: Free Press.

SHILS, EDWARD (1963), 'On the Comparative Study of the New States,' in *Old Societies and New States*, ed. C. Geertz, New York: Free Press.

SHIM, N. and A. DOLE (1967), 'Components of Social Distance Among College Students . . .' *Journal of Social Psychology* (73): 111–24.

SILBERSTEIN, FRED and MELVIN SEEMAN (1959), 'Social Mobility and Prejudice,' *American Journal of Sociology* (November): 258–64.

SIMMEL, GEORG (1955), *Conflict*, New York: Free Press.

SIMPSON, GEORGE and J. MILTON YINGER (1965), *Racial and Cultural Minorities*, New York: Harper and Row, (Second edition, 1972).

SIU, R. G. G. (1957), *The Tao of Science*, Cambridge, Mass.: MIT Press.

SOROKIN, PITRIM (1943), *Sociocultural Causality, Space, and Time*, Durham, N. C.: Duke University Press.

SOSA, ERNEST (ed.) (1975), *Causation and Conditionals*, Oxford: Oxford University Press.

SPIEGELBERG, HERBERT (1964), Phenomenology Through Vicarious Experience, in *Phenomenology: Pure and Applied*, ed. Erwin Straus, Pittsburgh: Duquesne University Press.

SPIEGELBERG, HERBERT (1965), *The Phenomenological Movement*, The Hague: Nijhoff.

SPIEGELBERG, HERBERT (1973), 'How Subjective is Phenomenology?' in *Phenomenological Sociology*, ed. George Psathas, New York: John Wiley.

SPOER, DOROTHY (1951), 'Some Aspects of Prejudice as Affected by Religion and Education,' *Journal of Social Psychology* (33): 69–76.

STAGNER, R. (1936), Fascist Attitudes: An Exploratory Study, *Journal of Social Psychology* (7): 309–19.

STAMPP, KENNETH (1956), *The Peculiar Institution*, New York: Vintage.

STANLEY, MANFRED (1978), *The Technological Conscience*, New York: Free Press.

STEMBER, CHARLES (1961), *Education and Attitude Change*, Institute of Human Relations Press.

STEMBER, CHARLES (1966), *Jews in the Mind of America*, New York: Basic Books.

STRASSER, STEPHEN (1974), *Phenomenology and the Human Sciences*, Pitsburgh: Duquesne University Press.

SULLIVAN, PATRICK and JOSEPH ADELSON (1954), 'Ethnocentrism and

BIBLIOGRAPHY

Misanthropy,' *Journal of Abnormal and Social Psychology* (April): 246–50.
SUNG, B. (1961), *The Mountain of Gold: The Story of the Chinese Americans*, New York: Macmillan.
SUTHERLAND, EDWIN (1949), *White Collar Crime*, New York: Holt, Rinehart, and Winston.
SUTTLES, GERALD (1968), *The Social Order of the Slum*, Chicago: University of Chicago Press.
TAYLOR, CHARLES (1971), 'Interpretation and the Science of Man,' *Review of Metaphysics* 15 (September).
TAYLOR, IAN *et al.* (1974), *The New Criminology: For a Social Theory of Deviance*, Harper and Row.
TAYLOR, RICHARD (1967), 'Causation,' in *The Encyclopedia of Philosophy*, New York: Macmillan.
THIO, ALEX (1973), 'Class Bias in the Sociology of Deviance,' *The American Sociologist* (8): 1–12.
TRIANDIS, HARRY and LEIGH TRIANDIS (1960), 'Social Class, Religion, and Nationality as Determinants of Social Distance,' *Journal of Abnormal and Social Psychology* (61): 110–18.
TRIMMER, JOHN (1950), *Response of Physical Systems*, New York: John Wiley.
TUMIN, MELVIN (ed.) (1958), *Comparative Perspectives on Race Relations*, Boston: Little Brown.
VON WRIGHT, GEORG (1971), *Explanation and Understanding*, Ithaca: Cornell University Press.
VON WRIGHT, GEORG (1974), *Causation and Determinism*, New York: Columbia University Press.
WAGLEY, CHARLES and MARVIN HARRIS (1958), *Minorities in the New World*, New York: Columbia University Press.
WALSH, DAVID (1972), 'Sociology and the Social World,' in *New Directions in Sociological Theory*, by Paul Filmer *et al.*, Cambridge, Mass.: MIT Press.
WALTON, ORTIZ (1972), *Music: Black, White and Blue*, New York: William Morrow.
WARREN, CAROL and JOHN JOHNSON (1972), 'A Critique of Labeling Theory from a Phenomenological Perspective,' in *Theoretical Perspectives on Deviance*, ed. Jack D. Douglas and Robert A. Scott, New York: Basic Books.
WAX, MURRAY and ROSALIE WAX (1976), 'How People Stop Smoking,' Unpublished paper.
WAX, ROSALIE (1971), *Doing Fieldwork: Warnings and Advice*, Chicago: University of Chicago Press.
WEBER, MAX (1946), *From Max Weber: Essays in Sociology*, translated by H. Gerth and C. W. Mills, New York: Oxford University Press.
WEBER, MAX (1947), *The Theory of Economic and Social Organization*, New York: Oxford University Press.
WESTIE, FRANK (1964), 'Race and Ethnic Relations,' in *Handbook of Modern Sociology*, ed. Faris, Chicago: Rand-McNally.

WHITE, DAVID (1950), 'The "Gatekeeper": A Case Study in the Selecting of News,' *Journalism Quarterly* (27): 385–6.
WHITE, MORTON (1955), *The Age of Analysis*, Boston: Houghton-Mifflin Co.
WHITE, NICHOLAS (1973), 'Origins of Aristotle's Essentialism,' *Review of Metaphysics* Volume 26, Number 1.
WHITEHEAD, ALFRED N. (1958), *Modes of Thought*, New York: Capricorn.
WHYTE, WILLIAM F. (1943), *Street Corner Society*, Chicago: University of Chicago Press.
WOODWORTH, R. S. (1921), *Psychology: A Study of Mental Life*, New York: Henry Holt.
YINGER, J. MILTON (1964), *Anti-Semitism: A Case Study*, New York: Freedom Books.
ZANER, RICHARD (1970), *The Way of Phenomenology*, New York: Pegasus.

Index

Ackerman, Nathan, 67
Adelson, Joseph, 82
Adorno, Theodore, 44, 80, 82, 83, 137
aggression, 78–80
Allport, F., 100
Allport, Gordon, 63–4, 65, 67, 70, 71, 78, 81, 84, 92, 140
anti-Semitism, 67–8, 79, 80–1, 84, 95, 102–3, 113, 120, 125, 136, 137, 140–1
Aristotle, 31, 35, 50, 120
Asch, S., 109, 110
Authoritarian Personality, The (Adorno et al.), 44, 80, 83, 84, 104, 136, 149

Ball, Donald, 55
Ballachey, E., 68
Barcus, F., 98
Barrett, Robert, 27
Bayton, J. L. McAlister, 87, 155
Beattie, James, 123
Becker, Howard S., 56, 95, 142
Benedict, Ruth, 125
Berelson, B., 96, 98
Berkeley, Bishop, 14, 33
Berkowitz, Leonard, 79
Bessie, Simon, 144
Bettleheim, Bruno, 79, 103
Black, Max, 85, 87
blacks, prejudice against: economics and, 112; education, 116, 132–3; employment, 89, 116; health services, 132–4; housing, 115; legal institutions, 92–3, 117; religious, 125–6; social position, 70, 71, 98, 118; stereotypes, 87, 94–5, 96, 99, 103–4

Blalock, Herbert, 3, 4, 5, 9, 103, 114, 126
Bledsoe, Jim, 51
Blumer, Herbert, 9, 14, 15, 16–19
Bogardus, Emory, 72, 89–90
Bogdan, Robert, 48, 55
Boguslaw, Robert, 13
Boys of Boise (Gerassi), 19
Braly, Kenneth, 87
Brewer, M., 98
Bridgman, P. W., 40
Brody, E., 98
Bugelski, Richard, 79
Bunge, M., 9, 12
Buss, A., 67

Campbell, A., 82, 101
Carr, David, 30
causation: action and, 7–8; interaction and dialectic, 10–11; investigation of various concepts of causation, 6–10; objections to interactionist assumptions, 11–13; social-correlation causation, 3–6
children's societies, 106–10, 127–9
Chinese, prejudice against, 88, 111, 121, 152
Chisholm, Roderick, 17, 38
Christianity: and anti-Semitism, 113; and causation, 6–7
Christie, Richard, 82
Cicourel, Aaron, 44
classlessness, 136–7
Cleaver, Eldridge, 93, 136
Collins, Barry, 44, 68, 71, 102
comparison, constant, 50–2

181

INDEX

conflict theory, 49
Cooper, J., 68
Corzine, Jay, 20
Coser, Lewis A., 49
Cowen, Emory, 79
Cox, Oliver, 67
crime, and symbolic interactionist research, 20–1
Crisis (Husserl), 33–4, 36–7, 39, 41, 45, 51
Criswell, Joan H., 110
Crutchfield, S., 68

Dahrendorf, Ralf, 49
deBary, W. Theodore, 110
degeneracy theory, 121, 122
Deloria, Vine, 96
Derbyshire, R., 98
deviance, and labeling theory, 19–20
Dimont, Max, 113
Dole, A., 97
Dollard, John, 111, 113
Dombrowski, J., 93

economic competition, 110–12, 129
education, discrimination in, 116–17
Ehrlich, Howard, 63, 71, 74, 93, 94, 100
Einstein, Albert, 39
Elkins, Stanley, 118
Elson, R., 96
Embree, Scotty, 109
Emler, Nicholas P., 85
empiricism: and causation, 5, 9, 11; and phenomenology, 31–3; validation, 58
Empiricus, Sextus, 3, 4, 9, 13
Engels, Friedrich, 10
Erikson, Kai, 19
essences: constant comparison, 50–2; determining possible essences of prejudice, 70–4; elaboration of, 76–130; essential relationships, 53–4; on functionalist sites, 76–8; and literature sites, 48; meta analysis, 54–6; objections to, 36–9; in other inquiry strategies, 39–40; phantasy variations, 52–3; phenomenology and, 29–31; what are they? 34–6; *see also* instrument essence
essential interactionism: essential relationships, 53–4; and expanded empiricism, 31–3; phenomenology and, 29–31; research suggestions, 151–7; verification and falsification, 56–8; and vicarious phenomenology

(*see also* literature sites), 41–2; *see also* essences, instrument essence
ethnocentrism, 81, 82–3, 84
Evans, R., 91
Ewens, W., 100

Farberman, Harvey, 20–1
fieldwork: constant comparison, 50–2; definitions of prejudice, 66–70; and essential relationships, 53–4; maps, 64–6; meta analysis, 54–6; phantasy variations, 52–3; verification and falsification, 56–8; *see also* literature sites
Flowerman, Samuel, 102, 138
Frank, Philipp, 143
Frazier, E. Franklin, 132
Freedman, Jonathan, 77, 131, 144
Frenkel-Brunswick, Else, 79, 80
Frustration and Aggression (Dollard *et al.*), 79
functionalism, 76–8, 131–6

Galileo, 39–40
Garfinkel, Harold, 29, 140
Gasking, D., 7
Geis, Gilbert, 20
Gerassi, John, 19
Gilbert, G., 87
Glaser, Barney, 43, 50
Glassner, Barry, 20, 56, 77, 109, 110, 128, 131
Goodman, Nelson, 31, 35–6, 57–8, 85–6, 87, 142, 145, 151
Gouldner, Alvin, 19, 20, 77
Greenblum, Joseph, 79
Greer, Scott, 149
Gregoire, Abbé, 122, 124
groups, human: changes, 8; structure, 8; and symbolic interactionism, 16, 17–18; *see also* children's societies, *specific ethnic groups*
Gurvitch, Georges, 29
Guskin, S., 95, 155

Hadden, Stuart, 51
Hanson, Norwood, 56, 85
Harris, Marvin, 114
Hartley, E. L., 97
Havinghurst, Robert, 127
Hegel, G. W. F., 10–11, 29
Heidegger, Martin, 40
Hesse, Mary, 141
Hirschi, Travis, 3
Hofman, John, 134

INDEX

Hogan, Robert T., 85
Holmes, David, 79
homosexuality, 43, 48–9, 99–100, 136–7, 154
Hovland, Carl, 79
Howard, David, 133
Hume, David, 3, 4, 5, 7, 15, 33, 85, 121, 122–3
Husserl, Edmund, 27–8, 29, 30, 31, 32, 33–5, 36, 39, 41–2, 45, 46, 50, 51, 54–5, 57
Hyman, Herbert, 3

Indians, prejudice against: North American, 96, 114, 121–2; South American, 120–1
Individual and Society (Litt), 29
instrument essence, 73–4; on functionalist sites, 76–7; interactions among techniques used for simplification, 100–4; in release of aggression, 78–80; and simplification, 80–4, 100–4, 135, 142; and simplifying affect, 92–3, 98–100, 138; and social distancing, 88–92; and stereotyping, 84–8, 94–6
interactionism: and causation, 6–10; and dialectic, 10–11; and indeterminism, 16–20; objections to assumption, 11–13; symbolic interactionism, 21–2; and idealism, 14–15; and symbolism, 16, 22; *see also* essential interactionism
intergroup competition, 106–10
intuition, 32–3
Invisible Man, 99

Jackman, Mary, 82, 144
Jacobson, L., 116
Jahoda, Marie, 67, 82
Janowitz, M., 79, 103
Japanese, prejudice against, 112, 113
Jensen, Arthur, 124
Johnson, John, 19
Jones, James, 63, 64, 65, 108, 115, 117

Kant, Immanuel, 29, 123
Karlins, Marvin, 87, 155
Katz, David, 87
Katz, Jack, 84, 95, 154
Kelsen, Hans, 4, 6, 7
Kendall, Patricia, 82
Kitsuse, John, 99
Klineberg, O., 68
Kluckholn, Clyde, 118

Kramer, B., 101
Krech, D., 68
Kutner, B., 88

labeling theory, 18–20, 95
LaGumina, Salvatore, 79, 111
LaPiere, Richard, 88
Larrick, N., 96
Lauer, Quentin, 57
Lazarwitz, Lila, 134
Lederer, William, 101
Lee, Alfred M., 77
legal institutions, prejudice in, 92–3, 117
Lemert, Edwin, 95
Lester, Marilyn, 51
Levin, David, 51
Levin, Jack, 67, 74, 78, 84, 96, 98, 108, 111, 132, 134, 140
Levinas, Emmanuel, 52
Liazos, Alexander, 19, 20
Linnaeus, Karl, 121
Lippmann, Walter, 84
literature sites: boundaries, 48–9; choosing, 47–8; constant comparison, 50–2; disadvantages, 44–5; essential relationships, 53–4; importance, 45–6; meta analysis, 54–6; methodological notes, 147–51; missing sites, 152–6; phantasy variations, 52–3; as research sites, 42–5; verification and falsification, 56–8; *see also under* individual authors and publications
Litt, Theodor, 29
Locke, John, 121
Lofland, John, 154
Logical Investigations (Husserl), 51, 55
Lohman, J., 70
Lundberg, George, 5

McCandless, B., 101
MacCrone, I., 125
McDonagh, E., 68
McGaugh, M., 68
McHugh, David, 84
McIntyre, Alistair, 12
MacIver, R. M., 5, 8, 10, 119
McWilliams, Carey, 112
maps: according to theoretical positions, 64–5; definitions of prejudice, 68–9; less useful than key informants, 148; way of prejudicing, 65–6
Martin, James, 68
Marx, Gary, 132

183

INDEX

Marx, Karl, 31, 136
Marxism, 11, 49, 112, 136–7
Massing, Paul, 113
Mead, George Herbert, 14, 16, 21–2
Merleau-Ponty, M., 46, 54
Merton, Robert, 70, 102–3
meta analysis, 54–6
Miller, Neal, 79
Montagu, Ashley, 95
Moreno, J. L., 17, 31, 110
Morris, Charles, 16
Morse, N., 100
Morton, Dr Samuel, 123
Mosher, D., 126, 127
music, as social phenomenon, 142–3
Myrdal, Gunnar, 99

Natural and Cultural Peoples (Vierkandt), 29
Nature of Prejudice, The (Allport), 63
Newton, Sir Isaac, 7
Nixon, Richard, 20

O'Hara, Robert, 96
operationalism, 40
Orne, M., 109

Park, Robert, 112–13
Peabody, D., 82
Pearlin, Leonard, 79
Perls, Fritz, 93
Peterson, W., 68
Pettigrew, Thomas, 118
phantasy variations, 52–3, 149, 151–2
phenomenology: and empiricism, 31–3; and literature as sites (*see also* literature sites), 42–6; and study of essences, 29–31; subjectivity of, 33–4; vicarious, 41–2
Phillipson, Michael, 30
Piaget, J., 127, 138
Pierce, Charles, 50, 85, 145
Pilcher, William, 70, 89
Pittman, David, 101
polygenetic theories, 122–4
Poole, W., 90
Popkin, Richard, 7, 120, 123, 124
Popper, Karl, 56–7, 86
Porter, J., 128, 138
Posterior Analytics (Aristotle), 35
prejudice: classlessness and, 136–7; definitions, 66–70; as distinct social phenomenon, 139; distribution of tasks, 112–15; economic competition, 110–12; entrenchment, 115–24, 129–30, 153; and functionalism, 76–8, 131–6; identifiability, 125–6, 130; inter-group competition, 106–10; normality of, 137–9; possible essences of, 70–4; in release of aggression, 78–80; simplification, 80–4, 139–44; simplifying affect, 92–3, 98–100; social distancing, 88–92, 97–8; societal control of, 126–8; solutions, 144–5; studies of, 63–4; target characteristics, 118–19; *see also* instrument essence; literature sites; maps; *under* specific ethnic groups; stereotyping
Prejudice and Racism (Jones), 64
Psathas, George, 128–9, 155

Quine, Willard, 35

racial prejudice, 64, 125–6; *see also* ethnic groups
Radke-Yarrow, M., 138
Rashevsky, N., 149
Razran, G., 94
Reid, Thomas, 7
Reitzes, D., 70
Richards, E., 68
Ricoeur, Paul, 46
Robb, J., 140–1
Rokeach, Milton, 91, 137
Rose, Arnold, 68, 79
Rosen, Bernard, 118
Rosenthal, R., 116
Rosenzweig, S., 78
Rudner, Richard, 27, 139

Saenger, Gerhart, 102, 138
Salter, P., 96, 98
Sanford, R., 79, 80
Santayana, George, 37
Sartre, Jean-Paul, 67–8, 72
Schur, Edwin, 20
Schultz, Alfred, 29
Scodel, A., 126, 127
Sears, Robert, 79
Secord, P. F., 94
Seeman, Melvin, 79
Selvin, Hanan, 3
Selzer, Michael, 95, 101, 155
Selznick, Gertrude, 144
Sherif, Muzafer, 49, 72, 78, 106–9, 129, 148, 152, 158–60
Sherman, Howard, 117
Shils, Edward, 50, 82
Shim, N., 97

Silberstein, Fred, 79
Simmel, Georg, 49, 134
Simon, Paul, 37
simplification, 80–4, 139–44; *see also* simplifying affect
simplifying affect, 92–3, 98–100, 105
Simpson, George, 81, 111, 112, 118, 125, 126, 137, 154
Siu, R. G. G., 142
Smith, Lillian, 92
Smith, P., 91
social distancing, 88–92, 97–8, 105
Social Psychology of Prejudice, The (Ehrlich), 64
Spiegelberg, Herbert, 31, 32, 33, 34, 41, 42, 53, 155
Spoerl, Dorothy, 97–8
Stampp, Kenneth, 114
Steinberg, Stephen, 144
Stember, Charles, 144
stereotyping, 84–8, 94–6, 100–2, 104–5, 115, 121, 137–8, 140–2, 145, 150, 153
Strange Fruit (Smith), 92
Strasser, Stephen, 36, 40, 46, 55
Strauss, Anselm, 43, 50
Street Corner Society (Whyte), 48
Sullivan, Patrick, 82
Sung, B., 111
Sutherland, Edwin, 20
Suttles, Gerald, 55

tasks, distribution of, 112–15

Taylor, Charles, 27
Taylor, Ian, 20
Taylor, Steven, 48, 55
Theory of Society (Vierkandt), 29
Thio, Alex, 19–20
Thomas, W. I., 6, 30
Triandis, Harry, 91
Tumin, Melvin, 103

Vierkandt, Alfred, 29
Von Wright, Georg, 4, 7, 12

Wagley, Charles, 114
Walsh, David, 45
Walton, Ortiz, 143
Warren, Carol, 19
Watergate conspiracy, 20
Wax, Rosalie, 55
Wayward Puritans (Erikson), 19
Weber, Max, 55, 111
Weil, A., 127
Westie, Frank, 68
White, Nicholas, 35
Whyte, William F., 48, 148
Wilkins, C., 88
Wolfson, Robert, 27
Woodworth, R. S., 78

Yarrow, P., 88
Yinger, J. Milton, 81, 95, 111, 112, 118, 125, 126, 137, 154

Routledge Social Science Series

Routledge & Kegan Paul   London, Henley and Boston

39 Store Street, London WC1E 7DD
Broadway House, Newtown Road,
Henley-on-Thames, Oxon RG9 1EN
9 Park Street, Boston, Mass. 02108

Contents

International Library of Sociology 3
General Sociology 3
Foreign Classics of Sociology 4
Social Structure 4
Sociology and Politics 5
Criminology 5
Social Psychology 6
Sociology of the Family 6
Social Services 7
Sociology of Education 8
Sociology of Culture 8
Sociology of Religion 9
Sociology of Art and Literature 9
Sociology of Knowledge 9
Urban Sociology 10
Rural Sociology 10
Sociology of Industry and Distribution 10
Anthropology 11
Sociology and Philosophy 12
International Library of Anthropology 12
International Library of Social Policy 13
International Library of Welfare and Philosophy 13
Primary Socialization, Language and Education 14
Reports of the Institute of Community Studies 14
Reports of the Institute for Social Studies in Medical Care 15
Medicine, Illness and Society 15
Monographs in Social Theory 15
Routledge Social Science Journals 16
Social and Psychological Aspects of Medical Practice 16

Authors wishing to submit manuscripts for any series in this catalogue should send them to the Social Science Editor, Routledge & Kegan Paul Ltd, 39 Store Street, London WC1E 7DD

● *Books so marked are available in paperback*
All books are in Metric Demy 8vo format (216 × 138mm approx.)

INTERNATIONAL LIBRARY OF SOCIOLOGY

International Library of Sociology

General Editor John Rex

GENERAL SOCIOLOGY

Barnsley, J. H. The Social Reality of Ethics. *464 pp.*
Brown, Robert. Explanation in Social Science. *208 pp.*
● Rules and Laws in Sociology. *192 pp.*
Bruford, W. H. Chekhov and His Russia. *A Sociological Study. 244 pp.*
Burton, F. and **Carlen, P.** Official Discourse. *On Discourse Analysis, Government Publications, Ideology. About 140 pp.*
Cain, Maureen E. Society and the Policeman's Role. *326 pp.*
●**Fletcher, Colin.** Beneath the Surface. *An Account of Three Styles of Sociological Research. 221 pp.*
Gibson, Quentin. The Logic of Social Enquiry. *240 pp.*
Glucksmann, M. Structuralist Analysis in Contemporary Social Thought. *212 pp.*
Gurvitch, Georges. Sociology of Law. *Foreword by Roscoe Pound. 264 pp.*
Hinkle, R. Founding Theory of American Sociology 1883-1915. *About 350 pp.*
Homans, George C. Sentiments and Activities. *336 pp.*
Johnson, Harry M. Sociology: *a Systematic Introduction. Foreword by Robert K. Merton. 710 pp.*
●**Keat, Russell** and **Urry, John.** Social Theory as Science. *278 pp.*
Mannheim, Karl. Essays on Sociology and Social Psychology. *Edited by Paul Keckskemeti. With Editorial Note by Adolph Lowe. 344 pp.*
Martindale, Don. The Nature and Types of Sociological Theory. *292 pp.*
●**Maus, Heinz.** A Short History of Sociology. *234 pp.*
Myrdal, Gunnar. Value in Social Theory: *A Collection of Essays on Methodology. Edited by Paul Streeten. 332 pp.*
Ogburn, William F. and **Nimkoff, Meyer F.** A Handbook of Sociology. *Preface by Karl Mannheim. 656 pp. 46 figures. 35 tables.*
Parsons, Talcott, and **Smelser, Neil J.** Economy and Society: *A Study in the Integration of Economic and Social Theory. 362 pp.*
Podgórecki, Adam. Practical Social Sciences. *About 200 pp.*
Raffel, S. Matters of Fact. *A Sociological Inquiry. 152 pp.*
●**Rex, John.** (Ed.) Approaches to Sociology. *Contributions by Peter Abell, Sociology and the Demystification of the Modern World. 282 pp.*
●**Rex, John** (Ed.) Approaches to Sociology. *Contributions by Peter Abell, Frank Bechhofer, Basil Bernstein, Ronald Fletcher, David Frisby, Miriam Glucksmann, Peter Lassman, Herminio Martins, John Rex, Roland Robertson, John Westergaard and Jock Young. 302 pp.*
Rigby, A. Alternative Realities. *352 pp.*
Roche, M. Phenomenology, Language and the Social Sciences. *374 pp.*
Sahay, A. Sociological Analysis. *220 pp.*

Strasser, Hermann. The Normative Structure of Sociology. *Conservative and Emancipatory Themes in Social Thought. About 340 pp.*
Strong, P. Ceremonial Order of the Clinic. *About 250 pp.*
Urry, John. Reference Groups and the Theory of Revolution. *244 pp.*
Weinberg, E. Development of Sociology in the Soviet Union. *173 pp.*

FOREIGN CLASSICS OF SOCIOLOGY
● **Gerth, H. H.** and **Mills, C. Wright.** From Max Weber: *Essays in Sociology. 502 pp.*
● **Tönnies, Ferdinand.** Community and Association. *(Gemeinschaft and Gesellschaft.) Translated and Supplemented by Charles P. Loomis. Foreword by Pitirim A. Sorokin. 334 pp.*

SOCIAL STRUCTURE
Andreski, Stanislav. Military Organization and Society. *Foreword by Professor A. R. Radcliffe-Brown. 226 pp. 1 folder.*
Carlton, Eric. Ideology and Social Order. *Foreword by Professor Philip Abrahams. About 320 pp.*
Coontz, Sydney H. Population Theories and the Economic Interpretation. *202 pp.*
Coser, Lewis. The Functions of Social Conflict. *204 pp.*
Dickie-Clark, H. F. Marginal Situation: *A Sociological Study of a Coloured Group. 240 pp. 11 tables.*
Giner, S. and **Archer, M. S.** (Eds.). Contemporary Europe. *Social Structures and Cultural Patterns. 336 pp.*
● **Glaser, Barney** and **Strauss, Anselm L.** Status Passage. *A Formal Theory. 212 pp.*
Glass, D. V. (Ed.) Social Mobility in Britain. *Contributions by J. Berent, T. Bottomore, R. C. Chambers, J. Floud, D. V. Glass, J. R. Hall, H. T. Himmelweit, R. K. Kelsall, F. M. Martin, C. A. Moser, R. Mukherjee, and W. Ziegel. 420 pp.*
Kelsall, R. K. Higher Civil Servants in Britain: *From 1870 to the Present Day. 268 pp. 31 tables.*
● **Lawton, Denis.** Social Class, Language and Education. *192 pp.*
McLeish, John. The Theory of Social Change: *Four Views Considered. 128 pp.*
● **Marsh, David C.** The Changing Social Structure of England and Wales, 1871-1961. *Revised edition. 288 pp.*
Menzies, Ken. Talcott Parsons and the Social Image of Man. *About 208 pp.*
● **Mouzelis, Nicos.** Organization and Bureaucracy. *An Analysis of Modern Theories. 240 pp.*
Ossowski, Stanislaw. Class Structure in the Social Consciousness. *210 pp.*
● **Podgórecki, Adam.** Law and Society. *302 pp.*
Renner, Karl. Institutions of Private Law and Their Social Functions. *Edited, with an Introduction and Notes, by O. Kahn-Freud. Translated by Agnes Schwarzschild. 316 pp.*

INTERNATIONAL LIBRARY OF SOCIOLOGY

Rex, J. and **Tomlinson, S.** Colonial Immigrants in a British City. *A Class Analysis. 368 pp.*
Smooha, S. Israel: Pluralism and Conflict. *472 pp.*
Wesolowski, W. Class, Strata and Power. *Trans. and with Introduction by G. Kolankiewicz. 160 pp.*
Zureik, E. Palestinians in Israel. *A Study in Internal Colonialism. 264 pp.*

SOCIOLOGY AND POLITICS

Acton, T. A. Gypsy Politics and Social Change. *316 pp.*
Burton, F. Politics of Legitimacy. *Struggles in a Belfast Community. 250 pp.*
Etzioni-Halevy, E. Political Manipulation and Administrative Power. *A Comparative Study. About 200 pp.*
● **Hechter, Michael.** Internal Colonialism. *The Celtic Fringe in British National Development, 1536–1966. 380 pp.*
Kornhauser, William. The Politics of Mass Society. *272 pp. 20 tables.*
Korpi, W. The Working Class in Welfare Capitalism. *Work, Unions and Politics in Sweden. 472 pp.*
Kroes, R. Soldiers and Students. *A Study of Right- and Left-wing Students. 174 pp.*
Martin, Roderick. Sociology of Power. *About 272 pp.*
Myrdal, Gunnar. The Political Element in the Development of Economic Theory. *Translated from the German by Paul Streeten. 282 pp.*
Wong, S.-L. Sociology and Socialism in Contemporary China. *160 pp.*
Wootton, Graham. Workers, Unions and the State. *188 pp.*

CRIMINOLOGY

Ancel, Marc. Social Defence: *A Modern Approach to Criminal Problems. Foreword by Leon Radzinowicz. 240 pp.*
Athens, L. Violent Criminal Acts and Actors. *About 150 pp.*
Cain, Maureen E. Society and the Policeman's Role. *326 pp.*
Cloward, Richard A. and **Ohlin, Lloyd E.** Delinquency and Opportunity: *A Theory of Delinquent Gangs. 248 pp.*
Downes, David M. The Delinquent Solution. *A Study in Subcultural Theory. 296 pp.*
Friedlander, Kate. The Psycho-Analytical Approach to Juvenile Delinquency: *Theory, Case Studies, Treatment. 320 pp.*
Gleuck, Sheldon and **Eleanor.** Family Environment and Delinquency. *With the statistical assistance of Rose W. Kneznek. 340 pp.*
Lopez-Rey, Manuel. Crime. *An Analytical Appraisal. 288 pp.*
Mannheim, Hermann. Comparative Criminology: *a Text Book. Two volumes. 442 pp. and 380 pp.*
Morris, Terence. The Criminal Area: *A Study in Social Ecology. Foreword by Hermann Mannheim. 232 pp. 25 tables. 4 maps.*
Podgorecki, A. and **Łos, M.** *Multidimensional Sociology. About 380 pp.*
Rock, Paul. Making People Pay. *338 pp.*

INTERNATIONAL LIBRARY OF SOCIOLOGY

● **Taylor, Ian, Walton, Paul,** and **Young, Jock.** The New Criminology. *For a Social Theory of Deviance. 325 pp.*
● **Taylor, Ian, Walton, Paul** and **Young, Jock.** (Eds) Critical Criminology. *268 pp.*

SOCIAL PSYCHOLOGY

Bagley, Christopher. The Social Psychology of the Epileptic Child. *320 pp.*
Brittan, Arthur. Meanings and Situations. *224 pp.*
Carroll, J. Break-Out from the Crystal Palace. *200 pp.*
● **Fleming, C. M.** Adolescence: Its Social Psychology. *With an Introduction to recent findings from the fields of Anthropology, Physiology, Medicine, Psychometrics and Sociometry. 288 pp.*
● The Social Psychology of Education: *An Introduction and Guide to Its Study. 136 pp.*
Linton, Ralph. The Cultural Background of Personality. *132 pp.*
● **Mayo, Elton.** The Social Problems of an Industrial Civilization. *With an Appendix on the Political Problem. 180 pp.*
Ottaway, A. K. C. Learning Through Group Experience. *176 pp.*
Plummer, Ken. Sexual Stigma. *An Interactionist Account. 254 pp.*
● **Rose, Arnold M.** (Ed.) Human Behaviour and Social Processes: *an Interactionist Approach. Contributions by Arnold M. Rose, Ralph H. Turner, Anselm Strauss, Everett C. Hughes, E. Franklin Frazier, Howard S. Becker et al. 696 pp.*
Smelser, Neil J. Theory of Collective Behaviour. *448 pp.*
Stephenson, Geoffrey M. The Development of Conscience. *128 pp.*
Young, Kimball. Handbook of Social Psychology. *658 pp. 16 figures. 10 tables.*

SOCIOLOGY OF THE FAMILY

Bell, Colin R. Middle Class Families: *Social and Geographical Mobility. 224 pp.*
Burton, Lindy. Vulnerable Children. *272 pp.*
Gavron, Hannah. The Captive Wife: *Conflicts of Household Mothers. 190 pp.*
George, Victor and **Wilding, Paul.** Motherless Families. *248 pp.*
Klein, Josephine. Samples from English Cultures.
   1. Three Preliminary Studies and Aspects of Adult Life in England. *447 pp.*
   2. Child-Rearing Practices and Index. *247 pp.*
Klein, Viola. The Feminine Character. *History of an Ideology. 244 pp.*
McWhinnie, Alexina M. Adopted Children. *How They Grow Up. 304 pp.*
● **Morgan, D. H. J.** Social Theory and the Family. *About 320 pp.*
● **Myrdal, Alva** and **Klein, Viola.** Women's Two Roles: *Home and Work. 238 pp. 27 tables.*

Parsons, Talcott and Bales, Robert F. Family: Socialization and Interaction Process. *In collaboration with James Olds, Morris Zelditch and Philip E. Slater. 456 pp. 50 figures and tables.*

SOCIAL SERVICES

Bastide, Roger. The Sociology of Mental Disorder. *Translated from the French by Jean McNeil. 260 pp.*
Carlebach, Julius. Caring For Children in Trouble. *266 pp.*
George, Victor. Foster Care. *Theory and Practice. 234 pp.*
  Social Security: *Beveridge and After. 258 pp.*
George, V. and Wilding, P. Motherless Families. *248 pp.*
● Goetschius, George W. Working with Community Groups. *256 pp.*
Goetschius, George W. and Tash, Joan. Working with Unattached Youth. *416 pp.*
Heywood, Jean S. Children in Care. *The Development of the Service for the Deprived Child. Third revised edition. 284 pp.*
King, Roy D., Ranes, Norma V. and Tizard, Jack. Patterns of Residential Care. *356 pp.*
Leigh, John. Young People and Leisure. *256 pp.*
● Mays, John. (Ed.) Penelope Hall's Social Services of England and Wales. *About 324 pp.*
Morris, Mary. Voluntary Work and the Welfare State. *300 pp.*
Nokes, P. L. The Professional Task in Welfare Practice. *152 pp.*
Timms, Noel. Psychiatric Social Work in Great Britain (1939-1962). *280 pp.*
●   Social Casework: *Principles and Practice. 256 pp.*

SOCIOLOGY OF EDUCATION

Banks, Olive. Parity and Prestige in English Secondary Education: a Study in Educational Sociology. *272 pp.*
● Blyth, W. A. L. English Primary Education. *A Sociological Description. 2. Background. 168 pp.*
Collier, K. G. The Social Purposes of Education: *Personal and Social Values in Education. 268 pp.*
Evans, K. M. Sociometry and Education. *158 pp.*
● Ford, Julienne. Social Class and the Comprehensive School. *192 pp.*
Foster, P. J. Education and Social Change in Ghana. *336 pp. 3 maps.*
Fraser, W. R. Education and Society in Modern France. *150 pp.*
Grace, Gerald R. Role Conflict and the Teacher. *150 pp.*
Hans, Nicholas. New Trends in Education in the Eighteenth Century. *278 pp. 19 tables.*
●   Comparative Education: *A Study of Educational Factors and Traditions. 360 pp.*
● Hargreaves, David. Interpersonal Relations and Education. *432 pp.*
●   Social Relations in a Secondary School. *240 pp.*
  School Organization and Pupil Involvement. *A Study of Secondary Schools.*

- **Mannheim, Karl** and **Stewart, W.A.C.** An Introduction to the Sociology of Education. *206 pp.*
- **Musgrove, F.** Youth and the Social Order. *176 pp.*
- **Ottaway, A. K. C.** Education and Society: An Introduction to the Sociology of Education. *With an Introduction by W. O. Lester Smith. 212 pp.*
- **Peers, Robert.** Adult Education: *A Comparative Study. Revised edition. 398 pp.*
- **Stratta, Erica.** The Education of Borstal Boys. *A Study of their Educational Experiences prior to, and during, Borstal Training. 256 pp.*
- **Taylor, P. H., Reid, W. A.** and **Holley, B. J.** The English Sixth Form. *A Case Study in Curriculum Research. 198 pp.*

SOCIOLOGY OF CULTURE

Eppel, E. M. and **M.** Adolescents and Morality: *A Study of some Moral Values and Dilemmas of Working Adolescents in the Context of a changing Climate of Opinion. Foreword by W. J. H. Sprott. 268 pp. 39 tables.*
- **Fromm, Erich.** The Fear of Freedom. *286 pp.*
- The Sane Society. *400 pp.*

Johnson, L. The Cultural Critics. *From Matthew Arnold to Raymond Williams. 233 pp.*

Mannheim, Karl. Essays on the Sociology of Culture. *Edited by Ernst Mannheim in co-operation with Paul Kecskemeti. Editorial Note by Adolph Lowe. 280 pp.*

Zijderfeld, A. C. On Clichés. *The Supersedure of Meaning by Function in Modernity. About 132 pp.*

SOCIOLOGY OF RELIGION

Argyle, Michael and **Beit-Hallahmi, Benjamin.** The Social Psychology of Religion. *About 256 pp.*

Glasner, Peter E. The Sociology of Secularisation. *A Critique of a Concept. About 180 pp.*

Hall, J. R. The Ways Out. *Utopian Communal Groups in an Age of Babylon. 280 pp.*

Ranson, S., Hinings, B. and **Bryman, A.** Clergy, Ministers and Priests. *216 pp.*

Stark, Werner. The Sociology of Religion. *A Study of Christendom.*
  Volume II. *Sectarian Religion. 368 pp.*
  Volume III. *The Universal Church. 464 pp.*
  Volume IV. *Types of Religious Man. 352 pp.*
  Volume V. *Types of Religious Culture. 464 pp.*

Turner, B. S. Weber and Islam. *216 pp.*

Watt, W. Montgomery. Islam and the Integration of Society. *320 pp.*

SOCIOLOGY OF ART AND LITERATURE

Jarvie, Ian C. Towards a Sociology of the Cinema. *A Comparative Essay on the Structure and Functioning of a Major Entertainment Industry.* 405 pp.
Rust, Frances S. Dance in Society. *An Analysis of the Relationships between the Social Dance and Society in England from the Middle Ages to the Present Day.* 256 pp. 8 pp. of plates.
Schücking, L. L. The Sociology of Literary Taste. *112 pp.*
Wolff, Janet. Hermeneutic Philosophy and the Sociology of Art. *150 pp.*

SOCIOLOGY OF KNOWLEDGE

Diesing, P. Patterns of Discovery in the Social Sciences. *262 pp.*
● **Douglas, J. D.** (Ed.) Understanding Everyday Life. *370 pp.*
Glasner, B. Essential Interactionism. *About 220 pp.*
● **Hamilton, P.** Knowledge and Social Structure. *174 pp.*
Jarvie, I. C. Concepts and Society. *232 pp.*
Mannheim, Karl. Essays on the Sociology of Knowledge. *Edited by Paul Kecskemeti. Editorial Note by Adolph Lowe.* 353 pp.
Remmling, Gunter W. The Sociology of Karl Mannheim. *With a Bibliographical Guide to the Sociology of Knowledge, Ideological Analysis, and Social Planning.* 255 pp.
Remmling, Gunter W. (Ed.) Towards the Sociology of Knowledge. *Origin and Development of a Sociological Thought Style.* 463 pp.

URBAN SOCIOLOGY

Aldridge, M. The British New Towns. *A Programme Without a Policy.* About 250 pp.
Ashworth, William. The Genesis of Modern British Town Planning: *A Study in Economic and Social History of the Nineteenth and Twentieth Centuries.* 288 pp.
Brittan, A. The Privatised World. *196 pp.*
Cullingworth, J. B. Housing Needs and Planning Policy: *A Restatement of the Problems of Housing Need and 'Overspill' in England and Wales.* 232 pp. 44 tables. 8 maps.
Dickinson, Robert E. City and Region: *A Geographical Interpretation.* 608 pp. 125 figures.
   The West European City: *A Geographical Interpretation.* 600 pp. 129 maps. 29 plates.
Humphreys, Alexander J. New Dubliners: *Urbanization and the Irish Family. Foreword by George C. Homans.* 304 pp.
Jackson, Brian. Working Class Community: *Some General Notions raised by a Series of Studies in Northern England.* 192 pp.
● **Mann, P. H.** An Approach to Urban Sociology. *240 pp.*
Mellor, J. R. Urban Sociology in an Urbanized Society. *326 pp.*
Morris, R. N. and **Mogey, J.** The Sociology of Housing. *Studies at Berinsfield.* 232 pp. 4 pp. plates.

Rosser, C. and Harris, C. The Family and Social Change. *A Study of Family and Kinship in a South Wales Town.* 352 pp. 8 maps.
● Stacey, Margaret, Batsone, Eric, Bell, Colin and Thurcott, Anne. Power, Persistence and Change. *A Second Study of Banbury.* 196 pp.

RURAL SOCIOLOGY

Mayer, Adrian C. Peasants in the Pacific. *A Study of Fiji Indian Rural Society.* 248 pp. 20 plates.
Williams, W. M. The Sociology of an English Village: *Gosforth.* 272 pp. 12 figures. 13 tables.

SOCIOLOGY OF INDUSTRY AND DISTRIBUTION

Dunkerley, David. The Foreman. *Aspects of Task and Structure.* 192 pp.
Eldridge, J. E. T. Industrial Disputes. *Essays in the Sociology of Industrial Relations.* 288 pp.
Hollowell, Peter G. The Lorry Driver. 272 pp.
● Oxaal, I., Barnett, T. and Booth, D. (Eds) Beyond the Sociology of Development. *Economy and Society in Latin America and Africa.* 295 pp.
Smelser, Neil J. Social Change in the Industrial Revolution: *An Application of Theory to the Lancashire Cotton Industry, 1770–1840.* 468 pp. 12 figures. 14 tables.
Watson, T. J. The Personnel Managers. *A Study in the Sociology of Work and Employment.* 262 pp.

ANTHROPOLOGY

Brandel-Syrier, Mia. Reeftown Elite. *A Study of Social Mobility in a Modern African Community on the Reef.* 376 pp.
Dickie-Clark, H. F. The Marginal Situation. *A Sociological Study of a Coloured Group.* 236 pp.
Dube, S. C. Indian Village. *Foreword by Morris Edward Opler.* 276 pp. 4 plates.
   India's Changing Villages: *Human Factors in Community Development.* 260 pp. 8 plates. 1 map.
Firth, Raymond. Malay Fishermen. *Their Peasant Economy.* 420 pp. 17 pp. plates.
Gulliver, P. H. Social Control in an African Society: a Study of the Arusha, Agricultural Masai of Northern Tanganyika. 320 pp. 8 plates. 10 figures.
   Family Herds. 288 pp.
Jarvie, Ian C. The Revolution in Anthropology. 268 pp.
Little, Kenneth L. Mende of Sierra Leone. 308 pp. *and folder.*
   Negroes in Britain. *With a New Introduction and Contemporary Study by Leonard Bloom.* 320 pp.

Madan, G. R. Western Sociologists on Indian Society. *Marx, Spencer, Weber, Durkheim, Pareto. 384 pp.*
Mayer, A. C. Peasants in the Pacific. *A Study of Fiji Indian Rural Society. 248 pp.*
Meer, Fatima. Race and Suicide in South Africa. *325 pp.*
Smith, Raymond T. The Negro Family in British Guiana: *Family Structure and Social Status in the Villages. With a Foreword by Meyer Fortes. 314 pp. 8 plates. 1 figure. 4 maps.*

SOCIOLOGY AND PHILOSOPHY

Barnsley, John H. The Social Reality of Ethics. *A Comparative Analysis of Moral Codes. 448 pp.*
Diesing, Paul. Patterns of Discovery in the Social Sciences. *362 pp.*
● **Douglas, Jack D.** (Ed.) Understanding Everyday Life. *Toward the Reconstruction of Sociological Knowledge. Contributions by Alan F. Blum, Aaron W. Cicourel, Norman K. Denzin, Jack D. Douglas, John Heeren, Peter McHugh, Peter K. Manning, Melvin Power, Matthew Speier, Roy Turner, D. Lawrence Wieder, Thomas P. Wilson and Don H. Zimmerman. 370 pp.*
Gorman, Robert A. The Dual Vision. *Alfred Schutz and the Myth of Phenomenological Social Science. About 300 pp.*
Jarvie, Ian C. Concepts and Society. *216 pp.*
Kilminster, R. Praxis and Method. *A Sociological Dialogue with Lukács, Gramsci and the early Frankfurt School. About 304 pp.*
● **Pelz, Werner.** The Scope of Understanding in Sociology. *Towards a More Radical Reorientation in the Social Humanistic Sciences. 283 pp.*
Roche, Maurice. Phenomenology, Language and the Social Sciences. *371 pp.*
Sahay, Arun. Sociological Analysis. *212 pp.*
Slater, P. Origin and Significance of the Frankfurt School. *A Marxist Perspective. About 192 pp.*
Spurling, L. Phenomenology and the Social World. *The Philosophy of Merleau-Ponty and its Relation to the Social Sciences. 222 pp.*
Wilson, H. T. The American Ideology. *Science, Technology and Organization as Modes of Rationality. 368 pp.*

International Library of Anthropology

General Editor Adam Kuper

Ahmed, A. S. Millenium and Charisma Among Pathans. *A Critical Essay in Social Anthropology. 192 pp.*
   Pukhtun Economy and Society. *About 360 pp.*

Brown, Paula. The Chimbu. *A Study of Change in the New Guinea Highlands. 151 pp.*
Foner, N. Jamaica Farewell. *200 pp.*
Gudeman, Stephen. Relationships, Residence and the Individual. *A Rural Panamanian Community. 288 pp. 11 plates, 5 figures, 2 maps, 10 tables.*
The Demise of a Rural Economy. *From Subsistence to Capitalism in a Latin American Village. 160 pp.*
Hamnett, Ian. Chieftainship and Legitimacy. *An Anthropological Study of Executive Law in Lesotho. 163 pp.*
Hanson, F. Allan. Meaning in Culture. *127 pp.*
Humphreys, S. C. Anthropology and the Greeks. *288 pp.*
Karp, I. Fields of Change Among the Iteso of Kenya. *140 pp.*
Lloyd, P. C. Power and Independence. *Urban Africans' Perception of Social Inequality. 264 pp.*
Parry, J. P. Caste and Kinship in Kangra. *352 pp. Illustrated.*
Pettigrew, Joyce. Robber Noblemen. *A Study of the Political System of the Sikh Jats. 284 pp.*
Street, Brian V. The Savage in Literature. *Representations of 'Primitive' Society in English Fiction, 1858–1920. 207 pp.*
Van Den Berghe, Pierre L. Power and Privilege at an African University. *278 pp.*

International Library of Social Policy

General Editor Kathleen Jones

Bayley, M. Mental Handicap and Community Care. *426 pp.*
Bottoms, A. E. and **McClean, J. D.** Defendants in the Criminal Process. *284 pp.*
Butler, J. R. Family Doctors and Public Policy. *208 pp.*
Davies, Martin. Prisoners of Society. *Attitudes and Aftercare. 204 pp.*
Gittus, Elizabeth. Flats, Families and the Under-Fives. *285 pp.*
Holman, Robert. Trading in Children. *A Study of Private Fostering. 355 pp.*
Jeffs, A. Young People and the Youth Service. *About 180 pp.*
Jones, Howard, and **Cornes, Paul.** Open Prisons. *288 pp.*
Jones, Kathleen. History of the Mental Health Service. *428 pp.*
Jones, Kathleen, with **Brown, John, Cunningham, W. J., Roberts, Julian** and **Williams, Peter.** Opening the Door. *A Study of New Policies for the Mentally Handicapped. 278 pp.*
Karn, Valerie. Retiring to the Seaside. *About 280 pp. 2 maps. Numerous tables.*
King, R. D. and **Elliot, K. W.** Albany: Birth of a Prison—End of an Era. *394 pp.*

Thomas, J. E. The English Prison Officer since 1850: *A Study in Conflict.* 258 pp.
Walton, R. G. Women in Social Work. *303 pp.*
● **Woodward, J.** To Do the Sick No Harm. *A Study of the British Voluntary Hospital System to 1875.* 234 pp.

International Library of Welfare and Philosophy

General Editors Noel Timms and David Watson

● **McDermott, F. E.** (Ed.) Self-Determination in Social Work. *A Collection of Essays on Self-determination and Related Concepts by Philosophers and Social Work Theorists.* Contributors: F. B. Biestek, S. Bernstein, A. Keith-Lucas, D. Sayer, H. H. Perelman, C. Whittington, R. F. Stalley, F. E. McDermott, I. Berlin, H. J. McCloskey, H. L. A. Hart, J. Wilson, A. I. Melden, S. I. Benn. *254 pp.*
● **Plant, Raymond.** Community and Ideology. *104 pp.*
Ragg, Nicholas M. People Not Cases. *A Philosophical Approach to Social Work. About 250 pp.*
● **Timms, Noel** and **Watson, David.** (Eds) Talking About Welfare. *Readings in Philosophy and Social Policy.* Contributors: T. H. Marshall, R. B. Brandt, G. H. von Wright, K. Nielsen, M. Cranston, R. M. Titmuss, R. S. Downie, E. Telfer, D. Donnison, J. Benson, P. Leonard, A. Keith-Lucas, D. Walsh, I. T. Ramsey. *320 pp.*
● (Eds). Philosophy in Social Work. *250 pp.*
● **Weale, A.** Equality and Social Policy. *164 pp.*

Primary Socialization, Language and Education

General Editor Basil Bernstein

Adlam, Diana S., *with the assistance of Geoffrey Turner and Lesley Lineker.* Code in Context. *About 272 pp.*
Bernstein, Basil. Class, Codes and Control. *3 volumes.*
● 1. *Theoretical Studies Towards a Sociology of Language.* 254 pp.
2. *Applied Studies Towards a Sociology of Language.* 377 pp.
● 3. *Towards a Theory of Educational Transmission.* 167 pp.
Brandis, W. and **Bernstein, B.** Selection and Control. *176 pp.*

Brandis, Walter and **Henderson, Dorothy.** Social Class, Language and Communication. *288 pp.*

Cook-Gumperz, Jenny. Social Control and Socialization. *A Study of Class Differences in the Language of Maternal Control. 290 pp.*

● **Gahagan, D. M** and **G. A.** Talk Reform. *Exploration in Language for Infant School Children. 160 pp.*

Hawkins, P. R. Social Class, the Nominal Group and Verbal Strategies. *About 220 pp.*

Robinson, W. P. and **Rackstraw, Susan D. A.** A Question of Answers. *2 volumes. 192 pp. and 180 pp.*

Turner, Geoffrey J. and **Mohan, Bernard A.** A Linguistic Description and Computer Programme for Children's Speech. *208 pp.*

Reports of the Institute of Community Studies

Baker, J. The Neighbourhood Advice Centre. *A Community Project in Camden. 320 pp.*

● **Cartwright, Ann.** Patients and their Doctors. *A Study of General Practice. 304 pp.*

Dench, Geoff. Maltese in London. *A Case-study in the Erosion of Ethnic Consciousness. 302 pp.*

Jackson, Brian and **Marsden, Dennis.** Education and the Working Class: *Some General Themes raised by a Study of 88 Working-class Children in a Northern Industrial City. 268 pp. 2 folders.*

Marris, Peter. The Experience of Higher Education. *232 pp. 27 tables.*

● Loss and Change. *192 pp.*

Marris, Peter and **Rein, Martin.** Dilemmas of Social Reform. *Poverty and Community Action in the United States. 256 pp.*

Marris, Peter and **Somerset, Anthony.** African Businessmen. *A Study of Entrepreneurship and Development in Keyna. 256 pp.*

Mills, Richard. Young Outsiders: *a Study in Alternative Communities. 216 pp.*

Runciman, W. G. Relative Deprivation and Social Justice. *A Study of Attitudes to Social Inequality in Twentieth-Century England. 352 pp.*

Willmott, Peter. Adolescent Boys in East London. *230 pp.*

Willmott, Peter and **Young, Michael.** Family and Class in a London Suburb. *202 pp. 47 tables.*

Young, Michael and **McGeeney, Patrick.** Learning Begins at Home. *A Study of a Junior School and its Parents. 128 pp.*

Young, Michael and **Willmott, Peter.** Family and Kinship in East London. *Foreword by Richard M. Titmuss. 252 pp. 39 tables.*
The Symmetrical Family. *410 pp.*

Reports of the Institute for Social Studies in Medical Care

Cartwright, Ann, Hockey, Lisbeth and **Anderson, John J.** Life Before Death. *310 pp.*
Dunnell, Karen and **Cartwright, Ann.** Medicine Takers, Prescribers and Hoarders. *190 pp.*
Farrell, C. My Mother Said. . . . *A Study of the Way Young People Learned About Sex and Birth Control.* 200 pp.

Medicine, Illness and Society

General Editor W. M. Williams

Hall, David J. Social Relations & Innovation. *Changing the State of Play in Hospitals.* 232 pp.
Hall, David J., and **Stacey, M.** (Eds) Beyond Separation. *234 pp.*
Robinson, David. The Process of Becoming Ill. *142 pp.*
Stacey, Margaret *et al.* Hospitals, Children and Their Families. *The Report of a Pilot Study.* 202 pp.
Stimson G. V. and **Webb, B.** Going to See the Doctor. *The Consultation Process in General Practice.* 155 pp.

Monographs in Social Theory

General Editor Arthur Brittan

● **Barnes, B.** Scientific Knowledge and Sociological Theory. *192 pp.*
Bauman, Zygmunt. Culture as Praxis. *204 pp.*
● **Dixon, Keith.** Sociological Theory. *Pretence and Possibility.* 142 pp.
Meltzer, B. N., Petras, J. W. and **Reynolds, L. T.** Symbolic Interactionism. *Genesis, Varieties and Criticisms.* 144 pp.
● **Smith, Anthony D.** The Concept of Social Change. *A Critique of the Functionalist Theory of Social Change.* 208 pp.

Routledge Social Science Journals

The **British Journal of Sociology.** *Editor* – Angus Stewart; *Associate Editor* – Leslie Sklair. *Vol. 1, No. 1 – March 1950 and Quarterly. Roy. 8vo. All back issues available. An international journal publishing original papers in the field of sociology and related areas.*

ROUTLEDGE SOCIAL SCIENCE JOURNALS

Community Work. *Edited by David Jones and Marjorie Mayo. 1973. Published annually.*
Economy and Society. *Vol. 1, No. 1. February 1972 and Quarterly. Metric Roy. 8vo. A journal for all social scientists covering sociology, philosophy, anthropology, economics and history. All back numbers available.*
Ethnic and Racial Studies. *Editor – John Stone. Vol. 1 – 1978. Published quarterly.*
Religion. Journal of Religion and Religions. *Chairman of Editorial Board, Ninian Smart. Vol. 1, No. 1, Spring 1971. A journal with an interdisciplinary approach to the study of the phenomena of religion. All back numbers available.*
Sociology of Health and Illness. *A Journal of Medical Sociology. Editor – Alan Davies; Associate Editor – Ray Jobling. Vol. 1, Spring 1979. Published 3 times per annum.*
Year Book of Social Policy in Britain, The. *Edited by Kathleen Jones. 1971. Published annually.*

Social and Psychological Aspects of Medical Practice

Editor Trevor Silverstone

Lader, Malcolm. Psychophysiology of Mental Illness. *280 pp.*
● **Silverstone, Trevor** and **Turner, Paul.** Drug Treatment in Psychiatry. *Revised edition. 256 pp.*
Whiteley, J. S. and **Gordon, J.** Group Approaches in Psychiatry. *256 pp.*